Further Journeys with a

SHAMAN WARRIOR

Gini Graham Scott, Ph.D.

iUniverse, Inc.
Bloomington

Further Journeys with a Shaman Warrior

iUniverse books may be ordered through booksellers or by contacting:

iUniverse
1663 Liberty Drive
Bloomington, IN 47403
www.iuniverse.com
1-800-Authors (1-800-288-4677)

ISBN: 978-1-4620-4416-0 (sc)

Printed in the United States of America

iUniverse rev. date: 09/06/2011

CONTENTS

1

MOVING ON

My previous training with Michael, the shaman I wrote about in SHAMAN WARRIOR and SECRETS OF THE SHAMAN, ended with my traveling through a gateway into another reality. Now I was ready to move on to the next level, which involved learning how to work more with the energies of this other world. It would involve another intense program of work, one which some people took months to learn, since they learned a little bit at a time. But Michael and his group had arranged for me to go through this training in an extreme immersion -- in a little over a week, since this was all the time I had left in L.A. before I had to return to my everyday commitments in San Francisco, which included law school and some new books to research and write.

"You should be able to do it," Michael said. "If you show that same kind of commitment you did in working on your gateway."

I was excited by the challenge. As Michael described it, I would have a chance to learn about the web of psychic connections he called the "circuit," which connected all people who had become psychically aware. I would learn how to tune in more to people's energies on a psychic and spiritual level. Perhaps most importantly, I would learn how to contact and work with these energy forms and spiritual beings from other dimensions of reality to gain access to this source of help in everyday life.

As Michael explained: "If you succeed in this training, you will learn how to obtain your own familiar, which is a kind of energy form bound to you, which you can call on for particular purposes. It takes a great deal of energy and commitment to achieve this level, to gain this kind of help from the other world. But once you do, you have truly advanced to a higher level of knowledge and power. Are you willing to do it?"

I said I was, and so I arranged to stay on at my hotel in Santa Monica for another ten days to continue my training. The atmosphere was ideal. I had driven down to L.A. with my portable typewriter, camera, stationery, and office supplies, and in my first 10 days there, I had turned my large room overlooking the ocean into a veritable office. At the same time, I had set aside a corner of my room for my shamanic studies, and it now housed the various tools which I had learned to use -- a small 9"x12" mirror in a frame used for gazing into other realities; a long black staff, which was a power object used to focus power in creating magical circles and opening gateways; and the small crystals I used for receiving energy. I also had brought along some photographs, drawings, charts, and written materials, which Michael had given me to use in meditation or better understanding the work.

I sometimes wondered what the maids thought as they cleaned up my room each day. Did they think the materials were all very strange? But since they barely spoke English, just Spanish, and I knew very little of that, I could never ask.

In any case, I felt very much at home where I was and decided to stay. So it was arranged. I would begin the next phase of my training the night after I created and went through my gateway. It was the 17th of December 1988, and I would have until January 1st to finish my training. The dates seemed significant. If I was successful, I would move on to a higher level of mastery at the end of one year and the beginning of another. It seemed like an especially appropriate time to make such a transformation.

On Saturday night, the 17th, I arrived at Michael's ranch house high in the canyons of Beverly Hills ready to begin. As at my previous trainings, I dressed in the usual ODF uniform, as did the others who were there -- a black shirt with symbols of our level of mastery on the collar and black pants, so we could better blend in with the elements when we worked outdoors at night.

As before, Michael had set up his living room to create a special magical space for our meeting. As I entered, I noticed the few small ritual objects Michael had placed on the long low coffee table in front of the couch -- a bowl of salt representing the element of earth, a chalice with water representing water, a censor with incense representing fire, and a ritual knife to cut a magical circle around us in the air.

I sat down on the couch, and in a few moments, Greta, one of Michael's students, came into the room from the kitchen. She explained she had just arrived from working as a paramedic on an ambulance, and she would assist Michael in the training that night. Then, she sat down in the chair across from me.

"Are you ready to begin again?" Michael asked.

"Yes," I nodded, and took out my notebook and pen, ready to write.

"Good," Michael said. "We have plenty to do. We'll start with the Shaman Warrior energy game tonight. We use it to develop an awareness of energy and improved psychic skills, and it will be a good introduction to this new work."

With that, Michael dimmed the lights and created a ritual circle around us, as he would each night to begin the training. Its purpose was to help us get more focused on the lesson for the night, as well as to keep out unwanted energies, particularly crucial now, since we would be doing advanced work with more powerful energies.

To make the circle, Michael first used his staff to draw a circle in the air. Then, he made a series of circuits around us in a counterclockwise direction, first holding the salt, then the chalice, then the salt and water mixed together, and finally holding the censor. Also, he drew a series of protective pentagrams in each of the four directions and above and below him to seal the circle. Finally, when he was done, it was like we were in a magical protective bubble, where we felt isolated and protected, almost like we were in another dimension, which the training was designed to explore.

Then, the ritual circle completed, Michael was ready to begin the first lesson. He lit a few candles and placed the board for the shaman warrior game on the table. The board was deep blue, and it featured a picture of a large circle divided into eight sections, like the pieces of a pie. Within each section, there was the image of a different animal -- a dragon in one, a snake in another, and a fish, spider, cat, eagle, stag, and wolf in the others.

"This is the Shaman Warrior game," Michael said. "Or more accurately, it's a series of games that nurture the psychic talent of the individual. So we use it as a training tool for intermediate students and a way to sharpen skills for all through regular practice. The reason for the eight animals is that these are totem animals, chosen for their mystic associations. Each animal is associated with one or more psychic or energy games of a particular type. Should you select that animal by spinning a spinner, that's what everyone plays."

Michael began to describe the play. "We use a betting process, and basically, energy is the stake. The reason for betting is that money is energy -- it's the symbolic representation of the energy you're expending and the goal you're trying to achieve. So the winner is determined by whoever has expended the most energy successfully, and that person wins the bet."

Michael took out some small draw-string bags with polished stones and poured them on the table. They sparkled in the flickering candlelight.

"The pieces are either polished glass or crystals," Michael explained, holding out a few pieces in the palm of his hand, so I could look at them more closely. "There are twenty-four pieces per player, a multiple of eight, which is a special number. Each person charges his own pieces at the beginning of the game."

"How does one do that?" I asked.

"You just hold them in your hands and project energy at them. It's like you would charge any object," said Michael. "Anyway, after the pieces are charged, we generally play three games. We decide that by spinning the spinner."

Michael put a small square spinner with the pictures of the eight animals on the table.

"After each game is determined by the spinner pointing to the animal associated with that game, we place our bets."

Michael dropped the pieces he was holding on the pie shape on the board with the picture of the eagle to illustrate.

"We bet by simply putting our charged pieces in the area with the animal spun," Michael explained. "Then, the bets are determined by the highest bidder, since everybody else has to match the high bidder to play. Finally, after the game, the winner is determined by the game master or the group. It's generally obvious who has won, so the winner is decided by consensus. But otherwise the game master decides. Then one of the best parts..." Michael chuckled a little. "The winner gets to consume the energy of all the other players by breathing in the energy they have projected into their pieces. Then, he gives their pieces back. Plus he consumes his own energy when he retrieves his own pieces from the board. So that's the incentive to win."

"It's like having an energy cocktail," added Greta. "It's really very energizing. It's like getting a psychic charge."

"Now let me explain some of the games," said Michael. "Then, we'll have a chance to play. You'll have a chance to match your energy against ours and see how psychic you are."

Michael pointed to the animal symbols in turn. "Basically, the qualities of the animals determine what games will be associated with them. For example, the dragon..." he pointed to the dragon "... is associated with the ball of energy game. In the game you have to project out your energy. It's like a duel, and it shares in the same qualities associated with the dragon, which is a fiery aggressive beast, who projects his energy out in the form of fire."

"How is the game played?" I asked.

"Oh, one person stands at one end of the room; the other person at the other. Then, they take turns projecting energy at each other. The idea is to hit the other person with your projected energy, while the other person attempts to ward this off by projecting a banishing pentagram or other symbol at it. Or he could dodge out of the way."

"So you can actually see or feel this energy coming and tell if someone gets out of the way?" I asked.

"Of course," Michael said. "You learned to see energy when you created your gateway, didn't you? And you were able to create or see energy darts thrown into that gateway, weren't you?"

I nodded.

"You've also been working on seeing into other realities since the beginning of your training, and you've been able to see various energy forms in nature, haven't you?"

Again I nodded.

"Well, this is exactly the same thing. Except instead of seeing the energy form around the person, you're seeing the energy projected from them. And you have to be quick, because the person may not just throw balls of energy or energy darts at you. Sometimes the energy can turn into rings or split in two directions. So it can get tricky."

"That's right," Greta commented. "For example, once when Paul and Michael were playing the game, Paul sent a ball of energy from the living room into the kitchen, and it curved around through there and came out and hit Michael in the back. He didn't see or feel it coming, so he got hit. I saw it, but since I was already looking in that direction, it was easy to see."

Michael pointed to the next image, the picture of the snake.

"This is associated with the radar in a blindfold game and other sensitivity games, because we think of the snake as being very sensitive. In this game, one person blindfolds himself and plugs his ears, so he can't see or hear anything. Then, the others move from their original position very quietly, and once they are in a new position, the individual tries to psychically sense their location. Whoever makes the most correct identifications wins."

"Does one have to know who's where?" I asked.

"If a player knows, that's really excellent," replied Michael. "But we just expect the player to locate the other person. That can be hard enough."

Michael pointed to the fish image.

"This one is associated with ESP cards and sensing colors. Also, we sometimes use Tarot cards with this. The basic idea here is to pick up what the card or color is when someone else turns up the card or looks at it. Then, the individual who scores the most correct hits wins."

The next image Michael indicated was the spider.

"This one is associated with hunting, since spiders go out to hunt and capture things. In this case, it's usually a more extended game in which we go someplace, such as to a shopping mall. Then, each player tries to project his energy out to create an effect."

"Like what?" I asked.

"You might try to get a person to move a hand or move from one direction to another in response to a projection of the will. Then, the person causing the greatest number of responses wins. Also, the spider image is associated with projecting the will into future time and with strategy games. For example, a person might focus his intention on having a certain event take place by a certain time, and the winner would be the person who has best achieved his intention of having the intended event happen. Or for strategy games, we might set up something like a match of chess, and then the players would draw on their psychic energy to help them know the best moves to make to win."

Michael went on to the next image, the cat.

"Since cats can be stealthy creatures and are good at hiding, we associate this image with the hidden bead game and with stealth games."

"Hidden beads?" I asked.

"Someone simply hides beads somewhere," Michael explained. "Then, the object is to psychically pick up where they are and find them. As for stealth games, this is stealth in the marital arts sense. One person tries to sneak up on another, and the other person tries to pick this up, as soon as he can."

Next came the eagle.

"We associate this with the projection of thought forms, since the eagle flies through the air, like a thought on the wind. In this case, what happens is that one individual writes down the thought or image he wants to project. Then, he imagines sending this thought or image out telepathically with his energy, while the others try to feel what it is. The winner is the person who can do this the best, which is indicated by how close the images are that others pick up. Or we might have a story-telling competition to stimulate the imagination, since this is another way of working with thought forms."

I noted Michael's comments in my notes and felt myself getting impatient, eager to play.

"How many more games?" I said.

"Just two more ," said Michael. "Then we'll play."

He pointed to the image of the stag.

"The stag is associated with games involving telekinesis, because of the associations with the stag's graceful movements. For example, some of the games we play with this involve dice or cards, in which the individual tries to cause certain numbers or cards to come up by using his intention or will. Still another game involves using a candle, in which the individual tries to move the flame of the candle in specific directions. And we also play a game using the crystal pendulum."

Michael pointed to a small wooden stand with four spindly wooden legs. A crystal about 1" long dangled on a string between them.

"The idea is to use your energy alone to stimulate this crystal pendulum which is suspended from the pyramid ," Michael explained. "You see..." he held his hand close to the crystal, but without touching it. "I project my energy from my hand and I move slowly enough, so there is no wind. Then, I focus on moving the crystal. Now watch..."

I looked closely and saw that the crystal seemed to sway slightly to the right and left.

"You can see it moving gently. And I haven't touched it. It's just my will. We also do this to work on moving the needle of a compass. It's used to develop the powers of telekinesis."

Finally, Michael described the game of the wolf.

"We play something we call astral tag, which can get rather wild and crazy at times. Basically, we use geoteleportation and conscious projection, and we have a chase. One person leads by projecting his consciousness and the others follow. We go from dimension to dimension, and the object is to discover where the other person is and catch him."

"But how can you tell where he is?" I asked. It was hard for me to imagine how one could even see or feel such thoughts, much less pin them down to a particular dimension.

"Oh, you can. You just learn to sense where the person is projecting his energy when you play. And the game helps to develop this sense." I looked at Michael a little dubiously. "Anyway, you'll just have to play to see."

Michael took three of the small bags of stones and poured them out on the coffee table in front of us.

"So, now you know all the games we play," he concluded. "It's a regular activity we use for training, and the betting makes it fun. Now we'll play a few sample games to show you how it works."

To prepare for play, Michael scooped up the dark stones on the table.

"I'll take the hematite," he said.

He gave Greta the translucent white amethysts, since she usually played with these, and he handed the remaining group of red glass stones to me.

"Now, you can take these stones and charge them."

I hesitated for a moment, not certain whether he meant for me to breathe energy into them or use some other method.

"Just put your hand over them," Michael explained, sensing my confusion, "and pour some energy in."

After I did this for a few seconds, he reminded me: "Now check one of the stones to see if you have enough energy in it."

But before I could react, Michael picked up one of the stones.

"Okay, this one is nice and charged. So now you're ready to bet."

After Greta picked up a stone, Michael continued. "Okay, now we'll decide which games we'll play. He spun the spinner three times, then announced the names of the animals which had turned up.

"Okay, that's it. We'll play the stag, dragon and eagle," he explained. "That means we'll be playing the pendulum, ball of energy, and projection of thought form games tonight. And now we'll bet on each. Bet based on how you feel you can do in each area. For example, if you feel really hot, bet more, and if you want, you can raise. Or if you feel less certain, hold back. But you have to meet the others' bets."

Michael plunked three of his stones on the section with the image of eagle.

"I'll try three on this."

"Better make it four," Greta said with a laugh. "I feel on tonight."

Michael and I likewise came up with four stones.

After we similarly bet on the games of the dragon and stag, Michael explained how we would play the first game of the eagle, which involved projecting our thoughts.

"Essentially, we'll be doing this partner to partner. You want to use simple thought forms, like basic geometric shapes or specific symbols or images. We'll each think of a basic image, and we'll each draw a picture of what we intend to project and fold it over. Then, we'll go around the circle, sending and receiving each image in turn, and we'll determine who was the closest in picking up the image. And if no one scores, we'll do it again until there is a winner."

"So who scores?" I asked. "The person who sends, or the person who picks up the image?"

"The sender does," Michael replied. "We assume the person who received the image got it, if it's close or correct."

Michael turned off a lamp to dim the lights. Now only two candles lit up the room. Then, he extended his hands to me, and we held hands.

"Now as we hold hands," Michael explained, "I'll project to you, and you want to open yourself to be as receptive as possible. Go into a meditative exercise and relax. After you receive, we'll talk about what you saw. I'll ask you about the images that passed through your mind, and try to remember everything you saw, even if it was fuzzy and not very clear."

"Okay ," I nodded.

Michael planted his feet firmly on the ground as he held his hands and gazed at me.

"Now I'll start sending by breathing out and visualizing that energy of the image reaching you. In turn, you will receive by breathing in. As you do, pay attention to any and all images that come to you. We'll go for about two minutes, which will give me plenty of opportunity to transmit."

"All right, I'm ready," I said, as I similarly sat up straight, my feet on the floor.

"Then, I'll start projecting," Michael said.

Now for about two minutes, there was utter silence. A myriad of images flashed through my mind -- a rock, some grass, a glass of water, a flower, a box, a stream. I didn't try to exercise any control. I just let the images come in, and I felt a little like I was peering into an ever-shifting kaleidoscope.

Finally, Greta called time.

"Okay, describe your images now," Michael said, and I went through my list. As soon as I mentioned seeing the box, Michael cut in: "Yes, bingo, that's it."

Then, Michael wanted to know if I saw anything like a castle, a house, or big square blocks.

"No," I said.

Michael explained the reason he asked. "I sent a lot of associated imagery with my main image. The reason I did so is because when you do this process, it helps to not only send your original image but anything associated with it to try to get across the idea. So when I projected the castle and house, I thought of rolling hills, and that's where your image of the grass probably came from. Also, I was trying to project an image of a solid square, and that could have been translated into your image of the rock. So, you see, these associations did seem to come across, and they helped you pick up my original image, the image of the box."

"But if I see enough images, wouldn't something possibly connect?" I asked.

Michael looked a little annoyed. "Look, you only saw six images, and one was right on. Two others were closely associated. So I would say that's a hit. Anyway, now try sending yourself."

This time, I tried sending to Greta. I thought of the image of two concentric circles, like two planetary orbits, and thought of the related images of pools, gateways, a target, and a fish in a lake. When it was over, Greta reported seeing a basketball court, sunlight, and images of summer, including a lake.

"That's pretty good," Michael said when we finished our comparisons. "As you can see these are all circular images, and there's even an exact correspondence in the lake."

Finally, to complete the round, Michael paired up with Greta, and after he described his images -- "a pile of wood stacked up, a cabin, some pine trees, an hour-glass, two large cones, a wagon from the old West, trees, horses, and a pyramid," Greta responded with excitement:

"What I was projecting was a wagon with horses. I saw a picture of a glyph from ancient Egypt showing a wagon pulled by oxen, and I was thinking of pyramids. So your wagon was very close, just a different time period. And your cones were close, too. And since I was also thinking of pyramids at some point, your pyramids were right on."

"So how do you decide who won?" I asked. "Everyone seems so close."

"Yes, it can be hard sometimes," Michael agreed. "And here there was no clear winner. Usually, the result is more definite. But when it's like this, we just do it again."

So, we tried the game for one more round, although this time, to speed things up, we only projected images for a minute each.

"And this time," Michael said, "the person who's closest to the exact image wins."

Again we held hands and projected energy, though in the reverse order. And this time, Michael was clearly the winner, after Greta picked up the freeway arrow he was projecting as an upside down triangle.

"So why should only the sender be the winner and not the receiver?" I asked.

Michael replied: "The receiver doesn't get points, because it's the strength of the sender that determines whether the receiver picks up anything. So if the receiver is not that good, the sender has to work that much harder. However, because of all the exercises you've been doing on sensitivity and gathering energy, that makes it relatively simple to play the game. That's why we were all so close in the first game. So you see, this game really does relate closely to our work."

Since Michael had won, he scooped up the pile of a dozen stones from the game section with the eagle.

"Now, as the winner, I breathe them in," Michael explained. "It's like a little charge of energy. If you're sensitive, you can notice the differences."

He held Greta's amethyst's under his nose, then breathed in the energy from my red glass pieces. "For example, her energy is sharper and sweeter, while your energy seems denser."

After breathing in the energy from all the stones, including his own, he handed them back. "Of course it gives the winner of one game a little bit of an edge on the next. After all, the winner has breathed in all that extra energy."

Michael grinned, and we went onto the next game, the game of the stag, using the pendulum. Michael placed the four-legged pyramid with the dangling crystal on the table in front of us, and explained the game in more detail.

"The idea is to reach through with your hands and hold them very near the crystal. We use a crystal because it's very receptive to psychic energy. But you don't want to touch the crystal or the table stand. Then project your energy out to make it move."

He put his hands on either side of the crystal to demonstrate.

"Also, move your hands very slowly, so you don't create any wind. And while you're watching..." he glanced at Greta and me, "you have to be careful how you move and talk, too. The crystal has to be moved by pure energy and will; by nothing else."

We nodded quietly, and Michael finished his explanation.

"Now, you can see how the crystal is just hanging there motionless. We use a crystal suspended by a string, because it's very sensitive to psychic energy. You want it to work with the ends of the crystal and get it to move in an obvious direction, and each time you score a point. But you can be disqualified for any heavy breathing or fast movements."

Michael moved the tips of his fingers to about a half inch from the ends of the crystal.

"We'll each go for two minutes," he said and began concentrating.

Greta and I watched silently, and in about a minute, the crystal began to oscillate slightly. Then, ever so slightly it seemed to push forward and back.

Finally, after Greta called time, she announced: "You got it to move six times," and Michael let go of his concentration with a rush.

Then, I tried, while Michael and Greta watched. I felt a tightness within me, as I held my hands stiffly by the crystal, and I imagined the energy rising up and spreading out from my core.

Soon I felt a tingly sensation, as if the energy was streaming from my fingers like a beam of light projecting into the crystal. Slowly, I began to move my hands. Would it move for me, I wondered? Or would anyone see it move? For a moment, I felt a little surge of energy, and then again and again. It was hard to tell if the crystal was moving or not, or whether I was just imagining it moving, since I felt so focused on this one image in front of me that everything in the background faded into black in the dim light.

Finally, Greta called time. "Well, you moved it nine times," she said, and Michael agreed.

"Pretty good for your first time," he said, "you even beat me. But different people are good in different things. Perhaps you are especially good in the skill of telekinesis, which is what's involved in this game. So maybe try applying this skill in other areas. See what else you might like to move."

Then, it was Greta's turn. "I'm usually pretty good at this," she said, as she positioned her hands at either ends of the crystal with a cocky confidence.

"How can you tell how many times it moves?" I asked, as we got ready to watch.

"Just look for the slight forward thrusts or vibrations," Michael said. "Each shift backwards or forwards counts as one." When it was over, Greta had in fact won.

"Twelve times," Michael exclaimed.

"You see, I knew I would be good," Greta said, and she scooped up the stones in the stag section of the board.

As she breathed in the stones, I thought about the symbolic meaning of what she was doing. It was like the breathing in of our energy was a further reaffirmation and build-up of her own power, and for a moment, I felt a twinge of resentment and annoyance, because of her cockiness, which seemed to say: "See, I told you."

But in another moment, I caught myself doing this, and I heard a little voice within me saying: "But it's only a game. It's only a game," and the feeling went away. Yet at that same moment, I also wondered: "But is it really just a game? Or does it tell us a little about how we and others approach life." It was something to think about.

But there was no time to do this anymore, because Michael was ready to announce the last game, the game of the dragon.

"This one can get pretty wild," he said, "since we'll be throwing around balls of energy. It's a little like playing dodge ball. We'll use partners, and each person will take turns throwing a ball of energy at the other. When the energy comes at you, you've got to catch it or jump out of the way, so it doesn't hit you. And you can't put up a full shield to play the game, because otherwise nothing will get through."

Michael blew out the two candles in the living room, so the room was plunged into total darkness, except for the faint reflection from a light in the hall.

"Now, the individual who isn't playing will be an observer and will help judge the game," he continued. "Although it will be clear once the ball is thrown whether the energy has scored a hit or not."

To demonstrate, Michael asked me to observe, and he and Greta positioned themselves at either end of the living room.

"Now we'll take turns extending our energy. I'll start by creating a ball of energy by visualizing it in my mind's eye. Then, I'll shoot it at her, and she has to ward it off, or it's a hit."

I watched intently, and I saw Michael's shadowy form stiffen in the darkness.

Then, before I could see anything else, I heard Michael cry out: "There. She's already got up her guard and fended it off."

Since I didn't see anything, I asked Michael to explain.

"I tried to project the energy around her as a ring. But she didn't fall for that, and she warded it off. So the energy didn't touch her, which is what it needs to do to score. Instead, it just bounced off and went around her, but didn't hit."

Greta got ready to throw this time, and I settled back to watch again.

In moments, I heard Greta call out: "I got you on the side," and Michael agreed. "Yes, you did."

I suddenly felt lost. Greta and Michael were both obviously seeing something, yet for me the room was just dark and shadowy.

"Don't worry," Michael assured me. "The energy moves very quickly. So sometimes when you are first doing this, it's hard to see. But even if you can't see the energy, when you play, you can feel it. And the game can really help to sensitize you to quickly seeing or feeling the energy that's out there and responding to it quickly."

"I'll try again," I said, and this time I concentrated on using the seeing exercises that Michael had taught me years ago, when I had first started the training. I let my eyes go out of focus, so I could look into the spaces in the air, not at anything in particular, and this time, I saw a slightly concentrated glow in front of Michael's chest in addition to a shimmery whitish glow around him. Suddenly, this concentrated glow seemed to move away into the air, and just as it did, I heard Greta call out: "I got it."

"So she's the champ," announced Michael. "She intercepted my throw," and with that, he announced that it was my turn to try. He would watch and I would play against Greta.

I got up nervously, still not sure what I was doing, or if I could see or feel the energy that quickly. I briefly recalled playing dodge ball at camp as a child, and I remembered having enough trouble dodging real balls when other children threw them at me. And now I was supposed to dodge energy balls. Somehow I felt a little like I was participating in some imaginary drama, in which Michael and Greta were both talking about some fragmentary visions they could see or agreed to see, while I was on the outside wondering if what they were seeing and talking about was real. Perhaps I had a glimpse of it, or just imagined I had a glimpse of it, but I wasn't sure. So as I got up and took my position across the room from Greta, I felt somewhat unnerved. I felt a little like I was trying to see and experience a unicorn running across a field at the same time that I was still wondering whether the unicorn really existed at all.

But Greta and Michael were obviously not concerned about such things, for they could see and feel the unicorn, and they acted as if they assumed I could or would shortly see it.

"Now you start," Michael called out to me.

I jerked back to attention and put aside my questions. Now I focused on projecting the image of a ball of energy at Greta's chest. At once, I saw her hands dart up in the darkness in front of her chest and make a pushing motion towards me.

"There, she's got it," Michael announced. "Now it's her turn to fire."

As Greta stiffened while she concentrated and got ready to shoot, Michael admonished me.

"Usually, you can't be so direct. It was so obvious the way you looked. We could easily see where you were projecting the energy, just by your attention, even if we couldn't see or feel the energy. So you have to be deceptive in the way you project it."

"Okay," I nodded.

Then I heard Greta saying: "Well, I'll be nice and do it simply, since this is your first time."

With that I suddenly felt a wave of energy come towards me and without thinking, I jerked up my hands.

"There, you intercepted," said Michael, and I suddenly had a feeling that yes, I could experience what Michael and Greta were talking about; I could see the unicorn. And I felt like another door to this other world of perception and feeling was opening up.

"So you're both tired now," I heard Michael say. Then, as my attention wandered, Michael's voice broke in again. "Well, now she got you in the butt."

I glanced over at Greta, not realizing she had even thrown an energy ball at me again.

"Well, it's there," Michael continued. "You can see the energy hanging there. So now, if you want, you can brush it off, and get ready to shoot."

This time, I tried looking one way, while I concentrated on projecting my energy in another. But apparently Greta was aware of this.

"No, she got it," said Michael, proclaiming her the winner.

So the game was over. I sat back down, feeling like I had just been up against s whiz player in ping pong, who could whiz smashes past me and stop anything I managed to get over the net. I reached for my notebook eagerly, like at least this was a known quantity.

"Now, this was just your first time," Michael said reassuringly. "You'll get better with practice. The game rests entirely on the ability to see as well as project. And the energy is moving very fast. So it can be very tricky. But as you learn to see and project better, you'll be better able to both send and respond, and the game can help you get better."

"Do you normally feel it or see the energy?" I asked.

"Either or both," Michael said. "For example, when you threw your energy, it was very clear. It was like a concentrated mass or cloud of energy that flew from your hands, and it was very easy to track."

"And I could feel it coming, too," Greta observed.

"Then, when Greta first threw at you," Michael continued, "she threw very fast. It was like an instant projection of energy, but you reacted at once, like you felt it and caught it, even faster than your eye could see and react. Then, when you missed the second one, what she did is throw the energy ball so the energy split, and it went in two circles to your sides. You see, as you get more sophisticated in working with energy, you can do that, and you can perceive or feel those splits. Then, you can respond to them, too."

"Is there any practical purpose to being able to do all this?" I wondered. "I mean, apart from just having fun, and playing the game."

"Of course," said Michael. "The game is just a way to develop and perfect these skills. Then you can apply it. For example, say you are out in the street in a crowd where two pickpockets are working together, and they have zeroed in on you as a subject. They're moving towards you, with the idea of one of them diverting your attention, while the other reaches in and grabs. Well, when you become sensitive to where all this energy is coming from, you can sense what's going to happen, as soon as they start focusing on you, before they even come near or try taking anything from you. So you can react in advance to protect yourself. Tonight we're just playing a game. But you will find this game, like many others, will help you become more aware of the energy that's the very stuff of life; it'll help you become more psychically astute."

"But how can you be sure of what you're seeing and feeling?" I asked. "For example, suppose you think you hit someone and the other person didn't see it? Or what if there is some disagreement about what two people see?"

"What makes the game work is that people are honest," Michael said confidently. "Also, even if the observer misses a throw, the other players can still see and feel what happened. For example, if I'm hit, I feel a certain pressure of energy hitting me. It's like getting a pie in the face."

"Or you might feel a sense of missing some of your own energy, like it's been pulled away. For example, when you hit me that's what I felt," Greta said.

"Anyway, just be patient," Michael said. "It takes some practice to really have that awareness and knowing. Then, you'll find that playing and judging the game is really a group thing, since everyone's skill is used in interpreting and feeling the energy."

Since Michael and Greta had both won their rounds, Michael called it a draw, and he began folding up the game and the pieces to put it away.

"So now you have an introduction to the Shaman Warrior game," he said. "You need some basic psychic skills to play, so it might be hard for the average person to play it. But we use it regularly and use it a lot, because it enables us to practice our skills. Plus it shows us the areas where we could use some additional work, so it's great for training. It gives you a sense of where you are psychically."

Michael snapped the game box shut and turned on the lights.

"So the whole idea of these games," he concluded, "is to develop the mind, body and spirit. For example, the stealth game I described earlier is particularly designed to develop the body, since the idea is to move as quietly as possible across a room without being heard or seen, while others try to listen and observe. Another game we play called "philosophy," is designed to stimulate the intellect in that each player in turn tries to come up with a gem of wisdom, and the consensus of the group or the game master decides whoever is the wisest."

"The game master?" I interrupted.

"Like what I did tonight," Michael said. "The game master just determines what the games are and oversees the judging. But in reality the games are decided by the consensus of the audience and the players.

"Finally," Michael went on, "we have many psychic games, such as you experienced tonight, to develop the spirit. Plus we're constantly adding to the games, because we believe it's important to keep challenging a person's skills and abilities. Otherwise, they can go flaccid and flabby, like the muscles. So the idea is to keep building in all ways -- by stimulating the mind through things like strategy games and puzzles, by stimulating the body through movement exercises, and by stimulating the spirit with psychic skills like the pendulum, thought projection, and the energy ball games we played tonight."

With that, Michael announced that tonight's lesson was over.

"Tomorrow we'll be talking about what it's like there out in the urban world for the shaman. As you'll discover, there's a whole world of psychic energy out there, a kind of a circuit you can plug into, as you become aware. And we'll talk about how you can connect with and work with that. Plus we'll have some interesting stories -- ghost stories if you will, as we talk about modern urban ghosts. Then, we'll do some energy exercises to help you prepare for your own trip into the field. After that," Michael concluded cryptically, "there will be much more."

I wanted to know more, but Michael told me to "just wait and see."

And so, thinking of the energy games we had played, I drove out into the foggy night. There was much to think about. My training had just started, and already I felt charged up by all the energy we had played with.

I stepped even harder on the gas, and my car shot ahead on the mostly empty late night freeway. I thought, "This is one more way of projecting energy." And again I gave the car another shot of gas.

2

LEARNING ABOUT THE
PSYCHIC CIRCUIT

In the afternoon, after what had become my morning ritual -- writing up my notes, I walked across the street to the Santa Monica beach. In the week or so since I had been here, the beach had become a kind of a friend I came to visit almost everyday, and like any good friend, I found the beach an ideal companion for trying out my new ideas and things I had learned to see how well they worked.

This time I thought I'd try out some of the psychic techniques we had played in the game. Would they work in an everyday setting? I walked up and down the beach to find out.

Now about 3:30 in the afternoon, the beach was relatively quiet. It was only about an hour away from the early winter sunset, and already there was a sense of hurry about the beach. The small sand birds scurried quickly across the sand; a group of seagulls whirled and tossed with growing speed, and suddenly rose up in a frenzied wave, moved several feet, then settled down again.

I saw a man in a brown windbreaker sitting on the steps of the lifeguard tower gazing into the surf, and decided to send him a thought form as we had in the eagle game to see if he would react. I concentrated on sending him the image of a campfire. I thought it came close to Michael's request to only send basic shapes or simple, concrete, and specific images. Besides, I thought, maybe if he sees this image, he'll feel warmer and take off his coat.

I imagined the flames leaping higher and higher, as I concentrated on sending the image. I saw sparks break away, then flicker and fall. I thought of some related images, as Michael had urged us to do -- a group of people around the campfire, the tree logs in a pile before they were cut, a forest fire growing out of control.

Then, the man in the windbreaker looked up and stared right at me. He sat up straighter and gathered his legs up under him, so he seemed almost perched on the platform around the lifeguard tower like a bird. Was he responding to me? I wondered. Did he pick up my image of the fire, and is that why he moved a little? Did he want to better watch it? Or did he notice my staring, and did that make him self-conscious.

I let my eyes go to glaze, so I was no longer staring at him, and suddenly I got the image of a flowing river overflowing its banks and dousing my fire. I glanced up to see the man still staring at me. Had he sent that image of the water to me to douse the fire? Was I picking that up? Was he trying to engage me in a battle of thought forms? I wasn't sure, but I felt unnerved by his eyes staring at me, like they were sending two beams of bright white light through me, so I turned away.

I continued my walk down the beach. A little further on, I saw a small white rounded pebble balanced precariously on the tip of a log, and I recalled the pendulum game we had played. What if I concentrated on the pebble moving or vibrating off, I wondered? I walked a little closer, held my fingers about an inch away, and imagined my energy pouring out of my fingers to dislodge the pebble. Just then, a gust of wind swept by, and the pebble fell on the sand. I glanced at the pebble lying there, then gazed out towards the ocean, from where the gust of wind had come. A success or a coincidence? It was an interesting question to think about, and I continued on down the beach, looking for some likely individual or group on whom to try out Michael's energy ball technique.

Then, I passed a couple throwing a small ball about. Perfect, I thought, and as they darted here and there on the sand, throwing and catching the ball, I concentrated on forming a ball of energy directly in front of myself. For a few moments, I held it there in my imagination, as if I was deciding the best moment to throw. Finally, just as the man lobbed the ball at his partner, I let go of my energy ball and directed it at him.

All of a sudden, at the moment I imagined it hit, the man turned and looked at me. He seemed surprised, startled, and he stared at me intently before turning back to his game. Had I somehow hit him with this energy, I wondered? Or did he just suddenly notice my presence and become self-conscious? I couldn't tell, and again, as I walked along the beach, I thought about the possibilities, recalling the question I kept asking ever since beginning my training: What was real? What wasn't? What was really out there? Or what was in my imagination? Or could my imagination itself create something real?

These were hard questions. Would I ever know the answers? Could I? Or would these questions ultimately have to give way to pure belief? It was something to think about.

Then, it was time to go back to my hotel and get ready to go to Michael's. The sun had set, and now a grayish cast was settling in over the beach. I turned around and walked back quickly. As I passed the place where the couple and the man in the windbreaker had been, it seemed like there was an energy hole there, for I felt I sense of emptiness as I passed. It was as if their presence had been subtracted from the environment; but a memory shell of their having been there remained. But would I have felt this, I wondered, if I hadn't known they were there in the first place? Michael said he could sense such things, that anyone could. But could I? Would I? What was real? What was not?

I hurried back to my hotel and got into the black slacks and black shirt with the ODF symbols I usually wore for these trainings. I had two silver stars on each shirt collar now, symbolizing that I had passed my fifth degree by completing a gateway into another reality. Yet still you're asking these questions, I thought to myself. You're still asking for proof; for some logical explanations, though these alternate realities defy proof, they defy logic.

I picked up my long black staff used to focus energy and power from the table. "Well, there may just be some things you can never ever know," I told myself, and I headed out the door. Tonight Michael would be talking about the urban psychic world I was becoming part of through my training, and suddenly my questions seemed incongruous. It was like I was going to visit someone while wondering if that person was there, as he or she came to answer the door.

When I arrived, Greta and Michael were already waiting for me in the living room.

"The door's open," Michael called out when I knocked.

I sat down across from him on the couch. After I set up my tape recorder and notebook, Michael did his usual ritual to create a circle of energy around us and began his lesson for the night.

"Tonight we'll be talking about living life as a modern shaman in the city," Michael began. "As you'll find there is a kind of hidden city out there, which is not readily apparent to most people, because it exists beyond outward appearance. It's a level of existence that occurs on a higher level or another dimension in the form of psychic or spiritual energy, and that's what we call the circuit. You'll have a chance to experience this soon in the field, and as you'll find, once you plug into this psychic level, you can always be part of it and use it as a regular state of consciousness.

"You see," he went on, "for most people, magic is something special -- something they use to feel special, gain help in a time of need, or achieve a special objective. For example, say a person wants to find a lover, obtain more money, or find a job. The person might use some magic for a little while, like putting on a pair of shoes. Then, when he's done, he puts it back. And anyone can do this, because everyone has psychic skills.

"But..." Michael paused to underline the importance of what he was going to say next, "...the shaman or sorcerer is different. He's unique, because he makes these psychic skills, this ability to work magic, an everyday part of his life. It's like the shaman is constantly in touch with this other world, and he knows he can tap into it at any time. In effect, this awareness of these other realities, this magical consciousness, has become a part of him, because he has developed his senses to experience it through training. So the shaman perspective is no longer a sometime thing, something he puts on like a special suit of clothes for a special occasion. Rather it's a living, functioning part of his life, which informs his whole point of view. So he, in effect, interprets the world through magical glasses."

I described how I had explored the beach and tried out the techniques from the game. "Is that what you mean?" I asked. "Trying to look at whatever you are seeing through psychic eyes?"

"Something like that," Michael said. "Of course, a shaman isn't on all the time. But he knows, whenever something happens, to assess anything in light of his knowledge of psychic forces. It's like being trained in a certain discipline, so you develop a whole new way of thinking; a whole new way of responding to things that becomes second nature.

"For example, cops often tend to be suspicious of things, even when they are off duty; lawyers are typically very reserved, controlled, and analytical; psychologists usually are very aware of people's feelings and are often searching for people's underlying motives. Well, a trained shaman is like that. He experiences the hidden reality that underlies outward appearances, and he can tune into that reality at any time, like turning up the sound on a radio that's playing in the background. He can suddenly hear what's there."

As Michael explained it, this change was of a qualitatively different order than becoming an expert or changing one's perspective in response to some other kind of training. Rather, as Michael put it, "Once an individual develops this trained psychic awareness, he or she becomes more evolved. This occurs because when you stimulate the pineal gland, this creates changes in the whole person. And once this evolution starts, it doesn't stop. The developed shaman can't suddenly turn off this awareness as if it doesn't exist, because he is aware that it does. He may not pay attention to it, but he can't deny it. It's different for the average person who might dabble in magic and then put it back. But the sorcerer or shaman has moved on to another level and can't turn back."

"Why not?" I asked. "If the shaman can stop paying attention, why can't he stop being aware completely?"

"Because that's not possible. Once you are aware, you start living a different kind of life. For example, there are many perceptions I take for granted, which others are not even aware of, such as using ESP and reading a person by picking up his energy. Also, even while I am acting on a physical level, I am fully aware of existing and operating at another level simultaneously, which is the level of the psychic circuit, the hidden level I spoke about. Once I have been part of this for sometime so it has become part of me, I cannot suddenly undo that and pretend it never happened."

Michael looked at me intently, and I suddenly felt very self-conscious, like he was about to put me on the spot again.

"All right," he said, "let me use a personal example to convince you. You grew up in New York. You spent 20 years there. You lived in Manhattan, in the middle of all that fast-moving energy. You took subways, walked with the crowds everyday. Can you ever forget that? Can you pretend you didn't live there?"

I thought for a moment, and noticed how I always felt like I was set at a higher pace than the other people in the San Francisco Bay Area who lived around me. So I always seemed to have more energy; I did things faster; I hurried through things to get them done.

"No, I guess part of me will always feel like a New Yorker," I said.

"Well, it's the same thing working with psychic energy. Once you unleash that awareness, once you are connected to the circuit and it becomes part of you, you will be forever hooked. So you can't go back."

"How is the shaman's life in the city special, besides having this special awareness?" Greta wanted to know.

"For one thing," said Michael, "the shaman is not primarily concerned with material things. His level of concerns is entirely different. Rather, he is more concerned with spiritual matters, and in achieving a psychic harmony whatever he does. And yet..." Michael paused for a few seconds thoughtfully, "...it's important to realize that in working towards these spiritual ends, a shaman or sorcerer can either be benevolent or he can use his special awareness to manipulate others towards destructive ends. The shaman's approach depends on the individual person, because the power itself is neutral, and with these new abilities, the individual can transcend many everyday constraints. We would of course encourage the benevolent uses, but the opposite is always one of the risks.

It's like any technology in the development of man's history -- industry, steampower, the automobile, nuclear fusion. We keep evolving to higher and higher levels of human achievement, and generally people use these new technologies for beneficial ends, and so the human race continues to survive. But there's always that risk that would lead to a blow-out. But so far, we haven't stopped developing. We've been willing to take that risk. And it's like that with psychic power. We keep evolving, and we hope that the shaman will use his evolved skills for generally beneficial ends."

Michael went on to describe the spiritual world which the shaman was constantly in touch with.

"It's a little bit like being aware of the fish under the surface of the sea. The average man in a rowboat may think he's is just being pushed about by the tides. as he rows with or against those currents. But at the same time, some of his movement may be caused by these large fish swimming around under the surface, which people can barely see or can't see at all. But the shaman is not only aware of these creatures. He can also contact and work with them, so he can use them to help him in making his journey.

"By the same token, the average person can miss seeing all sorts of things in his environment that affects and interacts with his life. For example, he can't see that certain individuals are especially powerful psychically and able to work magic, because on the surface, these people look like everyone else. Also, the average person won't be able to see the energies and entities that exist all around him, like the elemental forces. And he may see things as perfectly normal objects, when they really aren't normal -- such as seeing the image of a person on the street, when there's nothing there except perhaps a sign that looks like a person. You see, some energy out there may triggers that association, or the person may even see an urban ghost."

"An urban ghost?" I echoed.

"Yes," Michael said, nodding his head. "Real ghosts. But we'll talk about that later. What I'm mainly trying to emphasize here is the way shamans see things differently. There are so many things in the urban environment that people take for granted which influence them, but they aren't aware of their effect. It's like they have on blinders, so they don't see the psychic phenomena that's out there. At times, they may run smack into something psychic or do an occasional act of magic, that can get them wondering or thinking that they have tapped into some other world of reality. But mostly, they are shut off from this world, which the shaman can be in touch with all the time.

"So the major point is to understand that things aren't necessarily as they seem, and the purpose of this training as a modern shaman is to make you more aware of all these levels of reality that are out there in the environment all around you. This way you can be more successful in maneuvering through this environment and interacting with these other realities out there."

Michael held up a coffee table book with pictures of modern city streets. He flipped a few pages, and pointed to some pictures of gleaming silver skyscrapers, jammed up traffic, and people struggling to cross rush-hour filled city streets.

"You know, traditionally," he continued, "shamans have always been associated with primitive or traditional cultures. They have worked in isolated areas and out in the country. They have worked with local plants and animals, and many of those traditions have been passed on to us. But that was then. This is today, and now the city has become the symbol of modern times. It's the arena in which most people today struggle, seek fulfillment, or experience the denial of their desires. It's the material arena where they succeed or fail, just as the natural environment was once the setting for this.

"So now the modern shaman is in a new environment with new symbols. It doesn't mean that we can't use the traditional symbols. But now there are new ones, new meanings, to suit changing times. For example, today, most people still focus on the material level as they struggle to survive, though now you have corporate takeovers and strikes affecting managers and workers instead of hunters stalking animals and wars between tribes.

"Yet, despite these surface changes, the same kind of psychic forces still exist behind the scenes, though as in earlier times, most people don't see them; only the trained shaman or psychic does.

"So because of these other realities, this hidden world that exists simultaneously with the physical world, living in any city, even a big city like New York, can be just as metaphysical as living in the rural world of the past, or spending time alone on a vision question or out on the desert. However, because the fast-pace and materialism of the city and the rationalistic view of the modern world, it can be more difficult to uncover this hidden psychic world. So it takes an especially brave and committed person to do this. It's so much easier to live in the day-to-day world than to try to delve beneath the surface and see the spiritual realities that lie underneath, particularly since you can uncover spiritual dangers out there, and you can encounter not very nice spiritual beings that can take the form of monsters and ghosts."

Michael flipped through a few more pages of the coffee table book. He pointed to some pictures of fashion models giving a show in a luxury restaurant and some high-level corporate executives meeting around a large conference table.

"So you see, to the average person, the city is full of very ordinary things like people working, businessmen, dogs, cats, birds, goldfish, even winos and homeless people down on their luck."

He flipped to a page with a picture of a man in a shaggy tattered top coat sitting in an alley at night and warming his hands over a small garbage can fire. "But there's another dimension, and if you look closely enough, things start to change, and you get a glimpse of this underlying reality beneath the surface."

Michael turned the page to reveal the image of a bag lady looking out vacantly as she rolled her shopping card down the street.

"Now the first level of people perceiving something different consists of the crazies, psychopaths, and like individuals who are definitely not thinking in the norm with everyone else. Many of them in their madness may see into this hidden reality, because they have lost touch with the structure or blinders of normal everyday thinking. However, if they do see something, they are not in control. It's like they sometimes see what's out there, but it frightens them, and they don't know what to do with it. Yet they do see it, because their grasp on everyday reality is loosened."

Michael turned the page again, and this time stopped at the image of a Tarot card reader giving a reading to a passerby on a busy street corner.

"Then, there are the individuals who follow the ways of magic," Michael commented. "Sometimes they're called witches, psychics, magicians. But whatever they're called, whatever tradition they come from, they believe in more than the normal laws of cause and effect. Some have a certain amount of talent to call on and work with these powerful unseen forces. Some don't. And some, a minority, have a very strong psychic or metaphysical power. They live lives like the rest of us, and normally this power is hidden. But as you become aware, you can see it or feel it in these people, and perhaps you can develop that kind of power for yourself.

"This power is like that sense you have when someone powerful comes into a room. You can feel a kind of electricity -- a charge around the person. Or if you have that power, you have a radiance that follows you and let's everyone know you're in charge.

"Being in touch with this psychic circuit is like that. You can feel the energy vibrations that radiate throughout the room or put them out yourself so others feel them. Maybe think of the experience like tapping into a high power wire. As long as the wire is high and far away, the average person doesn't even know it's there. But touch the wire and you can feel it. Or connect a bulb, and see it light up. For there's this tremendous charge surging through the wires, and when you connect in, you can suddenly see it and feel it, and when you know how to use that power, you can sense where that current is going and what it's being used for, or you can tap into that energy and use it yourself.

"Or maybe think of tapping into that power like being a ham radio operator. When you have a receiver and know how to use it, you can hear all those people out there who are talking to each other on the circuit. Well, some of these operators will have more powerful transmitters, and some more powerful receivers, and some will be able to both send and receive more powerful signals. Likewise you can tune in and work with the circuit on any level; it depends on how well you are trained."

"What sort of things do you pick up when you tune in?" asked Greta?

"And how does what happens on the circuit affect things in everyday life?" I asked.

Michael answered both our questions. "You can pick up just about anything. People's motives, their plans for the future, what they have done in the past. It's like listening in on a telephone conversation, and much of what happens depends on the motives of the people and the groups involved. People can work with these psychic energies for benevolent or non-benevolent ends, though the average person not in touch with the circuit will never know."

Michael gave an example of an old man he had seen one time doing some magical work on the side of the freeway. Michael had pulled off on the side of the road to take a brief rest stop, when he saw the man several yards ahead of him in the shadows of a ramp leading up to an overpass.

"I could see the man holding an old book," Michael explained. "Then, in the distance I heard him chanting in other tongues, and at once I realized he was doing a magical working and that its purpose was not for the good. I could feel the dark energy that was radiating from him, and after a few minutes, there was a car crash on the freeway perhaps a dozen yards away. Then, I saw him stop his chanting and walk away after a brief glance at the crash. He seemed to have a satisfied grin, as if he was satisfied with his work.

"Now this is an example of black magic," Michael said. "Yet this is the 20th century, when we're not supposed to believe such things. And most certainly the people in the cars had no awareness of the forces affecting them, though I was aware of these emanations and sensed something bad would happen. Perhaps if the drivers were aware, they might have been able to stay out of this zone of danger where he was probably projecting his negative energy and so avoid the crash. But most people don't have this awareness, so they go about their lives, unaware of these influences. They have no knowledge or belief in this type of reality or in the power of the people who are part of this circuit. So they take no precautions. After all, why take them against something they are told isn't real?

"By contrast, I and others tuned into this circuit do take such things seriously. So just as I might take precautions against being mugged on the city streets, I take precautions against hostile individuals with psychic skills."

"What kind of precautions?" asked Greta.

"To avoid them or the hostile energy they have projected. Or sometimes, if there is time and it's appropriate, I might act to banish that hostile energy; I might act to diffuse their bad will and intent."

"Like the psychic police force," commented Greta, and Michael just smiled.

"Anyway," Michael continued, "this example of black magic illustrates one type of hidden magic that could occur and influence everyday activity. Also, there can be positive work, which is something many, perhaps most people, on the circuit try to do. For example, one time when I was driving on the freeway in the fast lane, I saw a woman whose car was broken down by the side of the road, and she stood beside it looking very helpless. But by the time I saw her, I was going too fast to stop, though I wanted to help her. So using my psychic abilities, I reached out to her, and I visualized some help coming to her immediately. Then, as I drove off, I saw in my rearview mirror that a tow truck was coming up the ramp of the freeway, and then I saw it pull over beside her. So I was able to give her a little psychic help."

"Couldn't it have been a coincidence that the truck was there?" I asked.

"No, I don't think so," said Michael. "I called on that truck to be there for her, and in a moment it appeared. Or at least I previsualized it coming moments before it was really there. In any case, this woman probably had no knowledge of the psychic assistance she received, and probably would not believe it if she was told, because most people aren't aware of such things.

"But whether people are aware or not, there are all sorts of different practitioners today of varying levels of ability and intentions -- New Agers, sorcerers, shamans, witches, Satanists, mystics, and metaphysicians of various types. In turn, if you can psychometrize and see or feel the environment around you, it is possible to be aware of the presence of these psychically active individuals and to gage the strength of their intentions for good or bad. And that can be important in knowing how to deal with that person or whether to stay around at all.

"After all, so much of this is hidden," Michael emphasized. "The occult stores, the bookstores, the organized groups are just one level -- like the tip of an iceberg. But the average person doesn't see any of this; only the person tuned into the circuit does. And this can sometimes create problems between those who are psychically aware and those who aren't, such as when an ordinary person does something to upset the person with these magical powers.

"For example, most people might not think the ordinary-looking person they are sitting next to on the bus has anything special about them. But I've seen or heard of some examples of people sitting next to someone on the bus, and then they push that person or insult them, and they get off the bus without giving their actions a second thought. But after that, they have some really bad luck for the next week."

I started to interrupt, but Michael cut me off, anticipating my question.

"Now you may wonder, was that a coincidence? But I don't think so. The psychically powerful person has simply sent out a negative energy charge in response to his bad treatment, and that force can linger for awhile, like a cloud around the person to whom it's directed, and so it serves to drag him down or make him feel slightly off. It doesn't matter if the person believes in the forces or not. They'll work anyway.

"This goes for positive charges, too, because as you have seen, not all forces are negative, though they all are potent. Thus, if someone does a benevolent helpful deed for someone else, who turns out to be psychically powerful, the person who was helped could send back a positive energy charge, which could help the other person feel better and have what seems like better luck.

"In short," Michael concluded, "by being tuned in you can pick up these different psychic energies, like being aware of the weather. Just as it's important to know what the weather is, so you have the right clothes and don't get rained on, so it's important to be aware of the psychic weather, so you can respond appropriately to that, as well."

Michael turned back to the coffee table book with photos he had been using to get us thinking about the psychic urban landscape, and he turned to a picture of a large rally. In it, someone was speaking on a large amphitheater stage and others were cheering or clapping.

"It's also important to realize," he said, "that the average person is capable of generating psychic forces, even though he may not be aware of this, especially if he is gathered together with others in large numbers."

Michael gave an example of when he had been in San Francisco about five years before shortly after Dan White, then a supervisor, had been sentenced for killing Harvey Milk, a gay supervisor, and George Moscone, the mayor of San Francisco. The killings had been very traumatic for the city, and when White got a light sentence, there was a great deal of resentment against the city and the criminal justice system. So a large crowd gathered to protest, while a large contingent of police appeared to contain the protest. Eventually, it turned into a ugly night of rioting, trashing, and head bashing, as people expressed their hatred for the straight establishment or the homosexual community. Meanwhile, as these outer events went on, Michael paid attention to the psychic energies unleashed by the situation. As he described it:

"Unlike most of the people who were there to express their hatred towards someone, I was there as a shaman interested in experiencing the forces at work and expressed by the crowd. What I saw as the crowd got angrier and angrier was that the atmosphere around them became smokier. It was like a darkness was gathering, and the angrier the crowd became, the darker it got. At the same time, I could feel a series of waves of tangible energy pass over the crowd. So the energy of this anger had literally risen up above the individuals below and it had become a living entity of its own. You could feel it, and maybe that's one reason the police held back, because it was scary to watch and feel this energy.

"In fact, the energy was so strong, that the average person could feel it. It was like the waves of congealed energy had become tangible, and you could not only feel this in the streets around the protest area, but the whole city was affected by the event. So no matter where they were, even if they were unaware of the riot, people were affected. They had this unconscious nervous energy, because there was something going on. And what was going on was a psychic trauma, which was transmitted through the circuit from living being to living being. So for that period of time, the energy of this trauma was very visible, for the whole city was affected, not just psychologically, but psychically. If you were aware, you could see it, because all of this negative energy had been compressed into a dark smoky cloud that hung over the city and moved across it in waves."

"Is this psychic influence like the hundred monkey phenomena?" I asked. I was referring to the story I had heard recounted again and again in which one monkey teaches other monkeys how to do something directly by example, so that gradually the custom spreads among those monkeys in contact with each other. But then, after the custom has spread beyond a critical point, say 100 monkeys doing it, there is no longer any need to teach by example. Instead, the activity spreads throughout the monkey population all over, as if it has traveled by some psychic or other non-physical link.

"Yes, this process is related," Michael replied. "There is this kind of psychic communication which is felt by the whole tribal community, once the communication reaches a critical mass. The reason this happens is because as we all cluster together in our social communities, whether they be cities or small tribal villages, we by our existence create a psychic network, web, or circuit, which we are all part of. Once you become psychically aware, you become aware of this pulse or feeling that connects everyone to this larger network. Even ordinary people who are not normally aware of this network are connected, though occasionally they may get glimmers of its existence, such as in that heavy feeling I described which spread out like a cloud over San Francisco. But people who are psychically aware and put out a lot of strong psychic energy, are not only more aware, but more connected, and they have more effect on what happens in this web, because they create a greater vibration through it."

"Then, what happens when you have this awareness of this network?" Greta wondered. "How do you use this connection?"

"Very easily," said Michael. "Someone who's aware can plug into it at any time. It's a little like turning on a radio, though for me and most people I know who tune into the circuit, it's mostly a background noise. We can feel the presence of others, but we don't tune into this circuit except in special circumstances. For example, I mainly just tune into it when I'm out on the street, and I have my psychic senses up to pick up on anything.

"In any event, when you do tune in on the circuit, you'll find that the individuals with real power stand out from the general noise in the background. They have a stronger, more powerful feel. There's a greater sharpness to their energy. So there's definitely a noticeable difference."

Michael snapped the book shut and turned to the blackboard behind him, where there was an image of a circle with five circles around it connected by five radiating lines.

"When you start off in practicing magic or shamanism," Michael continued, "this sends out a signal on the circuit. Your presence is felt, and others who are aware can feel you on this etheric or psychic level that interpenetrates with everyday reality. Then what happens depends on who picks you up, what your own feelings are, how you handle yourself, whether you are primarily working with positive, benevolent energy, and a variety of other factors."

He pointed to the diagram with circles on the board.

"This diagram will show what I mean by this circuit. The five outer circles represent the five senses, and the ordinary, conventional person is only aware of these basic senses and interacts within the limits of these senses. But once the sixth sense or psychic center is opened up, people become aware of another level of personal interaction, which is this circuit we have been discussing. As a result, they not only relate to others on the ordinary everyday plane of existence, but on the psychic level as well, which transcends the physical. In addition, they can relate to other beings on this higher level of existence that are part of this circuit."

Michael paused and pointed to a second diagram in which\ a center circle was connected to others outside it, and they were connected to each other by both straight and wavy lines. It looked something like this:

"What this represents," Michael explained, "is the way people interact when they have opened up their psychic center and are of greater or lesser psychic power. In this case, each person of greater or lesser psychic power, as represented by the circles, interacts with others around him on a physical level, represented by the straight lines. But each aware person can also interact on the psychic level, represented by the wavy lines of force, which connect all people. But while there may be this general connection, only those who have developed this awareness can regularly enter into communication with others on this level, because they have to be psychically open for others to notice them on the circuit. It's like your greater psychic development and openness makes you evident to others who have done the same.

"Or perhaps think of this system as like the ocean. Most people are at the bottom. They swim around, and they are concerned with chasing each other, eating each other, or just playing around with each other. But a few fish are powerful enough swimmers to rise to the surface, and these are like the individuals who work with magic. Plus there are some fish who rise to great heights, and they break through the surface to see another world above.

"Then, once on the surface, they can interact with other powerful fish who have similarly risen however they choose to interact -- positive, negative, it's up to the individual's choice. But the point is that once the individual rises up from the depths as a powerful shaman, or as a more powerful fish, as you will, he sends out a vibration that radiates in all directions along this higher level of being, and it travels like ripples of water upon the surface. In turn, others at this level or at the surface of the water are affected by these vibrations or ripples; they become aware that this other psychically developed being is now out there, and they can communicate back. Meanwhile, the people who are undeveloped, the fish who are at the bottom of the water, are totally unaware, because they have no knowledge of the surface."

"It sounds a little like Socrates' cave," I said. "He talks about people living in the darkness and seeing only the shadows on the wall; unaware of the light that exists above."

"I guess you could say that," Michael said. "Most people are asleep in the cave, and they need to realize there's another world of light. But when people do get up to the surface, when they climb out into the light and plug into the circuit, it doesn't mean they have plugged into a glorious, radiant world where all is sweetness and light. Rather it's a world of neutral psychic power. And once the person appears there, some psychically powerful people who are already there can respond to that person's vibration by being drawn to him in a positive, friendly way. However, the new person out on the circuit can also attract the sharks, who are attracted by this new vibration.

"So you have to be prepared for both, just as you would be on the physical level. For in effect, the rules of relationships and interaction are the same on both levels; it's just that in this spiritual or psychic world of the network, you are dealing with more power, and you are relating to people on a spiritual level, not in physical form. At the same time, both worlds are co-existing together, because we have both a physical and spiritual nature, and while we exist on the physical plane, we also exist as spirits on the spiritual plane simultaneously. In turn, the more aware we are of that spiritual world, the more evident our existence on that plane is for others. So the more potentially vulnerable you could be at the same time that you have more power. It's a central paradox. The more power you have, the more you are at risk. And yet the more power you also have to defend against that risk."

Michael paused for a moment as I caught up with my notes and then went on.

"It all balances out in the long run. The more power, the more sensitive you are, the more at risk, but the better you can defend yourself. However, the real problem which many people have as they develop their magical or shamanic skills is that they think they'll just work with these tools occasionally; they'll just make occasional trips into the spiritual world and then come back. But the point is that once you have developed your senses to a certain point, you can't go back, because you have this heightened awareness, so you live simultaneously on both levels of existence. You may intentionally lower or turn off your spiritual or metaphysical awareness at times, but it's still there to some extent. As a result, you are aware of both the physical and metaphysical as you go through the day, whether you want to be or not.

"For example, when I walk down the street, I'm seeing into both levels, whether I want to or not. That's why I sensed that strange energy that everyone was feeling all over the city when the riot happened. Or if there was a special energy affecting the whole nation, I could pick that up too. The reason I or anyone achieving a high level of sensitivity can pick up these larger energy currents, is because each individual is a cell in a many-celled connection of beings linked on the spiritual level. So a nation is not just a conglomeration of individuals, but a collection of spirits or spiritual beings that together make up one whole cohesive unit of beingness. It's like the nation, in fact the whole planet of human life, is a single connected organism on this spiritual level. So, with this greater attunement, you can sense these larger movements of energy through this single being."

"Does that mean people could sense when there is going to be an earthquake?" asked Greta.

"Yes, that too," said Michael. "Because there's this integrated connection between the spiritual and physical levels, and all people are linked to this spiritual web. For instance, shortly before a big earthquake hit in Armenia, I had a sensation that an earthquake was coming someplace; I just didn't know where.

"Then, too, because everyone is connected on this spiritual level, even though they aren't aware of this, they can be influenced in the way they act based on appeals to spiritual symbols which tap deep into the human psyche. For example, there have been individuals, who knowing this, have attempted to use metaphysical means to influence the course of history."

As an example, Michael described the rise of Hitler and the Nazis. "They weren't just a political movement," he explained. Hitler and many leaders were also part of an esoteric movement, aware of these metaphysical truths. So they were able to use these principles to invoke the very primal urges of the people to support their cause. For instance, they used magical symbols, rituals, and propaganda evoke not only the emotions of hatred and zealousness, but at the same time, they used these devices to unlock a great power within people that fueled these emotions even more, so they tapped into the essence of each person's being. In a sense, they were pulling on this core power which some in the Hindu tradition call the Kundalini, which can lie coiled like a snake within us. But then that power can be called forth to spread to all parts of the body, like a radiant beam of light energy.

"So when you draw on that energy from not just one person but from a collection of people, that energy from all of these people joins together and can be directed and manipulated to serve various group ends. The process is comparable to the creation of the cloud of hate I saw in San Francisco, though in the case of the Nazi's, that cloud of hate was magnified many times, as they had rallies, demonstrations, and other techniques they used to unify the nation behind their cause.

"In short, they were using the techniques of black magicians to get the people to respond on a very basic energy level, so they could then direct that energy to their own goals. Then, the result of channeling all this energy to their own uses had its expression on the material level, although in time, they ran into problems because they encountered some stiff military and political resistance. Additionally, there were many other individuals with strong metaphysical power on the circuit, who didn't like what the Nazis and Hitler were doing or had different ideas about what should happen in the world. So psychically these people took some actions to bring about the Nazi's defeat, and perhaps this contributed to many of the mistakes the Nazi's made that led them to fail."

"What individuals on the circuit?" I wanted to know.

But Michael thought it was time to get back to more practical, day-to-day effects of being in touch with the circuit, and he changed the subject.

"You can also be aware when you are in the presence of someone who has some psychic power, because of your own connection with the circuit. You can, of course, sense this personal power in other ways, such as reading a person's "hara" or energy center in the solar plexus, which we'll be doing when we get together again. One way to sense this power is if you feel a sense of a strong presence or tug on this psychic web."

Michael gave an example to illustrate. "This happened a few days ago when I was in the Beverly Hill library," he began. "There were about 200 people in the room reading books. Everything seemed very quiet, very ordinary. But as I was walking through, I got a strong feeling of another psychic presence in the room. I experienced this as a tug on the web, and I sensed the direction that it came from. So I turned in that direction. Then, as I glanced ahead casually, I saw a man at a table looking directly at me, and I could feel some power coming out of him. It's like he stood out from the rest of the group like a light bulb. So automatically, I immediately put up a shield around me, just in case, since I had no idea who this man was, and I didn't know anything about the source or intention of his power."

"What kind of a shield?" Greta asked.

"I just visualized a ring of energy around my waist at first," Michael replied. "Nothing complex. Then, when I felt a renewed surge of energy come from him, I put up the image of a banishing pentagram to bounce his energy back. I felt he was being a little intrusive on my presence. But perhaps he was doing so because he was aware of me, too, and sensed that I was also involved in psychic work."

"But what if he was just looking at you?" I asked, ever seeking some kind of proof. "How can you be sure he really was an especially powerful person?"

"Because I knew by my feelings," Michael replied with some annoyance that I was still asking for confirmations. "In any case, I confirmed my own suspicions by waiting until he walked away from what he was reading, and I went over to look at it. As I noticed, he was reading some books on the occult and witchcraft – not what your average person reads. Besides, he was dressed in black, and he looked like a sorcerer. In short, he was there on the circuit, and I felt it, and I proved it to myself." Michael glanced at me intently. "And hopefully to you."

"I've had that feeling myself when I've encountered some people," Greta observed, and Michael went on.

"So, what all of these examples about the circuit show, is that you want to try to be aware using your seeing, your feeling, your sense of energy, to notice the people and things all around you. Sense what's part of the background and what's part of the circuit. For example, go out and breathe in not just the night air, but try to feel the energies of the town you are in. Likewise, as you breathe in, try to sense the mood of the people, whether good or bad. And try to pick up with your breath a feeling of others around you who might have a achieved a similarly high level of awareness.

"In other words, you want to be as aware as possible all the time of the environment in which you move. And you don't want to just call on this awareness as a part of a ritual. Rather, make it part of your routine by becoming a part of that network so that you are aware of what's going on around you."

Then, Michael explained he had an exercise to show me which would help me become more aware.

"It's a training device we call 'Spy in the Sky,' and the idea is to move along the circuit and spot the other energies there which are more developed like your own."

Michael turned out the lights so the room was only lit by a few small candles. After I positioned myself comfortably on the couch, with my feet firmly against the floor and my palms up to be receptive, Michael quietly explained what he would do.

"I'll be guiding you over Hollywood and out to Glendale in the Valley. As we go, I don't want you to worry about seeing what's out there accurately. Instead, I'd like you to use your seeing or feeling to sense the energy. You want to experience the energy of the area as a whole. as a kind of energy blanket or cloud. Then, as you pass by, be aware of the people beneath this cloud, creating this cloud by the projection of their own energy. These projections are like little balls of light.

"At the same time, be aware of any bigger balls of light flying by. You may experience these as especially intense, especially powerful. Well, these are the individuals who are more developed psychically, and their energy has taken the form of these larger balls of light. Moreover, you can tell by the strength and quality of this energy whether the person is male or female, and how powerful he or she is, because each person leaves his or her own signature in this energy network. It's like leaving a handprint or a fingerprint -- no two prints are the same."

Then, Michael gave me some brief instructions to guide me along the way, leaving plenty of spaces in between for me to look around.

"You're traveling out of the house now, like a beam of pure consciousness... Now you're traveling along the canyon road ... Now you're flying along Sunset Boulevard... Now you're traveling on the coast road by the beach... Now you're moving along the freeway and you notice the houses below..."

Meanwhile, as I flew along, following Michael's voice, I tried to sense the feeling of the energy below, rather than focus on seeing particular landmarks or houses. As a result, everything below me soon became very fuzzy. Then, instead of seeing anything, I suddenly felt like I was moving through this cloud or field of energy which Michael had mentioned, and it seemed to move around me in a series of undulations or waves.

Here and there I noticed the energy was heavier or lighter, and then I saw the small pinpoints of light which Michael mentioned like street lights glowing in the evening fog, and some were even brighter, so they sent an energy beam back through the sky. The experience reminded me of hovering over a theater opening in which there was a beam scanning the horizon, except in this case, the fuzzy, meandering beam was radiating out from the small points of light which Michael said represented these psychic beings.

Then, Michael asked me to fly down even lower, so I could sense something about the lives of the people who were there.

"Again, don't try to see them," Michael cautioned. "Just feel them. Notice the quality of their energy. For example, does someone feel satisfied? Does someone feel pain? Then, see if you can tune in on the reasons for those feelings, and as you feel comfortable, feel those feelings yourself. For example, feel the satisfaction people have when they are winning or achieving something; notice their sense of loss when they haven't gained what they want."

Next , Michael asked me to stop at various sites along the way -- a park, a beach, the town of Malibu, the sprawling suburb of Glendale -- and at each stop, he asked me to sense the energy and notice the differences.

"Look at what you feel. Notice the quality of the light. What sort of textures do you feel? Is it heavy? Soft? Strong? Hard?"

Finally, Michael guided me back. As I returned to my normal state of consciousness, I felt like I had seen a kind of energy profile of the area, which reminded me of a relief map, with different heights and colors to mark the differences in the terrain below. Except in this case, the relief map was more like a large white filmy cloud, that had concentrations of whiteness and filmier and thicker sections here and there, to reflect the way the energy moved and shifted into different shapes and forms. And here and there through the cloud were bursts and sparkles of light, like sprays of pure energy, pouring out from the cloud and illuminating it with a brilliant luminescence.

After I described what I had seen, Michael observed: "Well, what you were seeing where these patterns of energy that form everywhere. It's like you were tuning into the network that exists apart and beyond the ordinary physical world. Then, from time to time, you experienced these more powerful psychic energies in the form of these bursts of energy or balls of light."

"But how is this trip different from ordinary astral or conscious projection?" I asked, describing a previous trip Michael had guided me on, in which I also flew over the hills of Hollywood and Beverly Hills and out to the ocean, while observing what I noticed below.

"The difference is that conscious projection focuses on the specific aspects of things. But this kind of travel is different, because you are concentrating on sensing the energy essence of things, rather than having a visual experience. So when you do this, you tune into the psychic circuit we've been talking about, rather than just focusing on the outward manifestations and forms. And that can be important for getting a general sense of how people are feeling or for picking up on the presence of people who are highly developed psychically. For example, you could get a sense of the mood of a city that way. You could even become aware of the location of a group of people working magically together by feeling that supercharged concentration of energy, when you tune into this circuit or blanket of energy."

Michael gave an example that happened to him about two years earlier when I was studying with him in the San Francisco Bay Area.

"When I tried this technique," he said, "I sensed that a particular magic group had established another branch, a kind of secret lodge, because I felt all this power when I was traveling through the circuit in the area. Later when I told one of the group's member's about it, she was at first very nervous, because the group was so secret. But then she confirmed it. I had been right."

Michael turned up the lights again.

"So you see, there are these subtle energies out there which you can perceive in various ways -- as lights, as feelings -- when you are tuned into the circuit. Some things, like the sorcerer I saw in the library are very blatant, and just about anyone can pick that power up with the slightest bit of awareness. But many other things are much more subtle, though you can sense them when you are highly trained, such as the existence of a lodge of people practicing black magic.

"And sometimes there are things you can pick up when you simply concentrate more deeply and discern what you are feeling. For instance, in many cases, I felt a negative intention coming from some people in a crowd. I couldn't see them, but I felt their presence. It was like their negative energy was sending out ripples through the crowd, and I could feel it hit me, like a kind of energy wave hitting my back, and so I focused more intently and swam deeper to try to identify the source of these feelings more directly."

"What sort of negative energy were you picking up?" Greta wondered.

"Maybe these were people who were just upset or angry about something," Michael replied." Maybe they were people who were feeling restless and frustrated because of the crowded street. Maybe they were people out there to steal, even people ready to respond and riot. The negative energy you pick up all depends on the situation. But with discernment, you can sense not only where this disharmony is, but perhaps even sense what it is all about, so you know if you need to take any immediate steps to protect yourself from the potential danger or whether it will just pass."

"Protect yourself how?" I asked.

"Well, you could use some of the psychic defense techniques we talked about earlier," Michael said, and I reflected back to the long lesson we had the previous week of my training and described in my earlier book SECRETS OF A SHAMAN. "But," Michael went on, "you could also change your signature or presence on the circuit as a way of concealing yourself."

I looked puzzled.

"Let me explain," said Michael. "When you learn to work with the "hara," the energy center located in the middle of your solar plexus, you become more conscious of how you feel to others, because you become aware of the shape of your own center as well as that of others."

Again, I thought back to the way Michael had described these centers as circles of light in the average person, which blossomed into mushroom light forms and later into dart or rocket-shaped forms as the person developed more psychically.

Michael continued. "Also, when you work with the hara, you become more conscious of your own feeling or signature out there, because you are better at seeing what other's centers are like and comparing them to your own. Then, because you are more aware of yourself and what you project out, because you are more aware of the trace you leave as you move about through the circuit, you can better sense what is outside and around yourself. Therefore, you can better pick up any dangers. At the same time, you can further protect yourself by changing your own signature or vibration on the circuit, so you become something else or literally disappear. It's like the chameleon on the tree branch who changes colors to blend in with the tree.

"Or perhaps think of it this way. Your own energy leaves a trail or footprint on the circuit, and once you become aware of what you look like, you can modify that look -- say by covering up the trail or brushing your footprints into nothingness. To do this, you must be tuned into the circuit; you must be able to perceive and make changes on this level. And to get that fine tuning, you must learn to open yourself up. For example, your channeling and color chakra exercises will help you do this."

I thought back to the previous week of training I had had. Now it seemed so far away, and I remembered I hadn't practiced these exercises for the past few days. I resolved to try again.

Then, as Michael described another incident where his awareness of the circuit helped him evade a sorcerer who was looking in on him mentally at 3 a.m., I had another question.

"But how can you be sure someone is really out there who has a negative intent or a particular level of power?"

I knew I was asking one of these prove-it-to-me questions, which probably couldn't be answered; yet still I sought some reassurance from Michael. It was like I was looking for explanations to the unexplainable, knowing it was unexplainable, yet still looking.

Michael glanced at me with some annoyance, as he often did when I asked such questions. It was as if he was throwing back the question to me with his unspoken reply: "How can you be so stupid?" or "Why are you here?"

But then, without saying anything, Michael replied: "You don't always get validation for these feelings you get when you are tuning into the circuit, just as you don't for other psychic insights and perceptions. In fact, much of the time you just feel a strong vibration or sense of difference in the level or intention of the consciousness around you, and you don't always have a chance to check it out, like I did in the library. So usually, you just have to trust your perceptions or feelings. But if you do verify when you can, you will find you are usually correct when you are plugged into this circuit. Then, this validation for those things you can check can help reassure you that your awareness, your intuition is correct at other times. In any case, that's the best I can do in helping you determine if your senses, if anyone's senses, are accurate. After that you have to trust and believe."

"Trust and believe." I had heard Michael say these same words to me so many times before. "Trust and believe." Ultimately most of what Michael was teaching me came back to that.

"I'll try," I said quietly, and Michael continued the lesson.

"So now we've talked about two of the major types of people who are out there on the psychic or astral level in the city -- the average individual and the people who have developed psychically. You can call them what you want -- shamans, sorcerers, occultists, psychics, witches. Another aspect of this circuit is represented by the crazies or psychopaths you may encounter from time to time. It's like the experience you had under the Santa Monica pier."

My experience under the pier. I had to think back hard to the week before to remember, because at the time, I had just thought of the experience as fairly ordinary. I had been wandering along the beach on my second day in Santa Monica, and it was the late afternoon, about four p.m., about a half-hour before the sun would go down since it was the end of December. As I walked under the pier, immediately, I felt enclosed by the darkness and the musty smell that pervaded the area. All around me I saw the posts supporting the pier standing like shadowy warriors, and I felt the same somberness and heaviness that

I had experienced a couple of times before, when I drove or walked through a cemetery at night. In both cases, the atmosphere felt very eerie and frightening, although no one was there and there was no visible threat of danger.

"How does my experience under the pier connect to this part of the circuit?" I asked.

"Very simply," Michael said. "You were sensing some kind of evil presence under there, although you didn't know this at the time. And you were experiencing that, because the Santa Monica pier has long been a known hang-out for assorted crazies and criminal types, and there have been many crimes under there. You see, there's a signature on the circuit associated with the mentally ill, and it's even stronger for the criminal mentally ill. They leave their trace, since they have a qualitatively different kind of energy from others. So when you were under the pier, you weren't feeling that way just because it was dark and perhaps a little smelly from the salt-water and leavings of the sea. Rather, you were experiencing the energy left there by some not so savory people."

Greta cut in. "Yes, that's very true. There have been a lot of rapes, tortures, murders, and all sorts of very violent crimes under there, and even the average person gets uncomfortable there. There's so much blood energy under that pier, it's incredible."

"So," Michael went on, "that feeling you got is a signature. It's the signature left on the circuit by multiple cases of craziness and violence. And you could sense that, because violence leaves its own distinctive presence, and you can tell the difference between that and the presence of a highly developed individual or sorcerer."

"Is that why when someone is killed in a house, other people often report feeling funny there?" I asked.

"Sure," replied Michael. "There's a signature there."

Then, Michael described how he had experienced these kinds of signatures of violence himself, when he worked many years before as a patrol officer for about two years.

"I spent a lot of time answering alarms and burglaries," he said. "And often, while I did so, I sensed the presence or signature of the criminals I was looking for. Then, they would be there, and that helped me track them down or capture them.

"The reason I could do this, is because you can feel this distinctive presence of the criminal, much like you can feel the presence of past violence or can distinguish the presence of another shaman or sorcerer. The truly evil or criminal individual has a distinctive aura and a distinctive energy level, and one advantage of the shaman over the average person is he can feel the presence of the truly malevolent person. He can feel the malevolence. Some ordinary people can do this, but most people don't have that extra sense. It's a little like having the sharp smell of an animal to smell a predator in the jungle. The shaman has that trained awareness, and he can protect himself accordingly."

"What about on a day-to-day level of dealing with people who seem honest but really aren't and have evil intentions underneath?" I asked.

Then, to illustrate, I described a traumatic experience I had when a man I met purported to be a book publisher and seemed enthusiastic about publishing a children's story I had written based on some dolls I had developed with a woman who made the dolls using a concept I suggested. However, over the next few weeks, after I introduced this man to the doll maker, he began introducing changes into my original concept. First, he made some changes in the character's physical features; then their name, and then he rewrote my original story. Finally, he suggested that I had supplied nothing to the project, and that the dolls and book had become a collaboration between him and the doll maker.

As it turned out, the man never had the money he claimed to produce the purported book, and so his threat to take the project away from me collapsed in a heap. However, due to all the confusion he sowed, the doll manufacturer which had offered the contract never produced the dolls. And later I found out this man had worked his way through several other groups in the publishing field by making false claims about who he was and what he could do, although eventually other people caught onto his game, and in time he left these groups.

"That's a classic example," said Michael. "At the time, you weren't sensitive enough to pick up his malevolence, and it would appear that neither were these other people, so he was able to ingratiate himself with people for awhile, before trying to bleed them like a leech. But once you get tuned into the circuit, you can notice such things and take the appropriate action, because you can tell the difference between the aura or energy of the criminal or madman and the average person or shaman, and you can even tell the difference between different kinds of psychically developed people."

"So what should I look for to make these distinctions?" I wondered.

"Well, you can start by paying attention to such things as the strength of the energy. Notice its weight. Does it feel light or heavy? Notice if it seems to be steady or scattered. Feel if it seems gentle and comforting, or if you get a sensation of danger. It's very hard to explain, because in the end, you'll get a sense of the energy of the circuit in a very holistic way that will signal you as to what kind of person you are meeting or feeling. Then, almost at once, you will both interpret and react to what you perceive or feel, so you can take the appropriate action.

"For example, one key difference is that the energy of the psychically developed person will feel stronger, more focused, and yet lighter, if that person uses his abilities benignly. But if the person is involved in things like the black arts, you might feel a heaviness in his aura. On the other hand, when the person is both malevolent and insane, you may experience the energy as being very scattered though very strong. And you may feel this kind of jagged, knife-like quality to the energy when there is a threat or danger.

"However, since each person is different, you may experience these energies in different ways. The main point is to understand there are these differences, so you can watch out for them. Then, as you become more discerning, you can better sense what you are actually picking up – an average person, a psychically developed person, a criminal or a crazy. Then, you will better know how to react."

And with that Michael concluded the lesson. As he explained, we would take a break, and then he would tell us about the other types of beings who inhabited the modern urban city along with the various types of humans he had just described.

"These are the ghosts of the modern city," he said, "and that's what we'll talk about next."

3

LEARNING ABOUT THE GHOSTS OF THE CITY

"Ghosts?" I said, sounding incredulous, when we returned from our break in the kitchen.

"Yes, ghosts," said Michael. "There are real ghosts out there. It's not just some people's imagination or some non-ghostly explanation, such as the claim some people make that

poltergeist phenomena is simply accumulated psychic energy from someone, usually a teenager, under a great deal of stress. So now we'll talk about ghosts."

I opened up my notebook and turned on my tape recorder again.

"Now," Michael began, "the first type of ghost some people encounter is the phantom pedestrian or derelict. This is essentially the person you see briefly who looks very real, but suddenly the person vanishes, because the person wasn't real in the first place. The vision was just a phantom or ghost."

"An illusion?" I asked.

"No, it's not just an imaginary vision, but of something real. For example, I and many individuals who have trained with me have seen individuals who appeared to be standing on the corner step off the curb, and then they vanished."

"But maybe they just lost the person in a crowd," I suggested. "Or maybe they just saw something that looked like a person, but it really wasn't when they got closer."

I described my own experience that had happened earlier that night on my way to class.

"I was driving in the rain and it was already dark. Then, as I pulled off the freeway, I saw what looked like a woman carrying a bag at the corner of the intersection. But when I got to the intersection, I saw it was a sign. So I could have easily thought this was a person because of the darkness and the rain. So how do you distinguish between what's real and what's not?"

"Well, in that case, what you saw could very well have been the sign, though it could be doubtful. So it could be worth it to check it out a little further. For example, was the woman you saw tall enough to correspond to the height of the sign?"

I said she was.

"Then, perhaps in this case you did see the sign as a woman. However, we have had numerous experiences where we have seen a person about to cross a street, and there is nothing there and nowhere to vanish to. They're not walking up the street and haven't crossed it. They're just not there anymore. And in many cases, there's no sign or anything like you experienced that they could be confused with, although in other cases, the sighting could be as doubtful as what you mentioned.

"So it's hard to say. For example, there's a chance that the woman you saw with the bag might have been a phantom of a pedestrian who got killed crossing the street without looking. It's one of the most common forms of death in this city. On the other hand, you may have just seen a sign. In any case, no matter what you saw or didn't, there are many, many cases where there is no doubt; where people do see these vanishing pedestrians or derelicts.

"And there's a very good reason why people do see such ghosts or spirits. For often these are wandering beings who have just experienced death."

"Wandering beings?" I glanced up from my notebook in surprise.

"Why are they wandering?" asked Greta.

"They're wandering," said Michael, "because it may be some time before they are aware they died, or some may know it, but they don't feel ready yet to move on. So they wander.

"For example, the skid row in a city usually has a lot of ghosts. They are people who died from exposure, and now they wander the streets as half-glimpsed phantoms. In fact, I've had many experiences of that myself. Many times when I was walking along in the area, I saw someone out of the corner of my eye, but whatever I saw vanished as I approached.

"These kinds of fleeting observations continually occur, and often people aren't aware that they have seen anything peculiar, because often, we're moving so fast in the city, that we don't stop to think about these kinds of things; we don't pay attention. So we don't look to see if the person we have just seen really crosses the street or ceases to be. We just assume that everything we see is perfectly ordinary and don't keep track. But under some conditions, it is possible to recognize that we have had a glimpse of such phantoms; we have had a look into this hidden netherworld of alternate realities and other beings."

Michael suggested I should think back to my experiences in seeing people on the street.

"But I'm not on the streets that much," I said. I explained that I usually worked at home or just hopped in my car to go places, so I hadn't really noticed such things very much.

"Well," said Michael, "if you do something where you are on the street a lot, such as working on an ambulance or on patrol as I have, you may become very conscious of this other reality, because of the experiences you have. For example, one common experience that many people on the streets have is walking along, and then they hear other footsteps. But when they turn to look, no one is there."

"But...but..." I started to interrupt, but Michael continued.

"Now, I know, you may try to explain this away. Just a mistaken impression, maybe because the person is nervous. But is it a mistake? Try telling that to someone when the footsteps seem to get louder and louder, but then he turns, and no one is there."

"Or maybe think about it this way," said Greta. "Some people tend to attract a great deal of ghostly energy to them. Everywhere they go, they seem to see or hear something. But other people see nothing, and nothing much seems to happen around them, such as in your case. But the reason has nothing to do with their lack of ability or psychic development. Rather it could be something about their aura or energy level, so the spirits don't respond to them and stay away. For example, a person could put out a sense of 'don't mess with me,' and so the spirits do just that. So maybe that's why you haven't had such experiences," said Greta.

"Anyway," Michael continued, "many people without any developed psychic skills have run into these ghosts. Often people try to deny them or find alternate reasons to explain what they have just seen. But these ghosts do exist."

Michael paused for a moment, and looked at me keenly, a little li ke a lawyer resting a case, and then continued.

"Now, who are these ghosts? One type are vagrants who have died. Some are people who have died and don't know where to go. There are murder victims and people who have died violently. And not only houses, but places associated with violence and death have ghosts. Like hospitals, for example."

"I know, that's true," said Greta, who had spent a great deal of time going into hospitals, when she worked for an ambulance company. "I've seen them myself."

She gave a few examples. "There was one hospital I went to that had a ghost in its elevator. The hospital was always having elevator problems, too. Commonly, one elevator was always broken down, when we took patients there each day. Also, there was one elevator that nobody wanted to get on. Again and again, we would see people refuse when it stopped, and they would get on another elevator and tell us we should wait too. As one person told us, the reason this elevator was so scary is an old nurse haunted the elevator, and when the elevator got stuck between floors she would appear.

"Well, one day, we got tired of waiting for the other elevators, so we took this elevator anyway. Then, we saw her. It was really gruesome. Her face just melted away. Her eyes were all popped out, and she looked disgusting. I can see why everyone wanted to avoid that elevator. But then, no one knows exactly why she was there."

"You see!" Michael said to me, as if I was a jury, and this was one more bit of evidence to prove his case.

Then, Greta gave another example. "This one involves a nurse that died of a heart attack. She called in an hour before her shift to say she was sick. Then, she had a cardiac arrest, and when the paramedics showed up to take her to the hospital, she was already dead, and they pronounced her dead in the emergency room. However, no one at the convalescent hospital where she worked knew she had died.

"Later that night, she appeared on the ward at her usual time, and her patients saw a half-form of her appear in their rooms. She was only there from the waist up, and she went around from room to room checking her patients. Well, every one of her patients rang the bell about 15 minutes apart, which is the time it would usually take her to go from patient to patient, and they called to say: 'You won't believe what I have just seen.' It was incredible. Everyone reported the same thing. So the other two nurses on the shift decided to check this out, and they waited for two hours. Then, they looked in on the patients she would normally check on her rounds, and they saw her do her shift. In fact, she did it for two weeks before she finally left."

"So she gave them two weeks notice," Michael commented, and we laughed.

"In any case," Michael continued, "you hear a lot of these stories occurring in the medical field, because the people there are dealing with death all the time. Also, you hear a lot of such stories in the field of security and police work, too, for the same reason. And it's important to realize that the people encountering such things are seasoned professionals, and they are expected to be serious, rational individuals. And these things are happening in modern facilities, too.

In fact, many trained professionals don't believe in such things, but that doesn't prevent this from happening to them."

Again Michael looked at me intently, and again I felt like a juror hearing a case.

"Okay," I said, and Michael went on.

"Now, there are other kinds of ghosts -- such things as phantom houses, cars, trees, and aircrafts. These are things that people see, even interact with. But then, these things disappear because they aren't real."

Michael gave an example. "For instance, when I was teaching in Berkeley a few years ago, a man I knew told me he was walking down the street one day, when he met a beautiful woman in long black hair. She looked very ordinary, he thought, in about her 20's and wearing a colorful rainbow dress. After they talked for a bit, she invited him to a party, gave him the address of the house, and left.

"That night he went to the location, and it was a very old house, a Victorian, and he walked inside, since the door was open. There he was met by this woman and several other people, and immediately, he found them very weird. The man didn't go into detail, but he said he felt very uncomfortable, when the woman kept urging him to go upstairs into her bedroom. But he felt there was something strange about the whole situation. So finally he left, though normally he might have jumped at such an opportunity. But in this case, he felt scared, though he couldn't understand why, and he didn't want to go upstairs.

"After he left, the experience bothered him. So the next day, he went back to check out the location. But he found no house there. The Victorian house was gone, and there was a very different house there instead. It had different architecture, a different number for the address, and when he asked a few people in the houses near where the Victorian was supposed to be, they looked at him strangely and said there were no such individuals there."

"So assuming he just didn't go to the wrong street, how would you explain that?" I asked.

"Well, he didn't make a mistake. It was the same street. He used the same directions he had already written down. So to explain it, I would say that the interaction he had with this woman and the house was like working with a gateway. He interacted with another plane of existence that exists adjacent to our own. So what he saw was a ghost woman and a ghost house. He experienced them for a brief moment in time, when they appeared through the gateway, and then they disappeared back into the gateway from which they came."

I glanced at Michael quizzically, but he ignored my questioning gaze and went on.

"Now this kind of experience is more common than many people think. For example, many individuals, especially hitchhikers, have had the experience of arriving in a small town on the highway. In fact, I've heard many of these stories from people in Texas. What typically happens is that the person stops off in a town, but he finds the experience very odd. He isn't sure what's wrong, but he feels very strange. Then, later when he goes back, he is unable to locate the town. Either he finds that no town exists there at all, or he comes back to the town, but it's different than the one he visited. There are different people, different buildings. He's in a different place."

Michael reminded me of his own experience, which he once told me about and I described in a previous book THE SHAMAN WARRIOR.

"You remember how Paul and I stopped off at that Safeway along the highway between San Francisco and Los Angeles. It seemed to be in the middle of this very isolated area. Just flat plains and farmland. We felt very weird, so we left, and when we came back, the place was gone. That's an example of this kind of things. You didn't believe me when I told you then."

So did I now, I asked myself. I wasn't sure.

Suddenly, Greta interrupted my train of thought. "There are also phantom shopping malls," Greta said. "I've heard lots of stories."

"Another thing is phantom cars," Michael continued. "An interesting manifestation of our high tech society. You're driving along, and these apparitions suddenly appear on the road."

Michael gave an example. "I was with a student and we were driving up a lonely canyon road in the early evening when it was still light, when a white Mustang started tail-gating us. We tried to speed up to get away, but it rammed our rear, and we were panic-stricken. Who was doing this to us? Then we looked back to see who was driving and we saw no driver. There was no one at the steering wheel. So we were even more frightened, and as we kept going, the car followed us closely. Then, as we came through hairpin turn, we suddenly noticed the vehicle was gone, and there was nowhere it could go, since there were no driveways or side roads off that turn. It was simply gone. And it didn't fall off the road either, since we would have heard that."

"So why should something like that follow you?" I asked.

"Who knows?" Michael said. "Maybe it didn't like us. Maybe it was feeling angry in general, and we just happened to be there. There could be any number of reasons for an unpleasant or out-of-the-ordinary interaction. The point is the experience happened; and while it did, the car seemed very real."

Greta then described her own experience with a phantom car, which appeared as the same white Mustang.

"I encountered it, too. It came up behind me several times and followed me. But in my case, it wasn't mean or vicious. Rather, it seemed to appear to me as a warning, like it was telling me when I should slow down or should watch out for something that was about to happen. For example, one time it prevented me from having a head-on collision. I saw the car behind me, looked around to see what was happening, and I saw this other car coming towards me, and I veered out of the way. Another time, I saw the Mustang, and I slowed down as I was going around a turn, and if I didn't, I would have hit a car that was speeding towards me."

"So these phantoms can sometimes be helpful as well as harmful," Michael said. "And remember, these are just mechanical objects we are talking about. But it's like they have a mind and a soul."

I glanced at Michael with a puzzled look. "A mind and a soul," I repeated.

"Perhaps," Michael said. "After all, human ghosts often appear because they are troubled or have links that keep them tied to a particular place, so they aren't ready to leave. Well, in the case of a phantom car, perhaps the car also experienced some kind of problem, such as going over a cliff or maybe it exploded. So, in a sense, it experienced the car equivalent of a very violent death. Maybe that's what happened to that white Mustang, both Greta and I encountered. Possibly it's at the bottom of the canyon. Or maybe it was destroyed in a head-on collision itself."

"That's pretty far out," I commented.

"Well, it's just a theory," said Michael. "You can make of it what you want."

Then, Michael changed the subject. "There are also stories about the ghosts of truckers, such as the trucker who helps people on a rainy night."

Immediately, Greta cut in with her own story of such an incident.

"Where I come from out near the Mojave Desert, there's a story about a trucker who appears on the road through the desert, on 395. As I heard many people tell me, if someone is going north on a rainy day and they break down, there's a truck that will come by to help them. But it's a phantom truck, and when people report it, they all say the same thing. They identify the truck, they give the name of the company that owns it, they give the license plate number. But it doesn't exist, because when the police have checked it out, there's no license issued to the car, there's no such license plate number. And in a few cases, when the police have called the company phone number, they find that the phone has been disconnected."

"What kind of reports have people made about being helped by this truck?" I asked.

"Oh, they get a ride into town," said Greta. "The trucker stops, and people get in, and he gets them to a place where they can get help. In fact, the California Highway Patrol in the area is very aware of this. They have written down the information people have given them on the truck. But then it doesn't show up in their computer, which means no registration has been issued on it in over five years."

I wrote down Greta's story without comment, though part of me was still asking questions. Could there be other explanations? Could these people have been mistaken? Could they have simply given the wrong name or license plate number for the truck? Yet, Greta seemed so certain and described her story so matter-of-factly, like this was simply another type of ghost. Why didn't I just accept that?

Then, Michael described still another kind of ghost, the rider on a motorcycle, and Greta chimed in with her own experience of such an encounter.

"I was passing an intersection near Torrance, where a CHP police officer was killed several months before," Greta began. "I pulled into the intersection, and suddenly, the lights turned red in all four directions, and right after that I spotted a CHP officer coming up the eastbound on-ramp. Then, he turned onto the freeway and disappeared into the traffic. What was so unusual about that is this was not a regular CHP officer, because all I could see was the uniform, but there was no body in it. It was just the uniform, and the officer's helmet, but nothing inside. And I'm not the only one who saw it. It was broad daylight, about two in the afternoon, and there were other people in cars on the street, as well as a few people standing at the light ready to cross. They all looked in the direction of the officer with a look of total shock."

"But what about..." I started to interrupt, but Greta continued on anticipating what I was going to say.

"And it wasn't just an illusion. I had a clear view of the entire ramp. There were no trees, no bushes, no signs in the way. And everyone else saw the officer whiz by, too."

Michael cut in. "So there, you have another example of modern ghostly phenomena. Clothing, but nothing there. This is like the modern version of some of the old stories you hear about armor moving, but then there's nothing in the armor. So here you have another example about how the average person has encountered a glimpse of this hidden city; he's seen some of the ghosts that haunt it."

I tried to remember back to note if I had ever experienced anything like the ghost stories that Michael and Greta were telling me. But all I could remember were seeing images of Dr. Jekyll and Mr. Hyde in the curtains of my bedroom when I was three or four, after my parents had read me the story. Then there was a time when I was running around the basement of my old apartment building, when I was about nine with a group of kids, and we heard footsteps coming after us. I had heard rumors of an old superintendant that haunted the building, but this time the real superintendant had shown up to kick us out, so those footsteps could have easily been his, although they sounded like they were coming from behind the wall. Then, as I grew up, I put all thoughts of ghosts and spirits out of my mind. But now, here I was, listening to a series of ghost stories, which Michael and Greta claimed were very true. It was like being projected back to my childhood again, when I quietly listened in school and at camp to these wondrous tales of mystical ghosts and their special powers.

"Now another type of ghost," Michael continued, "is the ghost of an animal," and I snapped back to attention. "Their ghosts sometimes hang around when the animal has been killed somewhere or if it misses its owner. For example, I encountered a cat ghost once when I was riding in a car with another patrol officer around three in the morning. We were cruising around various locations in Beverly Hills, when a cat suddenly ran out right in front of our vehicle. I heard the vehicle hit the cat with a thud, and I heard the crunch of the cat going under the vehicle. So we stopped immediately and got out with a light. But when we looked under the car there was nothing there. Then, we searched nearby in the grass and bushes, but nothing."

"Maybe it got out and crawled away," I suggested.

"No, if it had been a real cat," said Michael, it would be nearby or under the vehicle. Within seconds, we were out of the car looking for it. It couldn't just do a quick disappearing act like that. Not if it was a normal cat."

"I guess so," I said, and I remembered back to when my own cat had been hit by a car, and my parents and I had carried his nearly lifeless body from under the wheels, and thereafter took a few months nursing him back to health.

"Now sometimes," Michael continued, "it can be hard to tell whether something is actually a ghost, or perhaps it could be some form of elemental or spirit. For instance, in one patrol company I worked for, several patrolmen told me about some kind of spirit they encountered, which they called Captain Fear or the Electric Ghost, because it lit up the area when it appeared.

"They told me the story when I first started working for them, and as they described it, there was an old ranch in the Santa Clarita Valley, and for many years, people lived very quietly there. Then, a real estate developer came and built a cluster of new houses in a suburban neighborhood. But almost from the beginning of the project, there were mishaps, as if something didn't want the project there. For instance, a tractor parked at the top of the slope where he was building the houses suddenly had its brakes give out for no reason, and it started down the slope, although they were able to stop it before it crashed to the bottom. Then, a little later, when Paul got a job as a construction worker on the site, one of the worker's vehicles suddenly lost its brakes, and it crashed into a dumpster.

"At first, the workers at the site tried to ignore these incidents, but it became especially obvious that something strange was going on when the company hired the patrol company I later began working for to guard the site overnight from vandalism and theft. One security guard described how he began walking up the street from his car to the site, and he had left his car radio off. When he got halfway up the street, his car radio suddenly turned on very loudly. He went back to the car and shut it off and started back to continue his rounds. But once more, he heard the radio in the vehicle turn back on again."

"A vandal maybe?" I suggested.

"No," Michael said firmly. "The man had a clear view of the vehicle and no one was around. Then, later that night, as he was doing his rounds, he was showered by big rocks, although he could find no source for the attack. Later his relief officer experienced something very strange too. Now, this officer was a very tough fellow, very aggressive, and a very straight-laced, church-going type. He wasn't into anything occult or metaphysical. Just an ordinary normal guy. However, while he was on his rounds, he saw something strange inside one of the houses being built, and it scared him so much, he deserted his post and drove home. Afterwards, he refused to talk about what he saw. But he saw something, though he wasn't the kind of person who believed in ghosts.

"Then, after his experience, numerous other officers in the company reported seeing unusual glowing lights in the houses and had rocks thrown at them or experienced some of the other problems I already described. In fact, one patrol officer told me he was approached by these glowing lights while he was inspecting the site and received an electric shock when one of these lights touched him, which is how this spirit or whatever it is got the name of the Electric Ghosts."

"That's quite a story," said Greta.

"But that's not all," said Michael. "After I heard this story from the security officers,

I decided to check it out myself. So I drove there in my patrol car and parked my car on the slope. Then, I started walking. Now, I didn't know about the problems with the brakes or the tractor at the time, since I didn't meet Paul till later. But suddenly, as I was walking, I felt I should go back to my vehicle and park it on the flatter ground further down below or the brakes would give way. So I moved the vehicle. Then, as a precaution, I visualized a strong protective circle around my car, sealing it off from any psychic energies that might attack it. I got this strong vibration of danger from the area, and I felt I had to take these special steps just in case.

"Then, as if I was doing my regular rounds, I went out to check out the buildings being built and see if the spirit was there or if I could contact him. Well, as I walked from house to house, I felt the spirit was in the house ahead of me, as if it was moving to hide from me, and when I got to the end of the street, I look back and a saw things that looked like little balls of heat flying around my car. Then, they began bouncing against it, like gnats trying to get in. Then, I felt this sense of great agitation, like jagged ripples in the energy, as if they were angry because they couldn't get in.

"So I rushed back to my car, got in quickly, and drove out of the housing project. As I drove, I could feel the waves of energy following me, and as I picked up speed, so did these energy balls. I floored the car, wanting to get away from these things, and as I got to the gate, I visualized a strong protective wall of energy behind me as I left. In moments, I saw a flash, and I saw an intense vibration in this wall of energy, as these lights or beings or whatever they were smashed into it."

"How could you tell if this was a ghost or some other kind of energy form?" asked Greta.

"By going back, by checking out the place and the energy more closely. However, in this case, I didn't want to. I had enough. In any event, this is an example where you have both ordinary men and myself as a shaman encountering these unordinary beings, and as you can see, at times these beings can be perceptible to both, and as a shaman I was able to do something about them. I was able to use protective devices, such as the circle around my car and the wall, to keep them out."

"So what will happen to the people who move in there?" Greta wondered.

She described a case where some friends of a friend had bought a house back East, and over a period of time odd things happened. They found some of their china broken on the floor one morning; they heard a crash one night and found a shelf had collapsed; and subsequently they experienced other crashing noises and breakages.

"It's an unfortunate situation ," said Michael. "Probably the people who move in will continue to suffer from poltergeist phenomena for awhile, and anyone with psychic ability will probably experience this even more intensely. The reason for this is the energy there is already disturbed, perhaps because of some of the disturbances that occurred to the land in the course of construction. So it's likely the problem will continue until the ghost, spirit, or whatever is haunting the place gives up, or until someone who knows what they are doing takes some steps to clear out the place with some kind of cleansing or exorcism. But since many people may not believe in this ... " Michael looked intently at me, " ... nothing may be done, and so the problem may go on for much longer than it might otherwise.

"You see," he continued, "people keep trying to deny these kinds of things. They don't want to believe in this hidden city. It's hard enough trying to live in the real one and deal with all the real threats and dangers. Yes, it can be easy to deny these strange noises or lights; and often the average person doesn't even hear them. Yet, these incidents still continue. It's as if the hidden world is saying, 'Look at me...I'm here...Don't forget.' And so there are these continual glimpses of this other world."

Michael described another story from his patrol days to illustrate. This time, he received a call on his patrol car radio that a woman had seen a prowler in her backyard who was trying to break in, and his company alerted the Los Angeles Police Department, which dispatched a car with two men for back-up. At first, the incident seemed perfectly ordinary. Michael went over immediately; the woman let him in; and he checked through the house, though he found nothing amiss. The doors were all locked and there was no sign of a break-in. Then, suddenly, Michael began to hear odd noises.

"It sounded like there were boots walking on wooden planks," Michael said. "So I asked the woman if she had a deck or a wooden patio, but she said no, though there was an attic. So I went up to check it. I used my flashlight, and went up with my gun drawn. But nothing. Though I still heard noises, and the woman complained about them, too.

"Then, the LAPD arrived and after I explained the situation, we all went out to check the yard, since now it sounded like the noises were coming from there. The two cops from the LAPD were hearing this too. It was just like what happened in the attic. After we told the lady to stay inside, we searched around with our flashlights, but couldn't find anything unusual, though the noises continued.

"Then, suddenly, as we were out in the yard, the noises seemed to change in quality. Instead of sounding like footsteps on the ground, they seemed to acquire a hollow booming quality and their elevation changed as well. For now it sounded like they were coming from the roof. Then, they turned into loud booming noises, like a person beating on a drum to imitate the sound of footsteps. Soon the noise seemed to emanate from the air above the house, and in a few more moments, the beating became even louder and seemed to come from the clouds.

"Meanwhile, the policemen with me were hearing this, too, and we kept shining our flashlights higher and higher. But we saw nothing

-- just the wisps of fog illuminated by our beams, because it was a slightly foggy night."

"So we got ready to leave, and I asked the senior officer if he planned to write this up. 'Are you kidding?' he told me, and when we came back into the house, he told the woman that no one was there. But it was obvious the officers were a little shaken up by the incident. We had all heard something very distinctly, and the noises had suddenly ended up coming from the thin air, though we saw nothing.

"Then things got even weirder as we prepared to leave. I called in to get my next assignment, and my company said there were reports coming in of explosions all over the neighborhood near where we had been. So the police and I went on a search of the local area. When we went to a high spot to look for possible fires or evidence of combustion, we couldn't see anything. But we heard loud noises that sounded like exploding cannons. But nothing was there."

I tried to think of possible physical explanations of the phenomena, when Greta cut in.

"I actually saw the being."

Then, she described her own ghost story about the site. At the time, she was working patrol for the same company as Michael, although her shift was during the day, and shortly after Michael's experience, she received a report of a person going across the backyard and trying to get in through the door. She drove over and was joined by two officers from the LAPD.

"It was much like what happened with Michael," she told me. "We went around the back on foot, but saw nothing. We even looked in the soft ground for footprints, and checked the grass for broken grass blades, suggesting a person had been there, but nothing.

"Then, we heard some footsteps coming from about 20 feet away near some bushes at the rear of the property, and when we looked up, I saw a shadowy form which looked like a human being, though it was all fuzzy and distorted, like seeing something in a heat wave. The man looked like he was about 6'3", about 230 pounds, and the police officers said they saw the image of the man, too. But we decided not to tell the woman, and when the police wrote up their report, they said they didn't find anything. So this incident wasn't reported either."

"So you see," said Michael, "this is another confirmation for the existence of these things. But this report didn't make it into the official records either, because people have trouble with these things. They don't know to acknowledge them; they don't want to believe."

Michael had one more patrol ghost story to tell me. An alarm had gone off in a suburban house which had motion detectors, and Michael's security company sent him to check on this as a possible burglary. When he arrived, he met his LAPD back-up, and they entered through an open door. The alarm was still ringing in the first room they entered, but they could see nothing. Then, the alarm in the next room went off. But again, when they moved into that room, there was nothing.

"It was very strange," Michael observed. "As we moved about from room to room, the alarm would go off in the room ahead of us, but each time we checked -- and we looked in the closets, under the furniture, anyplace someone could hide -- we didn't see anyone. I even called my dispatcher after this had happened in several rooms, and she said something there was triggering the photoelectric motion detectors, and we seemed to be just behind it catching up. So we continued on upstairs, and eventually we got to the last possible room. But again, there was nothing. Our own presence was registering on these motion detectors, and so was the presence of whatever it is we were following. So this other thing was triggering these detectors, but it wasn't visible. And we never actually saw it."

I wondered if it could be the wind, or maybe even the sunlight triggering these detectors.

"No, no, that's not possible," responded Michael. "Remember we're in a closed house, and the windows are closed, and in many of the rooms, the blinds are drawn. Besides, these detectors are designed to pick-up the movements of physical bodies passing by them, and when something cuts across the beam that sets off an alarm. So if someone moves from room to room, the sensors go off in sequence, which is what happened. So all indicators were suggesting a prowler. And when we got to the last room, there was no where else to go. But nothing was there.

"Anyway, since then, other people living in the area have claimed this old house was haunted, and that's what I think it was. We were dealing with some sort of ghost or supernatural presence, since there is no physical explanation for what we saw."

"So why should this being choose that particular house?" I asked.

"It's hard to say, unless you know the history of the house, and even then, there could be various reasons. For example, sometimes the energy is there because something happened, such as a murder, or the person who lived in the house died there, or maybe the aura or energy of the person living there might attract something. In this case, the house was old and it was the home of a movie star who had a reputation as a fairly unpleasant, sleazy character. So perhaps he drew some kind of being there. But no one knows."

Then, Michael went on to talk about one last type of ghostly being in the hidden city, the vampire or being that draws its existence by sucking energy from others. Again, Michael had a patrol story to illustrate his encounter.

"I saw him several times around the Wonderland Park area in L.A. when I was on patrol," Michael began, "and Greta did too. He came out around twilight, and he appeared as the image of a man walking up the street, wearing a trench coat. He was very tall, about 6 feet, balding on the top of his head, clean shaven, and fat. But the strange thing about him was that he was all gray, like he had no blood in him, and he had these metallic-like eyes, like steel.

"I remember when I first saw him, I was driving down the street, and I saw him standing by the side of the road. He smiled at me as I drove by, and I saw he had these large canine teeth, and I wanted to move as far away from him as possible. I felt this really creepy energy around him, and it made me literally quake inside. I felt like he might even reach out and grab me, and I wanted to get away. Later, I saw him a number of times after that, since he lived in the area."

"How is he different as a being from these other beings you've been describing?" I asked.

"He's different," Michael explained, "since he's a real person, though different from an ordinary flesh and blood person. In the other stories Greta and I just told you, we've been talking about the presence of the spirits of individuals who have died or have had traumatic experience. So these are ghosts or phantoms which have come from other dimensions. But in this case, we're talking about an individual being who is physical enough to project a clear image. But it's also clear from his appearance, his grayness, and large canine teeth that he survives by draining the living energy from other individuals. He's one of a group of beings, human or otherwise, that exist by gaining their energy and sustenance from others."

Again, I wondered if there might be other explanations, such as a mistaken identification in the darkness. But again, Michael reminded me of the many sightings of this being by different people that were consistent.

"All this suggests this being isn't just some figment of the imagination, but seems to be real. Besides, there have been several books in which people have written about these vampires.

And I think after what I have seen, I have to agree. In any case, it's well known that there are psychic vampires, real people who draw in other's energy and leave them drained."

I nodded in agreement and indicated I had known such people.

"Well," said Michael, "in this case, there seems to be enough evidence observed by me, Greta, and others to suggest the possible existence of other more sinister and supernatural entities that do much the same thing as these living psychic vampires. But instead, they appear to be energy forms or beings that have taken on a sufficient physicality that they appear to be real."

Finally, Michael had one last type of being to describe, which he referred to as the "visitor."

"Essentially, this is the individual who is projecting his or her energy over long distances to visit an area. Sometimes, this energy can become visible, so you see it."

Michael reminded me of an incident I had described in my previous SHAMAN WARRIOR book. A woman was walking along the streets of Westwood, and Michael and Paul were about 100 feet behind her. It was the early evening, and the streets were relatively deserted. No stores were open. Then, suddenly, as quickly as she seemed to appear on the street, she disappeared.

"She just vanished," Michael reminded me, "and there was nowhere she could go. She was just a projected energy form, and when the person ceased her projection, the energy form disappeared, too."

I finished scribbling down Michael's last story.

"But with all these different possibilities, how can you tell what kind of being is what?" I asked.

"You use your ability to see, sense, and feel to determine this," Michael said. "The key is perception. Through seeing, we can become aware of the less obvious hidden aspects of the world around us. So we can see the energies, the forces, the beings that are there. As you learned tonight, some of them can be very strange and hard for the average person to see. But others cross over into everyday reality and become part of ordinary affairs, so they can be visible even to the average person.

"And unfortunately," Michael added soberly, "this picture of the hidden world, is not always a comfortable description, because there can be some fairly hostile and unpleasant beings out there, although others are quite friendly and harmless. Many people who work with psychic development aren't aware of all the different types of beings out there, so they don't understand the whole picture of what the modern city is like. But it's important to look at the whole picture, so we're fully aware of our spiritual as well as our physical environment. In fact, if you add to the ghosts and beings we've talked about tonight the elementals and energies in the field which we work with, you'll see the city has a very rich and varied tapestry with many life forms and energies, of which we and the animal world are only a part. It's like a vast populated jungle, in which we and the other animal forms occupy only the jungle floor and a short ways above it and under it. But if you climb up and beyond the trees or go down deep into the earth, you'll discover all sorts of other creatures and beings there -- and that's what I've tried to show you tonight, this hidden universe of beings that exists on another level, though we can see it at times if we're really aware."

To help me develop this awareness, Michael had another exercise to show me. "It's a more intense version of that 'Spy in the Sky' exercise we did earlier," Michael explained. "The idea is to look around and see what's out there on the circuit and tune in on this hidden universe. We'll be using a normal astral projection flight, but I'll use some special imagery to help you really feel this circuit and these hidden energies."

Again, Michael dimmed the lights, and Greta and I positioned ourselves so we were comfortable and receptive. I leaned back against the couch and let my feet rest firmly on the floor.

As I felt myself slide into an altered state of consciousness, I heard Michael's voice droning on, quietly, yet firmly in the background.

> "Just relax. Let your body relax. Feel your limbs relax. Let yourself drift. Now I'd like you to visualize yourself rising up in the air to about the ceiling. Then, look down from the ceiling and see your body sitting in the chair or the couch where you are. Now gently rise up through the ceiling, through the roof into the night air. Notice the house surrounded by a light blue cone of energy, which rises up about 20-30 feet above the physical top of the house. We are within this energy field. Allow yourself to be drawn up through this cone of energy and shoot out into the night air."

I was up over the house now, and as I glanced down, I heard Michael's voice continue on, from even farther away, echoing what I was doing, and then helping me to see more.

> "You should now be above the house looking down at the cone rising up through the roof. Now become very conscious of the energy. Look around where you are and see the other individuals with you, not as people but as billowing clouds of light energy. It's light bluish white

in color. Feel the life energy coming from it. Feel the energy in the air that surrounds them. See the energy as made up of thousands upon thousands of glowing particles. And visualize the air as being very thick, almost like we are in the water with all these suspended particles, and glowing lights are floating on the water. Notice that as we drift, every motion we make sends a ripple that disturbs these particles of energy."

I glanced about and had a sense of being in a heavy fog. But besides me, I sensed Michael and Greta being near me, of flying with me, like two shining beacons of light that broke through the fog. Then, from far away, I heard Michael's voice directing us to move on.

"Now I'd like you to turn, and looking out across the canyon, see these particles of energy stretching out as far as the eye can see, down across the canyon, over the hills, and across the city, and off into the distance. In some places it's denser than others, and if you look carefully, you'll see wisps of smoky areas where the particles are especially dense. And there's a feeling of motion as the energy moves and shifts."

As I glanced around, I felt a little like being in an airplane moving through the clouds. Every so often, they seemed to billow up, bunch together, and then float apart again. I began to drift aimlessly, and again, Michael's voice interrupted, directing me back on course.

"Now I'd like you to start flying down the canyon, looking below you. See the houses. At the same time, look into the houses and see the life energy of the people in the houses. Again, you see these blue white lights, and you see them glowing like light bulbs through the roof. Then, you see these lights or energies of these people in their individual rooms, and you feel them as you go by. Notice how dull in color they are, but still living like us."

I looked around. The lights sparkled like the lights of a city seen from an airplane. I thought of a colony of living, moving bees as I flew by.

> "And now," Michael was saying, "we're going to go down over the canyon over Beverly Hills, and we're going to turn left over Sunset, and then through the Sunset Strip area. See the streets below you. Notice the cars with people driving by. See the houses with the people in them, the buildings with lights. At the same time, look down from time to time, and see the people in the streets."

I noticed it seemed crowded. The traffic seemed to clump at each light, and small knots of people drifted up and down the street and came in and out of the stores.

Michael's voice droned on.

> "Now pick a person below you who is walking on the street, and see that person as not just a body. Rather see the light energy inside them. Then see the light energy of the people in the cars as they drive along and feel them. Notice sometimes how the colors are a little bit different from one person to another. Some are brighter. Some are dimmer."

Again I glanced around and saw a field of vibrating lights.

> "Now let's move east," said Michael, "and as we do, feel not just the energies or the people below you, but feel for other energies like our own powerful energies. Feel for other beings with the same amount of energies

as ourselves, or maybe even more energy out there, somewhere in the city.

If you look, if you feel, you'll begin to see that at certain points, out across this great city, you'll see individuals who glow a little bit more than the others. Pick up on these individuals, sense them. Feel them. Feel what kind of power they have. These are other magicians, and they may be very powerful people."

I noticed that there did seem to be a few more intensely glowing spots here and there. They reminded me of the spot lights turned on at an opening, announcing the event and inviting others to come to the site, as if drawn along the light.

"Now, look around you," Michael said, continuing the journey. "See the lights off in the distance of other individuals like ourselves who are aloft, and who are also looking and sensing. They're also flying out on this level as glowing points of light like ourselves, and some of them are very intense.

In fact, you might notice one off to the south that is very bright and very vivid. It's a little yellowish in color, and it seems to be watching us, as if it's unsure of who we are. It seems strong, powerful, perhaps the energy of a male, and he's very aware of our presence."

I saw the large yellowish clump of energy Michael was referring to. It seemed to flicker back and forth like the flame of a fire. Perhaps that's what Michael meant by it being unsure, I thought. Then, suddenly, the yellow ball of energy was gone, and I heard Michael directing us to start back.

"Turn around now," he said. "We're going to leave here and head back over the hills. Notice the feelings as we pass over the houses of the people. For example, in that white house, you might notice the energy of this young woman who seems so sad. Or notice the older individual on the hilltop as we pass over.

You will also notice as we pass over the terrain areas that glow a bit. You can feel the magic there, where some work has been done. Also, in some cases, you can see areas in the streets, where there are purplish trails where things or people have passed which have had a great deal of energy and have left their trail behind."

I saw what looked like a patchwork quilt of energy, with the glowing energy standing tall like ears of corn, with twisted purplish furrows around it. It was like fertile land awaiting the harvest.

Then it was time to go back.

"Now what I'd like you to do," Michael's went on, "is to follow me back up the canyon to the point where we can see the house with the cone again. I would like you to envision yourself floating down through the air through this cone, and from there, go back into the house and back into your body. Then, let yourself relax, slowly open your eyes, and envision yourself coming back to consciousness."

Then it was over. We were back.

"How did you feel," said Michael, as he turned on the lights.

"Very alert and energized," said Greta.

"Very aware and sensitive to everything," I said. "I felt like I could really see the energies around us take on a visual form."

"Very good," said Michael. "This exercise is to designed to not just look at things like in ordinary astral or conscious projection, but to really see and feel the energy, to interact with it, to experience its essence. That's why we visualize the other beings as energy, because it's easier to read that. So we see the people we observe as little balls of light.

"And what's especially important to us are the really big balls of energy, both below us on the ground or flying with us through the mass of energy particles. For example, I pointed two of these out to you in the vision. One was a powerful female energy, and the other was efinitely a male."

"How could you tell the difference?" I asked.

"By their energy," said Michael. "The female was a strong, but smaller glowing spark of energy. The male's energy was more compact, it was bright, but firmer."

"In any case," he continued. "The energy particles and waves we were going through is the astral level of the circuit. And out there, not only do we see and perceive other energies, but every move we make is felt by someone else. For example, just as we spotted other flyers nearby, others using the circuit could see us. And in a large city, you would expect this to happen. After all, we are not the only ones who are airborne on the astral and using the circuit."

"Would our visualization make others aware of us?" I asked.

"Of course, it would," Michael replied. "We were aware of them, weren't we?"

"Yes," I nodded. Then I wondered, "Were they aware of us before we were doing our visualization?"

"Some were, some weren't," said Michael. "You see, the visualization intensifies the strength of our energy, so you become easier to see for anyone on the circuit. You're sending your spirit forth as you guide yourself through the experience. But even at this lower level of energy, some can still pick us up. It's like you noticed as we passed through the by the houses. You could see the balls of energy below. Well, the more aware person can pick that up; the less aware person can't."

Michael paused for a moment as I noted the differences. "And now, one thing you can try in the future, when you go on these journeys again, is to reach down and use your feelings and your ability for psychometry. Use this sense of knowingness through contact to feel some of the lives of the people in the houses below. For example, I did this on a few of the people I pointed out on the journey – the old man in the big house on the ridge over the Hollywood Hills, the younger woman in the valley slightly below. The two were completely different energies; they had different essences and emotions. While he was fine, since he had a feeling of satisfaction, the woman had a feeling of sorrow and pain about her. So as you are flying about, you can really feel the people below. You can feel them suffering or being joyous, winning or losing, loving or hating, all of the emotions people feel. You just have to stop to see and feel and psychometrize to sense what's going on.

"Then, too, as I pointed out, you can use this exercise to pick up areas of more active psychic activity. For example, I pointed out some glowing areas, which weren't single individuals, but indication of psychic work. So you could see the clouds of energy left by this work, as well as the little traces where individuals of power passed by leaving a trail of energy, like the purplish trails of energy you saw."

I nodded, remembering.

"And so," Michael concluded, "as you have seen, this exercise is designed to help you get plugged into the circuit, and see and feel the energies out there, particularly the very powerful ones. In turn, this awareness will help you sense these other beings that we talked about, such as the ghosts and phantoms of the hidden city."

With that, Michael ended the lesson. I gathered my coat and hat and began to snap my notebook shut to go, when Michael reminded me he still wanted to give me some homework. Then, he described the four things I should do.

"First, I want you to practice your astral projection. Use the 'Spy in the Sky' technique we demonstrated earlier tonight to go up into the sky and fly around. Then, notice the sensations you feel. Also, try doing some sensing and feeling in your local area. For example, try projecting yourself into the bar downstairs in your hotel and feel how many people are there and what they are like. Then, go there physically and see how accurate you were. Also, as you move about, see if you can pick up on the energies of the more powerful people, as well as those who are average. But don't..." Michael eyed me carefully "...try flying here. You'll find this place is well guarded. We don't like intruding visitors."

Secondly, Michael asked me to practice my seeing exercises on some of the people I met or saw during the day.

"Try psychometrizing them. Reach out with your seeing ability and feel them and their energy. Sense what the person is like. Is he happy or sad? Is he powerful or not? Also, try to see the aura or hara of the person -- the energy field around them or the energy center within.

"And don't just see the energy, but try to pick up how it feels. For example, as you ask yourself questions about the person's energy -- is it well or not, happy or not, strong or not? Notice the feeling impressions you get, and record them along with any visual images you see. The idea of this exercise is to awaken your feelings and notice how your feelings and images match, so you can move from one to the other, like an immediate transfer from one sense to the other, like transferring from one line to another on the bus.

"You can also use people you know or people you don't when you do this. The point is to get out on the astral dimension and plug into this circuit, so you can really experience what's out there -- first on the dimension of ordinary reality and then you can go beneath to feel out the hidden city."

Thirdly, Michael wanted me to practice my breathing. "But this time, try to breathe in the energy of the city. And notice as you do, what you feel about the people around you. Breathe them in and notice their energy. Are they restful, agitated? Do they feel tense? Are they at peace? As you breathe, you'll notice different kinds of waves of energy. So try to discern the subtle differences in what you feel. Try to read the energy."

Finally, Michael wanted me to continue working on raising energy through the meditation and chakra channeling exercise he had shown me, when I first arrived for my training. The meditation involved spending a few minutes bringing my hand back and forth towards my pineal gland or third eye, while I imagined that I was sending energy through my hand until I could feel it coming closer and closer and becoming more and more powerful. The chakra exercise involved breathing different colors up through my chakras and experiencing the energy diffusing out through my body through the color associated with each chakra -- black for the lowest spinal chakra, yellow for the stomach area, red for the solar plexus, purple for the chest, green for the throat, blue for the third eye, and white for the crown chakra at the top of my head.

"You need to do these exercises," Michael explained, "because you'll be doing all of the other exercises which take so much energy. So you need to do these energy raising exercises to build yourself up."

Michael asked me if I had any questions.

"Just one," I said. "How can I tell if I'm accurate when I try psychometrizing people to get images and feelings."

"Don't worry about that," Michael said. "Right now you are just trying to feel whatever you feel and notice any visual phenomena. You don't have to pay attention to getting any confirmation right now. In fact, since you usually can't check when you're doing this, it's even better to wait until you get in the habit of doing this, because you'll be more relaxed and freer then, so the images and feelings will flow more freely. Later, when they do, you'll be more accurate. But you don't want to worry about that now. You want to concentrate on being aware and getting the perceptions first, for when you do, you'll find that the accuracy will eventually take care of itself."

Then Michael walked me out to my car, and he told me of the arrangements for the next lesson.

"We'll go out in the city and you can practice tuning into the circuit and all these energies we've been talking about as we travel around."

I said I could hardly wait, and I drove back to my hotel eager to experiment and see how all these techniques worked in actual practice.

4

A FIELD TRIP TO WORK WITH ENERGY TECHNIQUES IN THE CITY

The next day, Monday, was a free day, and after writing up my notes, I went to the beach to try out some of the techniques I had learned. It was December 26, the day after Christmas, and I felt a little like a kid who had been given a whole bunch of new toys, and now I was going to try them out.

I felt invigorated as I crossed the street to the beach, and as I felt the soft squish of sand under my feet, I concentrated on breathing in the energy of the air and the ocean around me. There was a cold snap in the late afternoon air, and I felt it tingle through me, like little jolts of energy charging a battery. As I jogged down the beach, I imagined I was breathing this air through the colors of my chakras, letting it stop at each level --black, yellow, red, and up, until finally, it radiated up and around me from the white crown chakra on top. Then, I let the energy ebb back down.

Soon, I was breathing the energy faster, faster, as I ran, until each breath in through all the colors came as I stepped ahead on my right foot, and each breath out through the colors came as I jogged ahead with my left. It was like having an energy current run through me, and instead of tiring when I ran, as I usually did after a few bursts of speed, I jogged on and on, feeling more energy run through me with each step. It was like I was some kind of battery or energy socket, and the current kept pouring through me as I ran.

Then, slowing down about a mile down the beach, I noticed some children playing with kites, and I watched the kites dart up and down in a series of swirls, whirls, and loops, as they were tossed every which way by the wind. For a few moments, they seemed to glide quietly, serenely. Then, suddenly, like a whoop, they would jerk and burst up or down, their tails trailing behind them, and there seemed no special rhythm or reason why they would go one way or the other.

Drawing on the energy exercises I had learned, I decided to track them, and I focused on breathing in the energy of the air and wind currents around them and feeling myself become one with a kite. Then, watching, feeling, I tried to sense where I as the kite would go next. In moments, I felt the wind lifting me, moving me, and suddenly, in tune with this ebb and flow, I sensed where the wind might pull me next. Then, I felt that movement, watched that movement, and stepped into the swirl myself.

It was amazing. Mostly I was right, and for that short instant I felt an intense connection with the kite in the air above me. It was like we two were flowing like one, and the wind was a mostly predictable but sometimes very erratic friend, who usually blew in a certain direction, but suddenly became moody, and sputtered about wildly. Then, he calmed down again.

I continued watching and sensing the kite's direction for a few minutes. Then, feeling drained by the intense connection, I let it go and continued down the beach. Again I sucked energy in as I walked, until I felt replenished, reenergized, and I began looking and feeling again.

This time, as I passed some individuals and groups of people on the beach, I tried to feel their energy as the little white balls of energy that Michael had spoken about. As each person passed, I noticed something different in the air around me -- like a little pinprick or small wave of energy had pressed against me. But was I just feeling this because I was seeing people and translating my perception of them into feelings? I closed my eyes and tried to notice if I felt anything or saw anything in my mind's eye suggesting someone had passed.

At first, it was hard to concentrate. My mind kept drifting off to the beat of the surf around me, and if people came close, I would hear their soft voices or the slight push of their footsteps in the sand. Then, I tried projecting my consciousness a little further away, so I couldn't physically hear anything, and I concentrated on directing my attention away from the pounding surf. Eventually, I felt like there was only me, encased in my own envelope of energy on the sand.

Then, having achieved that blissful, nothingness state, I waited, very receptive for those pinpricks or small waves of energy suggesting that someone was there. As soon as I felt their presence, I looked in that direction and opened my eyes. And yes, most of the time, someone was there. So I was somehow sensing the presence of these people, and they were far enough away that I knew it wasn't my normal hearing or sensing. I had somehow tapped into some deeper feeling sense that opened up this special door to feeling the energy.

After a few minutes of this, I felt drained, and got up and moved on. After doing some more breathing to feel more energized, I noticed the seagulls. It was almost the end of the day, about 4:30 p.m. now, and they flapped and swirled about noisily on the beach, variously whirling around in the air, landing, walking for a few feet, and taking off in a sudden flutter of wings once more. They reminded me of the unpredictable kites tossed in the wind, although this time, there was an animal consciousness, not just currents of the wind affecting their motions.

Could I tune in on them and sense their motions and where they would go next, I wondered? Again, I tried to concentrate on feeling the energy of these birds, and I selected a few birds to focus on, concentrating on each one in turn. Zeroing in on that bird, I tried to sense its energy, its very being, until I could imagine that I and this bird were one. Then, as it swooped and whirled, I tried to sense where it was about to go next and let my consciousness go with it.

It took awhile to make the connection, and at first I thought these birds were eluding me, as I felt my consciousness was going one way, the bird flying another. But gradually, my consciousness and the bird seemed to be coming closer and closer together, until soon, for a few moments, I felt like the bird and I were one, just like I had felt at one with the kite. And now, it seemed like the bird and I were flying and swooping together. For suddenly I did seem to know where the bird was going to go next and again, again, I darted up and down with the bird. But after a few swoops, I felt tired, and I had to let that connection go. However, by breathing in deeply again, by drawing the energy in through the colors, I felt revived, and I could tune in on another bird once again.

And so I continued to watch and feel with the birds until after sunset, as the prongs of golden and pinkish light dappled the sky. After awhile, the birds seemed to dart up with a very nervous energy, suggesting it was time for them to go, and I decided it was time for me to return home, too. So I let go of the birds, released the energy, and jogged back along the beach. Then, as the grayish curtain of evening settled over the beach, I crossed the street back to my hotel.

It was like walking back into the real, everyday world, and I was reminded of this as I darted quickly across the road before the next wave of traffic.

A few minutes later, I was going up in the elevator, looking out across the road to the now dark beach, enveloped in a grayish purple haze, and the beach seemed very far away. I was back in the real world. Back in my hotel.

* * * * * *

The next morning, promptly at ten, Michael came to my hotel room to pick me up, and like me, he was dressed in ordinary street clothes, not the black uniforms for group activities we had worn the previous night. The idea today was to blend into the ordinary and maybe not so ordinary people we would encounter or observe on the streets. So we both dressed casually in slacks and sweaters. Nothing should set us apart.

As we walked to Michael's car, a small gray four-door Ford with bucket seats in front, Michael described what we would do today.

"We'll be working with energy to try to feel people and things. You want to be able to read their energy to sense what they are about. We'll start off doing this as we drive on the city streets and on the freeway, and then we'll go to a bookstore that attracts some very powerful practitioners, since it specializes in occult and metaphysical literature. It's called the Bodhi Tree, and it's right near Hollywood," Michael said.

As we drove off, I described my own exercises of the previous day with the kite, the seagulls, and the people on the beach.

"That's wonderful," Michael told me. "It sounds like you're really starting to open up. Especially those connections with the kite and the seagulls. Now you'll have a chance to refine that. So beyond feeling people's presence or sensing what things and people may do, you can really tune into them to sense who and what they are. What's you've done is a very good start."

I felt a little disappointed. Somehow I had thought what had happened on the beach was close to phenomenal. It seemed so accurate, so real. Yet for Michael these were only ordinary everyday events for a practicing shaman.

"You have to learn to go much deeper," he added. "It's like refining your radar. You may think you've done fantastically well when you first do a broad sweep and pick up the image of something out there. But you've got to bring that object closer in on your focus. You have to zoom your radar right in on that, so you really know what you are dealing with. So the next step is to learn to zoom in."

We drove along the oceanfront road for a few minutes heading towards Wilshire, the wide central boulevard in downtown Santa Monica.

"Now you can start feeling for the different energies of cars and people," Michael suggested. "Just imagine that you are extending your energy or consciousness to do a kind of radar sweep, and notice the quality of the energy. For example, are the people fairly calm? Does it seem like the energy of an ordinary day? Or do you feel any spots of tension or activity?"

I glanced around. I saw a scattering of people walking along the streets or into the stores. There were some cars waiting with us at the intersection for the light, while cars on the road to our right poured into the intersection and turned onto the road we were on.

"It looks very ordinary," I said.

"Don't look. You want to feel," Michael reminded me. "For example, I feel a little tension ahead in the downtown area. It's like some kind of disturbance might be happening there."

Michael drove a few more blocks and turned onto Wilshire.

"I used to use this radar technique a lot when I was on patrol," he explained. "It was a good way to feel for trouble spots, before I even came to then."

Just then a police car drove past us in the other lane, and a few blocks further ahead we saw another police car off to our right.

"There, you see," said Michael. "There was probably something happening downtown, and I was picking that tension up. You wouldn't usually encounter so many police cars in this area, so this suggests I was sensing something going on. However, now the energy feels much lighter, so whatever was happening seems to be over."

Michael circled around and drove back along the ocean front road. He drove slowly, close to the right.

"Now I'm reaching out and feeling the energy of the people as we go. I'm trying to notice the energies in people's haras."

Michael was referring to the energy center in the solar plexus he previously described as a whitish ball of light.

"Now you try it," he suggested. "Then, tell me what you feel."

I saw a group of women with shopping bags standing on one corner. Several men in business suits walked nearby.

"Everything seems fairly calm," I said tentatively.

"Yeah, things are mostly light right now," Michael agreed. "But there are a few exceptions."

He pointed across the road to a tall man in his early 20s who was walking along the park that ran alongside the beach.

"That guy in jeans has a much heavier feel. He seems pulled down, maybe even troubled. He has a darkish aura."

I glanced over quickly as we drove by. I noticed man's clothes seemed a little faded, maybe even shabby, and he had a slow, casual, even lazy step, as if he was wandering around sightseeing or with no particular purpose.

"Is it the way he looks that gives you that impression?" I asked.

"Maybe a little," Michael acknowledged. "But mostly, it's the way he feels. Even if you can't see it, you can sense his aura. It's like a feeling or sensation I get in my gut or I have this sense of knowing. It's hard to explain. But as you keep doing this, the process becomes automatic. You focus your attention in on someone, and all of a sudden you have a sense of who he is and what he's about. Keep doing this for awhile, and in time you'll experience this, too."

Michael turned back onto Wilshire and headed towards the freeway.

"Now you might notice," he commented, "that as we're moving further east, things are feeling lighter. It's like we're moving further away from the tension we felt earlier, away from the higher pace of activity in the center of the city. You can feel that shift in the energy all around us. It feels looser, more diffused -- like all these little energy particles we saw on that visualization last night are further apart; they're less concentrated; and you can feel that in the air."

"Perhaps," I said, trying to feel what Michael was talking about.

Then I leaned back against the car seat, as Michael headed up the ramp to the freeway. Yes, perhaps I did feel more relaxed now than I did earlier. Perhaps I did feel more of a sense of uplift. I opened the window and let the breeze flow in. It felt so warm and soothing, like it was blowing in the soft morning sunlight outside. Then, I gazed ahead on the freeway, as Michael told me to pay attention and look at the cars ahead.

"Now what you want to do," said Michael, "is to really feel the different types of cars out there. Sense the energies of the people driving.

Get a feeling of who they are. Notice if there's something different about a car that makes it stand out."

I glanced about. Nothing seemed unusual - just blips of moving cars, all going about the same speed in front of and behind us.

"What do you mean different?" I asked, "And how should I feel the cars?"

"It's like sending out radar and noticing if anything has an especially unusual look on the screen -- like it's moving too fast or too slow; maybe it seems much brighter or darker than usual; or maybe it's fading in and out or waving back and forth; or perhaps it just feels strange.

"In fact, this process of feeling is a little like what police officers do. When they're cruising the freeway, they're in a predatory relationship with the other drivers out there, since they are looking for lawbreakers to give tickets. In doing so, they can become very sensitive to the energy of the cars out there. For instance, they can feel when a group of cars are about to come into view, or they can sense when someone may be coming too fast ahead of the pack.

"Conversely, if you're driving..." Michael suddenly slowed down a little and pulled over into the right lane, "you can use protective radar to sense for police officers. It's like a slightly heavier, more direct energy. Or maybe you might get a sudden feeling like I did to slow down. And then often..." I noticed a police car whiz by on the opposite side of the freeway "...you may see a police car there!" Michael acknowledged the appearance of the car. "Usually it will be on your side of the road. But some officers are good at shielding themselves, so they don't put out as heavy a vibration, so you may not feel them as readily."

I glanced behind us and watched the police car recede in the distance. Then suddenly, I felt the car jerk forward as Michael stepped on the gas and pulled back into the left lane.

"Now, look ahead," Michael told me. "I'm feeling a little tension ahead of us."

I looked up. Nothing seemed that different. Just a dozen or so cars within view whizzed along and a few cars eased onto the freeway.

"Now it may be nothing," Michael continued, "but one thing that criminals do is they try to appear as normal as possible before the crime.

But a police officer who can feel the person will feel something beneath the surface. It's not just the person's body movements, but a sense of what the person feels like. He sees the person on the street, and he feels right or he feels wrong. It's a little bit like that on the freeway. If you feel, you can pick up these things."

Michael stepped on the gas a little harder and we sped on, gaining on a group of cars that seemed to be traveling like a pack ahead of us.

"Now one way to sharpen your feelings," Michael continued, "is to put a circle of energy around yourself. You can do it wherever you are, or like now, I put one around the car. It's not just for protection, but also for creating a sensory envelope around yourself. That way you can feel when people pass you. For example..." Michael passed a few of the rear cars in the group that had been ahead of us, "I can notice a special feeling when we pass cars. There's a kind of heaviness." He pulled away from the small cluster of cars in the rear. "And now that we're in the open again, the energy feels much lighter."

I did feel a lifting sensation, although I wondered if it was because I could see the car we were passing.

"Sure, your seeing might contribute to that feeling," Michael said. "But sensing the energy is more than that. It's like being in a crowd in the city. Even if you close your eyes and plug up your ears, you can still sense when there are a lot of people around you by feeling the lightness or heaviness of the energy around you. It's the same way on the freeway. You can feel a difference in the pressure of the atmosphere around you, depending on whether you are in an open freeway or it's full of cars.

"And perhaps that sense derives from our hunting/gathering days. The hunters couldn't always see the game. But they could sense whether it was around or in what direction it was going. Then, they could follow that feeling to the game. That sense helped them survive. I think that same kind of feeling has lingered for us today. We live in cities; we drive on freeways. But we can still reach out with that inner radar and feel."

Michael suggested I close my eyes and try to feel what the energy was like around us as we drove.

"Just tell me if you feel like we are passing a car or not as we drive. Hold your hands on your ears so you don't hear anything, and look away, so you're not influenced by any changes in light as cars pass. Then just feel."

I tried doing this for a few minutes, and reported if I sensed a car around us or not.

"Well, you were about 75% right," Michael said when we finished. "So you see, you did do much better than chance. You did feel something."

We drove on for a few more minutes and turned off of the Santa Monica Freeway onto the San Diego Freeway going north. Now the traffic was a little heavier, and soon a pick-up truck was traveling close behind us.

"Now I'll hit the truck with a banishing pentagram," said Michael. "He's driving too close, and I want him to stay back. You can use any banishing symbol to do this."

Michael focused on sending the image to the driver through the mirror, while he kept his eyes on the road. It was like splitting his consciousness, so one part was driving, the other sending a message to the driver. A moment later, I saw the driver fall back a few feet, but after a few seconds, the truck driver caught up to us again.

"Well, it doesn't always work if the other driver is determined," said Michael. "But if you step up the charge it might. For instance, now I'm increasing the strength of the banishing pentagram. I'm seeing the image more strongly. I'm focusing on sending it with greater strength and intent."

This time, after a few moments, the truck pulled away from Michael and moved into the left lane.

"And there, he's gone!" exclaimed Michael.

But did the driver really feel something, or did he just move over because he felt Michael was going too slowly, I wondered. I asked Michael about this.

"Don't you feel something if someone gazes at you, even if you don't see him directly looking? Michael shot back at me.

I nodded slightly.

"You feel uncomfortable, don't you? You want him to stop, or you may even move away out of his line of vision. Or even if you are not directly aware of someone looking, you may still feel this sudden desire to move and get away. You may not know why, or you may suddenly find another reason to explain your moving, such as getting up to close the window or check the door.

It's like you don't want to acknowledge this force that's urging you to move, or you aren't aware of it. And maybe you might have other reasons for moving. But the point is, you experience some sort of tension as a result of someone else's willed intent, and so you move."

"I guess so," I said tentatively.

"Well, it's the same thing here," Michael said. "I was sending this guy the message: 'Get back. Get away.' I was sending him my energy, so he would feel some pressure and want to get out of that line of fire, so to speak, and move away. And as you saw that's what he did. For whatever reason, shortly after I began my projection, you saw him move.

"In any case," Michael concluded, "it's useful to use these energy projections and protections when you're driving, just like when you're in a crowd. It helps you keep you alert to other people's energies, and it helps to keep others away and give you space. It helps you better maneuver. You feel freer; you feel easier. It's like having a shield of energy around you, so others stay out of your space, so you can move more freely and safely. Anyway, it's something I do as I go places almost automatically. It's like second nature. Practice with this, and it'll become like that for you."

We drove on for a few minutes silently, and I watched the cars around us intently, for now I was coming to see the freeway in a totally new way. So often I drove in a glazed fog, lost in thought, my mind drifting off into space, while I let my body respond, as if on automatic pilot.

But now I felt keenly awake and alert. As I looked about, I thought of each car as a shimmery packet of energy, almost like it had an aura like each person. Or again, was I only just imagining all this?

Just then, Michael's voice broke through my train of thought.

"Now feel ahead in the traffic," Michael asked me. "Do you notice anything?"

I glanced ahead. Just another cluster of cars, I thought. "No, nothing special," I said.

"Well, one person feels very tense up there," Michael said. "And I'm picking up a bluish car." He leaned forward and the car spurted ahead. "We'll go up to see."

In a few minutes, we had closed in on the pack.

"He's up a little ways," Michael commented, and he plunged into the herd of cars. He began to weave in and out in the traffic, and I felt like a private eye on the track of a car.

"There, now we're closing in," Michael said and just a few cars ahead there was a light blue Ford.

"That must be it," Michael said. "I can feel a single male occupant, and I can see some tension in him."

"What's different about him?" I asked, as we pulled up even with his car on the right.

"He has an aggressive energy," Michael said. "He's putting out an out-of-my way energy, and you can feel this all the way down the freeway."

Was he? I glanced in the car as we drove by. The man looked like he was perhaps 20 with dark hair and a stubby beard. Maybe he did look a little on the tough side, I thought.

"Now don't look at him too closely," Michael said, and I turned away. "You don't want to make him nervous, which might interfere with his driving."

"Just by looking at him?" I asked.

"Sure," said Michael. "Our looks have great power. The Indians knew this when they developed their stalking technique. They were very careful not to look directly at an intended prey or to think aggressively about their prey, so they didn't give a forewarning. You see, if you think loudly, people will hear you. For our thoughts project images; they project energy. That's why you can usually tell when someone has seen you even when you're both very far away. Whether or not you actually see where his eyes are looking, you can feel the connection. It's real, because of the energy transfer that's taking place. So that's why you want to watch when and where you're looking."

"Okay," I said, and looked away from the blue car. "But how did you sense the man's qualities?" I asked.

"These kinds of sensations can be very subtle," Michael observed. "But as you work on your skills, they become more finely tuned. So you can better pick up finer sensations out of the background, and then translate them into what you mean. At first, you generally just get the most powerful things when you try to sense, such as the presence of nearby objects, like these cars just ahead or besides us. But as you become more sensitive, you can pick up more subtle things from a further distance off.

"But you have to keep stretching yourself. So at first you may not experience something at all as you push yourself a little further out; but then, you'll start picking up those vibrations and you'll be able to identify them more exactly. It's like a dog smelling fear or other smells belonging to particular people. Most people don't sense such things. But you can train yourself to be more like that dog to pick up finer and finer vibrations."

Michael turned off the freeway onto Sunset Boulevard going east. It was a broad and windy road, and we drove along for awhile silently, as I lazily scanned the road ahead. There were just a few cars immediately ahead of us, and now and then a car whizzed by to our left.

Soon after we passed a sign that said Beverly Hills, Michael suggested: "You can start feeling for the different energies of cars and people again. We're in a much tighter area now; it's much more confined than being on the freeway. So now, imagine you are extending your energy or consciousness to do a radar sweep until you interact with another energy. See if you can feel the presence of other drivers or pedestrians before you see them. So notice if you feel anything along the side streets, before we come to them. Just reach out and feel. Then, you may notice some little bumps or blips in the energy ahead of you. It'll feel a little like you have hit something. That's what I'm doing now."

I gazed at the large hedges we were passing, occasionally punctuated by a long sweeping driveway. At times, I could see a hint of a large mansion in the distance.

I tried to project my energy out beyond the hedges. As Michael passed each street or driveway, I looked to see if anything was there. But at first I felt uncertain, like I was making random guesses. Sometimes a car would be there and sometimes it wouldn't.

"Just feel ," Michael reminded me. "Just feel and don't guess. Relax into your feelings. Imagine we're driving through a field of energy, and feel for the points of pressure; the points where clusters of energy particles come together. Also, be aware of the gaps; the places where the energy is more diffuse."

This time there was a car behind the bush as I imagined.

"Very good," said Michael, reassuring me that this wasn't just a lucky guess. He asked me to sense if something was there or not a few more times. "Then, we can try to get more precise," he said. "For example, try to sense if the car is a regular car or a police car; or if the person is a female or a male."

Again, I tried to concentrate, but now I found it hard to do so. It had been so much easier when I sensed for things around me when I was on the beach, where I could see something in front of me while I was standing still. And even on the freeway, when I projected my energy, I could see the cars. But now, we were racing along about 50 miles an hour, and Michael wanted me to project my consciousness out to feel something I could only see for a matter of moments. I was starting to feel scattered and diffuse.

"Then, just relax for a while," Michael said. "Get back your energy. Besides," he reassured me, "even when someone is trained, his skills aren't always there. Anyone can have off days. Or if your energy is low, you may not be able to pick up too much. It takes a lot of energy to use these techniques, as you have seen. So sometimes, you just have to relax and let go. Then, when you feel replenished, you can begin again."

Michael suggested I just breathe in some of the energy around us for awhile, and I did. As I relaxed, Michael spoke of some of the practical applications of using these energy techniques on the road.

"First of all," he said, "you can use these techniques to feel ahead for a sense of danger or tension. Then, if you get a feeling that something is wrong, you can take some corrective action. Or if you feel things seem fine, you can relax. For instance, you might pick up that a driver is going at a very high rate of speed and coming around the bend in the other lane, though you can't see him. So you could slow down, or move over more to the right, so you don't have a collision. Or if you're driving rapidly over the speed limit, you might sense that intensity or aggressive energy that suggests a police officer is ahead. Then you can slow down so you don't get a ticket."

Michael slowed down for a light and stopped. "Now an interesting thing about intersections," he commented as we waited. "Often you may find a lot of negative energies hanging around here, because of the negative energy projected out by drivers interacting with each other. For instance, one person doesn't stop completely or speeds through a light as it's changing, which nearly creates an accident and gets another driver mad. That kind of energy can grow, as it's fed by other drivers who arrive at that intersection and have some problem. Then, once created, that energy can hang around, and it can latch onto someone passing through. So that person could become anxious himself or lose concentration, and perhaps even have an accident or a near miss, if the conditions are ripe for this. By contrast, if you're aware of this negative energy, you can pay more attention and perhaps avoid a potential accident. Or if you do have the accident you can take some action to make it less serious.

The light changed and Michael drove on again.

"But if I think there's going to be an accident," I asked, "couldn't my sensing it actually create it. In other words, if I think something will happen, maybe I might act in some way to bring it about."

I described an incident that had happened to me about two years before, when I was driving home across the bridge from neighboring Marin County into San Francisco. It was a cold, rainy night, and I sensed that I was going to be in an accident. But still I drove on, knowing I had to get home. Then, about half-way down the bridge, even though we were creeping along at about 15 miles an hour, the car in front of me suddenly stopped, and, since I wasn't paying much attention to anything except the rain fogging my windows, I crashed into the car. A moment later, the car behind crashed into me, while the car in front lurched against the car ahead, which hit another car. Altogether, five cars were involved in the snafu, and as the police signaled us to drove off the road, since no one was seriously hurt, I wondered if my thinking about my accident had led me to have it, like the proverbial self-fulfilling prophecy. So maybe I wasn't pre-viewing the event at all?

Michael pooh-poohed my concerns. "You can try to rationalize such events if you want. But there is no such thing as coincidence. If they fear a disaster, most people do what they can to take precautions, not create the event, so they can avoid the problem occurring. For example, when I feel some negative energy ahead or feel a premonition that something might happen, I act or drive more cautiously. Then when it doesn't happen, I feel I've averted it. I acted to change the events of the future based on a sense of what might happen in the present

"Thus, your thinking of danger may not have caused the accident you experienced at all. Rather, just own what you experienced as a genuine intuition. You felt it, and then it happened. That's a good indication you were really picking something up.

"So believe in your intuition and power, and you can use these skills when you're driving, when you're shopping, wherever, to take the necessary steps. For instance, if you feel the dark energy of some nut out there with a gun or driving like a maniac, get out of the way."

We drove on a little further, and soon were driving along the Sunset Strip, heading into downtown Hollywood. Now there were nightclubs, restaurants, billboards along the way.

"The point of this whole lesson," Michael continued, "is when you develop your sensitivity, you recognize that all things around you have an energy signature. And just by feel, you can read your environment, the people around you, the cars on the road, everything. You can sense when things are right or wrong. You can get an energy picture of everything just by feel."

Michael turned at the light onto a side street, and continued. "In fact, this feeling is a skill that many people already have; it just isn't formally developed. For example, if someone's looking at the back of your neck or following you down the street, even the average person is likely to feel something amiss and turn around and look. He may not know what he feels, but he senses something, because there's an energy beam going through.

"Some people can be particularly sensitive to this, even though untrained. For example, many criminals are especially attuned to the energy they experience when they're followed or observed, because they're already nervous and high strung, since they have their senses up due to their fear of being caught. It's like they have this extra charge of adrenalin that tunes up their whole system, like an animal being tracked by a predator in the brush. So for sheer survival, they're extra alert, and if anything feels wrong, the criminal won't do the job or he'll quickly run. And as I've described cops feel this heightened awareness, too, when they're out on a chase.

So the scene of a crime is like the world of the jungle, the arena of the predator and the prey, and both are relying intensely on their intuition. They're sensing the energies of each other. Though these energies are really subtle, they're very real; they leave a particular mark. For example, the cop gives out a strong, hunting energy; the criminal a scattered, nervous, anxious feel. These are subtle differences perhaps. But when you're trained or otherwise very aware, you can pick up these energies."

We passed a group of teenage boys in a souped-up low rider car.

"Now here's a good example," Michael said, pointing to the boys in the car, as the driver tore away at the light. Their wheels screeched, and there was the smell of burning rubber as they sped away. "Lots of times, while driving, I've felt this really aggressive energy, and when I look up or the car comes into view, I'll see this carload of hot rodders, or gangbangers as we sometimes call them here. They have a real predatory feeling, like a wolf pack or other predator, looking for trouble. Or sometimes I'll feel this predatory energy, but it's more solid, more direct, and when I see the car, it's a carload of cops. So there are these distinct signatures, based on what people are doing, what they're feeling, what's their intent, and you can get to know these differences.

"Then, once you're aware of these signatures, you can, if necessary, act to change your own. For example, criminals tend to gravitate towards a person they feel would be an easy victim, and not just because of the way the person walks. Rather, they get a feeling from the person's energy that he or she feels like a victim, because their energy seems weak, diffuse, scattered, unsure, or otherwise has that victim feel. By knowing this, you can pay attention to your own feelings as you walk down the street and ask yourself: do you feel like a victim, or do you feel like you're in charge? Then, should you feel the victim, you can change, and once you get rid of the energy of the victim and feel in charge, criminals will tend to stay away."

I reflected on what Michael had just said, and remembered my experience a few months before when I had gone on a business trip to New York. One evening I had gone exploring on foot in out-of-the-way places by the docks and along 9th and 10th Avenues.

"It was pretty rough there, I guess," I said. "But I didn't feel like anyone would bother me, and no one did. I guess I was putting out a sense of confidence; of don't mess with me."

"Exactly," said Michael. "You can feel when someone's nervous and scared. Likewise you can feel when they're in control. And it's not just the look -- it's the feeling deep inside. People can pick that up. They aren't even aware of what they are doing -- but they're sensing the emanations from the hara, the energy center within. So that's one more reason to develop this awareness of energy -- you not only become more sensitive to the energies of others around you, but to your own, and that gives you tremendous control. That's because you can create yourself by crafting and shaping your own energy, so you in effect create the energy signature you want. And you're not just making surface or image changes. You're changing the you from within."

Michael pulled into a drive-in McDonald's, and we stopped briefly for snacks, while Michael explained what we would be doing next -- visiting the renowned New Age bookstore in West Hollywood -- the Bodhi Tree. Now he wanted to prepare me for that visit.

"This isn't just like going into any store," he began. "Here you'll find a concentration of New Age people, many of them well-developed psychic practitioners. When we go in there, we'll be looking for psychic signatures, people who stand out psychically over the common herd."

Michael took a few bites of his fish sandwich, then continued. "Now, when you walk in, as in going into any occult or metaphysical place, you want to put up a little shield. You may normally shield yourself anyway, but it's especially important here, because it's a place where there's likely to be lots of high energy psychic power. When we go in, we won't know what the terrain or psychic energy is like. So it's important to have your shield up, until we can find out and make sure it's safe to be more open. Otherwise you can get hit with all kinds of very powerful energies which you don't want to receive."

"Okay," I said, visualizing a small egg-white body of light forming around myself.

"Not yet," said Michael as we drove off. "Wait until we get there, just before we go in, to put up your shield."

"Okay," I nodded, letting my image go for now.

After a few minutes of driving along several wide L.A. boulevards with miles and miles of low-lying shops, condos, gas stations, discount centers, hamburger chains, and Thrifty drug stores, Michael announced: "We're here."

I looked across the road to see a long Spanish-style stucco building with a heavy wooden door in front of a stone archway. It reminded me of a Moorish palace.

Just then Michael pulled into a parking place diagonally across from the shop.

"Parking magic," he exclaimed. "It's a good thing to have in a city like L.A."

Then, we got out of the car, and I put on my shield.

"Now, I want you to just observe at first," Michael said, as we approached the heavy wooden door. "This is a good setting to do this, because as you're browsing, it gives you a good excuse to be near the person, so you can better seek or feel their energy."

We walked in through a small hallway with a few piles New Age newspapers and flyers describing New Age events. Inside about a dozen people browsed lazily through several rooms with rows upon rows of books. At first, they seemed like very ordinary people, dressed in casual L.A. style, such as the first few people I noticed -- a tall slightly scruffy looking tall man wearing jeans and carrying a backpack; a short squat woman with long blonde hair wearing a colorful poncho; a short haired man who looked like a junior executive wearing a white windbreaker. I glided quietly up and down the aisles after Michael, just looking, getting a general overview of the scene.

After we completed the circuit of the main room and three connecting rooms, Michael motioned for me to stop by a corner where there were a collection of books on shamanism. He pointed out my own book SHAMAN WARRIOR, and asked me to glance back at the room we had just walked through.

"Well, what did you notice about the energy?" Michael asked me.

What did I notice? I suddenly felt on the spot. Everything had seemed so ordinary on the surface, yet I knew that wasn't what Michael wanted to hear. He wanted me to dig deeper, to really feel and go beneath the surface appearances to sense the energy underneath.

I tried to do so on the spot. I imagined my energy reaching out; I imagined my consciousness moving around the room like a beam of light trying to see what was there.

"Well, it seems quiet and restful," I finally said. "It feels like some people are really searching for knowledge about an inner reality; about themselves."

I felt like I was merely scratching the surface by just stating the obvious, but my comments seemed to satisfy Michael.

"That's fine," he said. "Now just pay particular attention to the people." Notice those who seem especially powerful."

I glanced around the room and saw three people -- a short wiry black man at the end of one row, the tall slightly scruffy looking man a little further away down one aisle, and a short blonde woman in a strawberry sweater.

"Now try to see beyond their outer appearance," said Michael. "You may see an aura emerge, but go beyond that and try to see the hara, the energy center. Notice how well developed it is. That will tell you something about how psychically developed and powerful the person is."

I remembered back to Michael's earlier lesson about haras. The hara of the average person, he had told me, would be like a bright glowing ball of energy in the center of the solar plexus. Then, as the person developed psychically, that ball would expand and form a mushroom-shaped form, and the longer and more stretched out the wings of the mushroom, the more developed the person. Finally, in the most developed person, the mushroom shape would elongate further until it formed into a rocket or missile-like shape, representing the more focused and therefore the most developed hara.

I glanced back and forth from person to person, trying to pick up this kind of imagery. But nothing. It was as if their clothing acted as a shield against me, shutting out my gaze. So everyone still looked very ordinary; like I could be in any bookstore in any mall. I felt frustrated, like I should be seeing more than I was.

Suddenly I felt Michael's tap on my shoulder. "Now follow me. Look," he said. He directed my attention to the tall scruffy looking man who was now standing in the center of a long aisle intently reading a book. "Just pay attention; then we'll talk about this later."

Michael left to wander around the store on his own. "We can meet in about 20 minutes," Michael said. "Just keep looking, and we can compare what you see."

Then, he was off, and I gazed at the tall scruffy man. After a few moments, feeling self-conscious that he might notice me watching, and not seeing anything special about him I wandered away. Casually, slowly, leisurely, I walked up and down the aisles. As I looked at each person, I tried to see the haras Michael talked about, though I found I couldn't, at least not here. Instead, I came away with a lot of visual impressions, like snapshots of people caught for a photo album, or pinned butterflies to be studied later.

I wondered if perhaps I wasn't seeing in depth, because there was so much to look at and I wasn't sure where to look. So maybe that's why I got a lot of fragmentary images, like the baby in John Locke's example initially confronted a booming, buzzing confusion, before he began to sort them out into the appropriate categories and learned the rules for doing so. Now I felt like that baby, not sure of what to look at and see, so the images of people, shelves, books, and magazines flooded in, and I wasn't sure when to stop to focus and look below the surface.

Even so, a few people stood out because of what they were wearing, such as a woman wearing a long black skirt, black sweater, and necklace of red and black beads. Then, I remembered what Michael had told me, "Don't be misled by surface appearances," so I sought to put aside these outside cues that I usually used to get some insights into the person within. However, that made the whole process even more confusing, for not only was I trying to reach beneath the surface, without being sure of the markings, like a ship captain lost at sea, but I was trying to overlook many of the markers I did see, fearing these external markers could easily lead me astray. It was like I trying to tell myself: "Don't think about the elephant," and fighting my tendency to think about just that, at the same time that I was not sure what to think about in its place. No wonder I couldn't see within -- I needed someone to guide the way.

Finally, after about 15 minutes of grappling with an explosion of thoughts and images, I retreated to the magazines and flipped through them. And for a few moments, it was like taking a vacation from all this uncertain looking.

Then, Michael found me there. "Now, I want you to look at one last thing," he said. He pointed out the woman in the black skirt who was standing a few yards away looking at a book.

"Powerful, isn't she?" he observed, and I suddenly thought of the irony of his comment. Here I had been trying to put this woman out of my mind, because I thought I had been misled by her distinctive clothing which made her look like the Hollywood image of the powerful witch. And now Michael was saying that in fact, she was exactly that.

I glanced at the woman again, this time intently. And this time, spurred by Michael's direction, I did see and feel the image of a hara emerge, like a glowing fountain of energy, with bright sparks radiating from the wings of the mushroom, and for a moment, I felt a rush of power surge through her like an electric charge.

"I guess she is," I replied.

"Okay, well now look away," he told me. "You don't want to make her self-conscious by too much looking."

I quickly broke my gaze, as Michael instructed. Then, he motioned for me to follow him to the counter. He had a few things to purchase, and then we could go. While we waited, he joked with the short woman in the strawberry sweater about traffic in L.A., and after making his purchase, a small jar of incense, we returned to his car.

"Now's let's talk about what you experienced," Michael said as we sat there.

I explained my difficulties.

"Okay, next time I'll draw your attention more to the people who stand out ," Michael said. "Eventually, you'll be able to pick this up directly yourself. You'll feel their stronger signature coming out loud and clear."

Then, Michael pointed out the four people who had stood out for him and what had drawn his attention, so I would be more aware of such things in the future.

The first was the tall scruffy-looking man, who looked like an ordinary hippie-type to me.

"What I first noticed about him," said Michael, "was his fuzzy aura. It had this strange shimmer or shake to it. On the surface, he seemed to be dressed very casually in his loose-fitting jeans, tan jacket, and his beard made him look very friendly -- like a big teddy bear of a man. But then, I noticed he didn't feel quite right -- like his energy was out of whack with his appearance, and when I looked closely, he was reading a book about black magic, which helped to confirm my impression.

"So I look at him more closely. I did my seeing on him, and his aura had this dark brownish color, and there seemed to be this unusual concentration of energy low down around his pelvic area. And there were fibers coming out of this very fuzzy shaky aura."

"What does that mean?" I asked.

"Well, when you see such things, you have to interpret those impressions against the meanings of these images for you, since there's an interaction of the energy a person is putting out with your own symbolic interpretations of how you see and feel the energy. In this case, I felt he was a somewhat disturbed person. It was like he had this unhealthy focus or obsession in his sexual center, and perhaps that's one reason for his interest in black magic -- as a route to sexual power."

"Hmmmm," I said, impressed at how much Michael could sense about this person when I could tell nothing. Then I wondered: "After you see all this, how can you check it out? How can you tell if you are accurate?"

"In this case you can't tell precisely," Michael said. "There were some indications, such as his book on black magic or his nervous jerky movements, which seemed to correspond to his shaky aura. But otherwise, you have to pretty much go by your impressions and build up a sense of overall confidence in your accuracy from previous experiences doing this and checking out what you have done. For example, I've done this in many other cases where I have been able to check after I've met a person and I've been right on. So in time you get this sense of when you are right. So you have to rely on your own intuition; on your own belief."

Then, Michael described the next person, the short blonde woman in the strawberry sweater.

"What was so special about her?" I asked.

"Again you have to look beneath the surface," said Michael. "Externally, she looked very ordinary. And she was. She told me she was a housewife, while we were waiting on line. Yet she was also a spiritual seeker, and I sensed she has been looking because she has experienced some unhappiness. Externally, she seemed to have a very open, light, sunny aura, and it was fairly strong, as well. It was a kind of goldish-red color, which has this brightness and strength. Yet, I could also sense an inner sadness in the little fibers of darkness I saw inside her hara. I also sensed a feeling of reaching out, of searching, of asking the questions: 'Why? Who am I? Is there anything else? So this shows you the importance of looking past the surface and sensing the essence within."

The third person Michael spoke about was a woman I hadn't seen at all -- a tall woman with curly black hair. He characterized her as "a classic psychic, with an interest in metaphysics, but not very strong."

"What gave you this impression?" I asked.

"Her aura was a combination of light blue and purple, which I usually pick up when someone has achieved some level of psychic development. But as I tuned into her hara, it had a sharp, spiky feeling, a little like a cactus, and her feelings seemed to be all pulled into her body, like she was surrounded by an energy of fear. It was like she was putting out this message: 'Don't mess with me.' But at the same time she wasn't completely certain that people would buy this message. So she also put out this feeling of fear. Then this undercut her psychic powers. So she did have some psychic abilities, but I sensed she wasn't that strong and not that powerful, because of that curtain of fear."

Finally, Michael spoke of the woman in the black skirt who looked like the classic Hollywood witch.

"She was very definitely the most powerful person there," he said. "I could sense that immediately, even before I tried to feel her aura or hara. For example, she was very aware of us as soon as we came in. She kept glancing our way, as if she could sense we were here for a special reason, not just to look at the books. Then, she moved around in relation to us. You may not have noticed this, but as we moved about, she seemed to want to keep us in sight or at least within feeling distance, and as we moved from room to room, so did she.

"Then, when I did tune in on her energy, it seemed a lot more focused, as well as very intense in its strength. Also, her aura was distributed fairly evenly around her, and it radiated out this even strength.

"You see," Michael explained, "as an individual grows in strength psychically, their aura becomes more energized. Fr some, this energy gets more concentrated in some areas of their body, so when you see them, this area stands out and is especially strongly illuminated. And the more powerful the individual, the more illuminated they become. In her case, this strong aura was radiating out from her all over, as if she had developed this strong psychic and balanced state."

"And her clothing?" I asked. "Did her appearance have anything to do with what you picked up?"

Michael laughed. "No, though I know what you're thinking. This lady dresses to look especially powerful, to send out the signal, 'I'm a powerful witch.' Well, in her case, the image is true. Now someone else might walk around dressed that way. But if they weren't true to their image, you can pick that up. I've already illustrated this with two of the other people we talked about. As you've seen, if the outer image doesn't fit the person, the aura and hara won't match. If you're sensitive, you can sense the difference.

"But in her case, she was dressed to fit her image. And perhaps that fooled you. You were thinking if she's dressed to look like the classic witch, then certainly she's not. You were trying to shut her off, so you wouldn't be fooled. And so you were.

"In short, what I've been trying to show you is that you have to look past the external appearances to the real spirit of the person underneath. Sometimes the spirit and the outer being will be totally one. But at other times, that won't be the case. That's why it's so important to use your seeing and feelings. That way you can see and feel past these external appearances, like zeroing in through the outer shell of an atom to the component parts of that atom that lie underneath. Or maybe think of this deep sensing as tuning into the genetic coding within each individual, which is like the physical counterpart of the inner spirit. You want to strip off that outer layer to see that essential being that lies deep inside."

With that, Michael started the car and headed back towards my hotel.

"Suppose you were looking at my aura and didn't know me?" I asked, as we drove along Wilshire towards the freeway. "What would say about that?" I was almost afraid to hear, after all this talking about the inner hidden person underneath, but curious to know.

Michael gazed ahead at the road and drove on for about a minute in silence. Then, quietly, he began, and I scribbled down his comments in the jerking car.

"Well, you have a lot of energy. You stand out. I sense a certain amount of stress and tension, but a very open feeling, not at all defensive. There's also a very business-like, purposeful feeling, and no negative feelings. It's just a very active, almost hyperactive energy, since I get a reddish feel with some yellow."

Michael turned onto the freeway, then continued. I listened raptly as he continued his energy portrait.

"However, your energy is not entirely even. I sense a lot of energy accumulated around the top of the head; but it's getting more even, focused, and stronger since I've known you. But I don't feel this knowledge is natural to you yet. You're still resisting, still questioning. Yet I've been seeing changes in your level of ability, too. For instance, when you first started your gateway..." Michael was referring to the work I had previously done in the field to advance to my fifth degree, described in SECRETS OF THE SHAMAN, I didn't see any energy. It was like you were blocking it; maybe doubting what you were doing out there. But then you started breathing, and the energy came up. By contrast, when Paul, who has been working with these techniques for years, went out to demonstrate how to do this gateway, the energy was already there and it was more evenly distributed around him.

"So ideally, that's the energy state you want to reach. And when you get to that level, you will no longer need any exercises to bring up your power. It will just be there for everyday workings. Then, you can always use your breathing to bring you to an even higher level for more powerful acts of power. Your energy level suggests you are starting to develop this, and as your own energy level rises, you can get your power going faster. And that means you can see and feel better, because you can get the voltage up faster. So the more you do, the easier this sensing becomes and the more powerful you'll become. The more you can see and feel, the more you can do."

I felt encouraged by Michael's comments, and as we hurtled down the freeway, I imagined the cars we passed like little balls of energy and felt like driving on the freeway would never be quite the same.

A few minutes later, Michael pulled into the parking lot in back of my hotel. I started to get out, but Michael motioned for me to wait. He had a few last comments.

"Now it's one thing to have power," he cautioned me. "We've been working on developing that. But the spirit that directs the power, that focuses it and drives it, is equally if not more important. You need a strong will, and you must learn to focus it clearly, for that's what makes a person really powerful -- a combination of strong energy and a directed will. And, of course, you must use your power with good intention, so you don't end up having your negatively charged energy and will boomering back at you.

"You see," Michael continued, "the real key to using power is learning to focus your will to manipulate and shape that inner power. Many occultists, magicians, and others working with power just focus on getting power. But then, they don't stay focused in their intentions and their lives. So though they could be very powerful, they become very diffused. Their power dissipates out, and you can see the results in how they live their lives. For example, there is a lack of timing, an undirected purpose, a general sense of drifting in and out of life. Then, this drifting quality can help to undermine their power, because this work with focused energy is so central to all we do. It's not just like a magical hat to put on from time to time, when you decide there is something you want to achieve. Rather to be truly powerful you need to work on having not only that high level of energy but that focus of will to use and direct it in all areas of your life. In short, you need to make that power an essential part of you -- not just an occasional toy to play with out in the field."

I said I would try and hopped out of the car. Michael walked me to the door.

"Now remember to practice trying to feel people. Try to get a sense of them by reaching out with your energy to contact them. Then see what you see in your mind's eye. Notice what their aura looks like. Get a sense of how they feel, and notice if anything feels out about them, like an inner energy that's out of phase with the outer image they give out. You just have to reach out and taste. At first, you may have to keep thinking about doing this consciously. But in time, it will be something you do as you go about your daily activities, so you can really sense who people are."

"Okay, I'll try," I said again, and Michael quickly reviewed our plans for later that evening. We would go to a mall to practice reading people by sensing their energy. Then, Michael would demonstrate how the focused will could have a powerful effect.

"It's like we're all part of this huge energy web and it's all connected," said Michael. "You can see the strands and pull them or weave them if you know how."

So tonight I would learn a little more about maneuvering within the web. I waved goodbye and went upstairs. As I gazed out across the road to the beach and the ocean as the outside elevator climbed higher, I thought about how this world out there was like a solid city of shapes and forms, but underneath lay a hidden world of energies and forces underneath. So what was real?

5

EXPLORING THE ENERGY
AT A SHOPPING MALL

After writing up my notes from the morning, I met Michael at his house for our trip to the mall that evening. Greta was already there, talking about her hectic day on an ambulance.

"We had this most amazing patient today," Greta said, and she described her struggles with a co-worker to haul a man who weighed 350 pounds down the stairs of a rickety duplex onto the truck. "It was like hauling a tub of lard," Greta said. "Then, when we finally got him settled, he complained about being tired. Anyway, I'm bushed."

However, the coffee revived her, and when we were ready to go, Greta was her usual go-go bundle of energy again. We piled into Michael's car, me in the front, Greta in the back, and before we drove off, Michael concentrated silently for a few moments to put up a protective circle of energy around the car. I hadn't noticed this before, and when I asked him about this he told me:

"Oh, I always put up a circle around my car before I go out. When you consider that driving on the highway is one of the most dangerous things you can do, it makes sense to do a little magic to protect yourself."

Then, we were off through the winding canyon road to Mulholland, the high road in the hills cutting across the city. We had a long way to get to this mall in the valley, near Sierra Madre, and I appreciated the scenic night view along the way. As we drove high in the hills, I could see the lights of the valley stretching alongside us like a black carpet with sparkling white lines marking the roads

Michael and Greta began reminiscing about the days long ago, when they had both worked on patrols in the hills. They spoke of some eccentric Hollywood stars and millionaires who kept strange animals, built unusual structures, barricaded themselves behind high gates, and sometimes called to report odd apparitions and ghosts.

"It was like loony tunes, sometimes," observed Greta.

Then, she pointed out some of the places where lovers parked on my right.

"Of course, Mulholland is very famous for that, though most people don't know about the ghosts."

Then, we were on the freeway heading south, and Michael showed me some more psychic tricks of the road along the way. As he wove into the right lane between two cars, he cautioned me: "Try not to think too loudly if you're going to squeeze in and the driver behind seems aggressive. Then, he may try to not let you in. Or if someone is driving too slowly, I might urge him along psychically."

As Michael explained, "Sometimes I send psychic energy at a person to get him to move. I visualize sending the energy to him as I focus on him. Also, at times, I might try to feel how many people are in a car. I've found it can be a very valuable patrol skill to know this.

"It's also very useful to sense the energy ahead of you and behind you to sense any disturbances. Then, you can try to evade this. For instance, if a person is coming up fast, you can look up in time to get out of the way."

I glanced around feeling a little paranoid with all these suggestions about freeway cautions. Then, as a truck driver came barreling on fast behind us, Michael quickly darted out of the way to let him by, and I could see why he kept emphasizing all these precautions. It was a little like living in a jungle on the L.A. freeway, and like the ancient shaman used his magic to help his tribesmen hunt and beware of stalking beasts, now the modern-day shaman might use the same powers for protection on the freeway. It seemed a crazy thought to have, but as if to confirm my thinking, Michael added:

"So what's important with all this freeway violence is to sense the intent of the other drivers, before you come up on them or they come up on you. For example, if the driver is drunk, you can tell this, because the energy feels more scattered and disorganized, due to the effects of the alcohol. If the driver is more aggressive, the energy will feel stronger, more intense."

"But can't you tell that from the way the person drives?" I asked.

"Not necessarily," said Michael. "The person could be driving along, seemingly normal, and you can pick up something strange about his energy. Many cops do this all the time. They zero in on someone who feels not quite right. And this is before the person does anything to give themselves away. Then, the person will do something, which will confirm the feeling. For example, the drunk will start weaving; the aggressive guy will start speeding; and you know your feelings are right. So it's good to know these things."

Just then, the lights of a fast-moving car came up behind us, and tailed us like a bird dog.

"I'll put up a wall to slow him down," Michael said, and a minute later, the car pulled into the right line and sped away.

"There, you see," exclaimed Michael, "He's taking off. He probably got tired of running up against my wall."

Then, Michael sped up, and I described my image of the freeway jungle.

"Well, it's true," exclaimed Michael. "If you lived here, you'd know. The freeway seems to bring out the feelings of prey or predator in everyone, and it helps to use your psychic skills to survive."

I glanced around and now saw the gleaming white headlights whizzing by and behind us like the eyes of cats in a jungle. Then, ahead, I saw the sign for Sierra Madre, and Michael drove off the freeway ramp. I felt very relieved to be back on the street, and in a few moments, Michael pulled into the parking lot of the shopping mall. We were finally there. It was about 7:30 p.m.

Michael led us through the wide sliding doors and down a long corridor to the central atrium. The shopping center spread out before us like some glittery secular shrine, with people scurrying back and forth down the long sweeping aisles and into the rows of shops. Some people with large bulky packages crowded onto one of the central escalators, which stood side by side like two long metal feeders, moving people up and down.

Michael headed up one of the stairways to the second level, and he motioned for us to join him by the railing overlooking the atrium below.

"Now we have about an hour and a half till closing time," Michael began. "We'll be observing and experiencing the energy. First, get a general sense of the energy, and then we'll zero in." He looked at me. "Now what do you feel?"

I glanced around. Everything looked fairly ordinary. People walking, talking, a few laughing. Some teenagers jostled each other on the escalator. A few children played in the mini-playground with a sandbox and wooden horses. I felt a little on the spot, unsure what Michael expected.

"It just feels fairly average," I said. "Low key, relaxed."

Michael gazed around. "Yes, I guess you could say that. Anyway, now I'd like you to do a special kind of seeing. I want you to look for each person's double."

"Double?" I said surprised.

"Yes, double," Michael repeated. "You've seen it before. When we were out in the field, it's that afterimage which you can usually see behind the person working in the field."

I thought back to those times in the darkness, when someone from the group would stand about 20 or 30 feet away wearing dark clothes and calling up the energies of nature around his or her circle. As the person moved, those of us watching would usually see a whitish fuzzy shape that looked like a gauzy outline of that person slightly set off from the blackness beyond.

"Yes, I remember," I nodded.

"Well, everyone has a double," Michael went on. "We don't usually see this, because we aren't doing any special looking, and it's much easier to see in the darkness at night, such as when we're out in the field. But if you use your seeing exercises and really look, you can see these doubles in the light, too, and especially the dimmer indoor light that we have here. So now, go look."

I gazed across the atrium and focused on the escalators going up and down. I watched a man in a raincoat go up; I saw a woman in gray slacks and a beige sweater go down.

"I'm not seeing anything different," I admitted. "Just people looking a little out of focus, since I'm trying to look through them, not at them."

"That's a good first step," said Michael. "Now you want to gaze at the area right behind each person, perhaps a few inches away with some people; up to a foot or two with others. Then, look for a gauzy sort of image. It may be very faint. You may see it as something you can see through. It may seem slightly luminescent.

"However it emerges, one particular thing to notice is how close it is to the person. You'll find the double tends to be much further away in kids, because they tend to move much faster, they have so much more energy. It's as if they outrun their double, and it stays further behind. But as the person gets older, the double generally seems to come closer, because the energy of the person seems to be slowing down. In fact, the double comes even closer to a person as he or she approaches death, and at the moment of death, the double blends with the person, for the individual and his ghostly or spiritual essence become one -- so the two come together."

Michael fell silent again, and again I looked back across the atrium to the escalators to try and see. Then, as I let my eyes gently go out of focus, I heard Michael's voice quietly guiding me, suggesting what I might see.

"Just look at that couple below walking."

I glanced over to where Michael was gazing in the center of the atrium. A man and a woman in their 20s were walking along slowly holding hands. She was tall and strode along firmly, while he hung back slightly.

"Now look," Michael urged. "You can see the double of that couple. It's the shadowy image of each person that's right behind them."

"Yeah, it's right there," I heard Greta whisper loudly beside me.

For a moment, I did see a flickering, shadowy image, although just as quickly, it disappeared, and I saw the couple firmly in focus again. Did I really see their double? Or did I imagine it? I wasn't sure.

But there wasn't much time to think about this, because now Michael asked me to pay attention to the man in the gray coat getting on the elevator.

"Now you'll notice his aura is very close to him," Michael said. "That's because he's much older. His energy is much slower. So the double clings to him much more closely."

As a group of teenagers, two boys and two girls, squeezed onto the escalator laughing, Michael asked me to pay attention to them.

"This time," he said, "don't just look for distance, but look for strength. And as you'll notice, the double in these teenagers is much brighter. That's because they have so much more energy. It's like the energy is pouring out of them and illuminating their double or ghost. So they're not only moving faster, which keeps the double away, but they're moving at a higher energy rate, and you can see that in the double, too."

Again, Greta said she could see the image clearly, although I noticed only the fuzziest hint of an afterimage.

"Just keep looking and don't worry ," Michael reassured me. "It can take more time to learn how to see clearly in these lower light conditions."

He next pointed at three young children playing in the sand box and on the horses below.

"Now here the double is even farthest away and brightest at all."

As we watched, one little girl in a bright red sweater bounded up from the sandbox and ran about in a loop. The two other children jumped up and ran after her, then returned to the sandbox.

"It's almost like they're playing tag, and their doubles are running around after them trying to catch up," Michael observed. "In fact," he continued in a hushed tone, as if he was about to reveal some long held secret, "you know those fantasy people children sometimes report? Or sometimes you hear a child talking to someone. Or the child may talk about having a special, imaginary friend. Well, often what the child is talking about is really his ghost. The ghost is far enough away so he can see it or feel it as a separate person apart from himself. So it can become a special friend or companion to the child."

I continued to gaze at the children playing for a while, and I thought back to my own childhood when I was 2 or 3. Yes, I remembered, I did have some imaginary conversations with some of the people or spirits I saw around me. Sometimes late at night when I couldn't sleep, I would go into the bathroom, sit on the floor, and await my special friend. Then, he would usually pop up behind me, and I would turn and have a conversation with him, until my parents noticed I was up and told me to go back to bed and go to sleep. Or at other times, I would see someone in my bedroom hovering around me, and I would start chatting excitedly, until my parents heard me and called in for me to shut up. So was that the double that Michael was talking about now?

Or was it just an imaginary friend I had created to have someone to talk to? I didn't know.

Suddenly, I felt Michael's tap on my shoulder.

"Now I'd like you to move around breathing in the essence of the people around us. Just breathe in deeply, and sense how the people feel."

We began moving along the upper corridors, trailing behind one and then another person or group. Others passed by from the other direction as we walked. Meanwhile, as I breathed in deeply, Michael kept up a running commentary, pointing out things I should notice and feel.

"Now see that older guy in a trench coat. He has a heavy feeling, doesn't he?....Now notice those little kids. They have a much higher vibration...Now look at that couple coming towards us. Notice the difference in their energy. She feels much stronger. He looks much weaker, doesn't he?"

Then, stopping by the railing, Michael had another technique for us to try out.

"Now I'd like you to reach out with your own energy. Just imagine you are extending your fibers of energy from your belly and sense what the energy of the area is like. We'll start with the area generally, and then tune in on feeling the energies of some people."

I glanced across the atrium. Some boys about 12 were darting in and out of the crowd. Other shoppers, mostly women in slacks, a few men in suits, walked by leisurely but briskly.

I tried imagining and reaching out the energy fibers as Michael suggested, and I felt a racing in the pit of my stomach.

"Well, it feels busy," I said.

"Yes," Michael agreed. "Kids and teenagers often have a very frenetic feel. They have more life energy. They're freer, and they can transmit that feeling to the whole area around them. But adults tend to be calmer; they put out less energy ."

I asked about the reasons for using all the different techniques. "I feel like I'm just picking up what I'm already noticing by seeing," I said. "Then, when you've asked me to breathe in or feel, I'm getting the same kind of message."

"That's fine," said Michael. "That's helping to confirm or intensify your initial impression. But sometimes you may sense something different, because your breathing, your feeling, they each go a little deeper. It's like first seeing the energy, and then going through that outer shell to experience and feel that core within. Or think of it this way. When you use your seeing, it's like using a camera. You start off with a simple camera. Then, you get all kinds of filters, which enable you to see even more. Using your breathing and feeling are like that. You're becoming more and more sensitive to the vibrations out there."

Michael then asked me to use the same reaching out technique to focus on a few people individually. "But you want to be gentle when you reach out," Michael cautioned. "You want to just touch their aura or energy field briefly, feel it, then move away. Otherwise, the person may feel uncomfortable, like their energy has been interfered with, and you don't want to do that."

We began walking around the second floor corridor again. As we passed groups of people, I picked out one individual in the group and imagined sending my energy fibers out. I felt a pulling in the pit of my stomach, and for an instant, I felt a brief jolt or surge of pressure, as

I passed and looked at that person, as if I had made a connection.

"Now notice exactly what you feel," I heard Michael saying, as if he was completely aware of what I was experiencing, without my saying anything.

Just then a burly security guard with a mustache passed.

"His aura feels a little heavier or more solid," I commented.

Greta laughed at my comment. "They usually do. It seems to go with that line of work."

She described some of her experiences in noticing the energies of some of the patrol officers she had worked with and compare them to other people she met. "I think the work hardens you. Then that attitude shows up in your aura."

"Now let's try an experiment," said Michael.

He motioned for us to follow him to the railing where we could see the center of the atrium. The escalators were across from us, and off to the left there was a small cluster of round white tables and chairs for people who wanted to stop and rest, and perhaps snack on something from a nearby restaurant.

"Now we'll reach out and touch someone with these energy fibers for a little while, and see if they notice. This will show you how you can reach out over even a great distance, in this case, about 100 feet or even more."

We leaned over the railing watching, with Michael between us.

"Now gently," Michael reminded us. "I'll pick out someone, and you can both focus on touching him, too. It'll have to be someone who's not moving too quickly, so he or she will be more receptive to feel this very subtle touch."

We watched the people walking and scurrying about below. A young couple strolled by and Michael rejected them.

"They're too involved in each other," he said. A businessman with a briefcase rushed by and walked up the up escalator. "Definitely too fast," Michael said.

Then a bearded man in a colored T-shirt strolled by, who looked like the perfect candidate, I thought. But Michael rejected him too.

"His energy is too scattered," Michael explained. "He'll never notice us."

Then a man in a rumbled jacket and glasses who looked like a college English professor walked by and stepped onto the up elevator.

"Try him," Michael said.

So, as the man rose up across from us, we concentrated on sending out energy fibers from our bellies to gently touch him. Suddenly, when he was about three quarters of the way up, he turned and glanced around, making a quick scan of the atrium.

"There, he felt something," said Michael. "He's aware of something touching him. So now release."

We broke the connection, and moments later, the man, now at the top of the escalator, turned back and looked ahead. Then, he exited the escalator and blended in with the crowd, so we could no longer see him.

"Couldn't he have just looked around anyway?" I asked.

"No, no," Michael shook his head. "That man definitely felt something, and he was trying to see what it was. You don't normally expect a person to suddenly look around like that."

"Yes, I felt the connection," Greta affirmed. "I felt my energy touch his, and at that moment, he seemed to jerk, and then he started looking."

We all glanced back over the railing.

"We'll do one more demonstration to illustrate this," said Michael.

His eyes scanned up and down the atrium for a few minutes. Then, pointing quickly to the cluster of tables, he told us to notice a woman with long dark curly hair who was sitting alone at the far table. She was smoking a cigarette, had a small bag beside her, and gazed out at the area around her, as if lost in space.

"She's perfect," said Michael. "She's by herself, quiet, open, and very receptive."

Michael fell silent, and we concentrated. As before, I imagined my energy fibers reaching out to her, extending across space, and Michael and Greta did the same. Then, suddenly, as we were concentrating, she uncrossed her legs, looked ahead, crushed out her cigarette, and opened her bag.

"There again! She felt our energy and reacted to it," Michael exclaimed. "So now release."

Again I wondered about the direct connection. Was she reacting to us or just reacting as she might anyway?

Michael glanced at me with some annoyance. "Look you can never prove this absolutely. But this is another piece of evidence which seems fairly convincing. We watched her, we sent out our energy, and just when you would expect it, she responded by breaking the gaze which she had had for several minutes and looking away in our direction. That seems like pretty strong evidence to me."

Michael then suggested we try out all these different techniques in the stores around the mall, and afterwards he would have one last technique to demonstrate -- looking at different people's haras.

"Use any techniques you want," Michael suggested as we headed down the corridor.

"Seeing, breathing, reaching out generally, or sending out your fibers to touch one person. And see what you feel. Notice the subtle differences between people. Sense if anyone stands out."

We went into a jewelry shop, and watched several people looking at jewelry, then into a shop with crystals and assorted magical paraphernalia. A girl in a leather jacket with her boyfriend, also in leather, stood out, and I watched her for a few minutes.

"Well, what do you think?" said Michael.

Again, I felt on the spot, like Michael was judging me.

"She seems to have a stronger, freer energy," I suggested. "She feels independent, self-confident, sure of herself."

But was I picking up this sense from the techniques we had just practiced, or from my impressions from seeing her appearance and the way she moved. I still wasn't sure. The impressions from all the different sources seemed to jumble together. Yet, my uncertainty didn't seem to matter to Michael.

"Yeah, Michael agreed, "I feel that, too."

Michael led us over to the crystals, so we could feel and sense them, too. There was a case of crystals of all different sizes.

"Just put out your hands or project your energy," Michael told us. "You can use the same techniques we used on objects as well as people. For all objects have an energy essence. And places do, too. Just reach out and feel."

"And touch someone..." Greta commented softly, alluding to the telephone commercial, and we all laughed.

As we gazed at the crystals, I noticed, or perhaps more accurately, felt the store owner hovering in the background looking at us strangely.

"I'm sure he must think we're a little weird," observed Greta.

"Yes," Michael agreed, and we returned to the atrium railing, so Michael could do his last demonstration -- seeing the haras.

Now Michael wanted me to do the same kind of observing we had done earlier at the Bodhi Tree, but this time he thought it would be easier to do, since we would have a grandstand view of everyone at the mall. Though the people we observed would be a little further away, we could observe from a more detached, neutral position, where we could watch more leisurely, without the fear of being so readily noticed ourselves.

"So you should be more relaxed and comfortable doing this now," Michael said.

I leaned across the railing and got ready to watch, and Greta, just a few feet away from me, did the same.

"Now, just gaze at anybody you want and try to see the hara. Let your seeing go out of focus as you gaze at each person's center and look for that glowing white energy ball, mushroom, or rocket-like shape we talked about. Mostly, you'll find that people have average energies here, so they'll be round glowing balls, like dots in their center. But sometimes we've seen more psychically developed people here. Many of them are drawn to the crystal shop we just went to. So see what you can see."

At first, I didn't see anything except ordinary people walking back and forth, and Michael gave me some further instructions on how to look.

"Think of it this way," he said. "Visually, you are seeing the emanations of each person's energy coming from his solar plexus, or you are picking up those emanations with your feelings. Then, you are associating what you are seeing or feeling with the shape of the person's hara or power center in your mind's eye. This way you have a frame of reference to interpret or express what you are seeing or feeling, and you can use those symbols or images to translate what you are seeing or feeling into something you can work with. So don't worry if you are seeing the hara or using your imagination to create it from what you are feeling or sensing about the person. It's a symbolic representation you can use to clarify what you are picking up about the energy of the person you are seeing."

Then, Michael fell silent and watched with us. The crowds of people were a little sparser now, since it was getting late, only 30 minutes before the mall closed for the night, and people seemed to move more slowly, languidly. The running children were gone now, and even the few teenagers seemed quieter. Also, many people now carried heavy packages, so perhaps they moved more slowly for that reason, too. Whatever the reason, everyone seemed to have less energy now or were even tired, or maybe I was getting tired, too.

"Now concentrate," I heard Michael saying, and I snapped back to attention.

A man in a sweater was going up the escalator now, and I focused on him. Slowly, I saw a soft whitish glow emerge near his waist. Was I finally seeing this energy ball which Michael spoke of, or was I just creating it and projecting it in my mind?

Then, I shifted my gaze to a tall man in a mustache who was hurrying across the floor below us. A little glow around him seemed to bounce and vibrate slightly as he moved.

Suddenly, I heard Michael cry out: "Now, quick, look. On the escalator."

I looked and saw a slim man in a long brown coat carrying an attache case. He seemed to be looking to the left and right, and I noticed he seemed rigid and alert.

"I think he's aware of us," exclaimed Greta. "I picked him right out."

"Yeah, I noticed him immediately, too."

"What's the matter? What's going on?" I asked, puzzled.

"Don't you see that man?" Michael said. "He's got an incredibly well-developed hara. A tightly formed mushroom shape. And you can see how sensitive he is. He's sensed us looking at him. And now he's looking around."

Just then, the man came to the bottom of the escalator and began striding away from us down the long first floor corridor between the shops. In a few moments, a large tree-like plant with thick floppy leaves, like elephant ears, was between us.

"There you see how crafty he is," Michael commented. "He knows someone is tuning in on him, and he's sought to put a barrier between us, so it's harder for the psychic energy to get through."

"But how..." I stumbled over the words, confused and feeling Michael and Greta's sudden excitement.

"Because the obstruction deflects or breaks up the beam, like radio waves," Michael tolde me. Then, turning to Greta he said, "Quick, let's try to follow him. Let's see if we can psychically pick him up."

Then, Michael and Greta were off, and I raced after them. They charged down the upstairs corridor, walking rapidly, almost at a run, then raced down the escalator, leaping from step to step, and ran through the first floor corridor. I was about 10 feet behind, trying to keep them in sight. I felt like I was in a detective hunt, as I ran after them.

After a few minutes, I couldn't see them anymore. I wove in and out of the crowd looking for them. Finally, at the far end of the corridor, I saw Greta.

"We picked him up to the right," Greta commented. "I even said 'hello' as I passed him, though he didn't say anything. Then, he went into a men' s store. Michael's over there now."

"Oh," I said, still amazed and uncertain about what was going on. It sounded like we had caught some kind of psychic quarry.

Then, Michael popped out of one of the stores on the horseshoe turn at the end of the corridor.

"He just left the store," Michael said quickly to Greta. "I was about 20 feet away from him, so he didn't see me. But I'm sure he picked us up psychically."

Just then, I saw the man again go into a record store, make a loop and come out.

"It seems like he's trying to get away from whatever he's sensing, because he's not sure what it is. Yet, because he's so powerful, he's picking something up."

The man walked away from us down the corridor and began climbing the stairs to the upper level.

"See if you can follow him," Michael said breathlessly. "I'll see if I can keep him in range psychically from underneath."

Greta went rushing off towards the stairway, while Michael strode rapidly down the corridor. I followed behind, feeling like the kid sister trying to keep up with the boys. Meanwhile, as we raced along, a few people glanced quizzically at us and moved out of the way.

"Hey, what's happening man," I heard a lanky black man with a radio say as we passed.

I caught up with Michael half-way down the corridor, where he had stopped and was gazing up at the second level walkway.

"I felt his energy till about here," Michael told me. "Then, I sensed he turned and went out of the store."

Michael walked slowly to the central atrium near the escalators where we had first seen the man. A few minutes later, Greta joined us.

"I saw him leave by the side door," Greta said. "Then, he went out into the parking lot."

"There, I knew it," exclaimed Michael. "He sensed some kind of presence, and he wasn't sure what he was up against psychically. So he had to get away."

I glanced around the atrium and along the corridors. There was only a sprinkling of people left, since it was about 10 minutes before closing.

"But couldn't he have been just wandering around shopping, like an ordinary person?" I wondered. "Maybe he wasn't even aware of us psychically and just decided to leave."

Michael looked at me with annoyance, like I was totally stupid.

"Don't be silly," he said. "The man was very aware of us, and a very powerful magician, too. Just wait till we get to the car, and then I'll explain."

Quietly, I followed Michael and Greta on the escalator to the upstairs corridor, which led to the upper parking lot. Michael pushed the door to the lot open and looked around. Then, closing the door, he turned to us, sounding glum.

"No. He's not here anymore. I feel he's gone. I had hoped we might even meet him after all this. He might have appreciated knowing us and knowing what we were about. Then, he would have realized there was no psychic danger from us, no reason to run away. We were just tuning into him on the psychic circuit, and he definitely picked that up, though he didn't know what was going on psychically. I guess if I was in his position, I would have taken off, too. After all, there were three of us, and just one of him."

"But I wasn't really tuning into him," I commented. "I was just following along."

"Then, two to one," Michael commented. "In any case, he could sense this other power around him. So he felt it judicious to get away, at least until he could check out the energy we sent his way, which is probably what's he's doing now. He's probably trying to sense us out and tune in on us psychically to figure out what was going on."

Then, concerned to get us home before this powerful psychic could find us and perhaps track us as we were trying to track him, Michael hurried us back to the car in the lot at the other end of the mall. So we walked back through the almost deserted mall rapidly.

In a few minutes, we were back in the car. I was glad to be back and eager to hear Michael's explanation. I felt like I had been tagging along at the fringes of some strange, exciting adventure, and I wanted to find out exactly what was going on.

As he drove out of the parking lot and onto the freeway, Michael began. "Well, we picked this guy up as being sensitive, when we were doing the hara and reaching-out exercises. When as we reached out, he started looking around, which distinguished him from the others, who weren't paying any attention. Then, almost right away, he became nervous and agitated, as if he could feel something, though he didn't know what. Then, he looked up, almost at us, as if he could sense the energy was coming from around us."

I acknowledged I hadn't been aware of any of this, and Michael continued.

"Now the next thing that happened," he said, "is that once this man became aware of something, he took some steps to evade this by getting a physical object between us, which is one of the most basic ways of deflecting psychic energy. When you feel someone looking at you, you get a solid object in the way. Then, too, he was moving briskly, so he definitely wasn't shopping, though he probably had been. Then, when we went downstairs to follow him, since he was moving very quickly, he moved to the end of the corridor and ducked into the stores ."

"But couldn't he have been just doing some last minute shopping?" I asked.

"No... No..." Greta jumped in. "I saw him there. I even said 'hello' to him. And he was definitely moving around very nervously, not really looking at anything. I sensed he was trying to shield himself from whatever psychic energy he was picking up and was trying to get away."

"That's right," Michael agreed. "We got a sense he was intending to leave. We could feel him broadcasting his thoughts loudly. And one reason we could feel his intent so strongly is because he was feeling so anxious. That feeling radiates. It's like a dog is able to pick up fear.

"Then, to confirm what we were picking up psychically, Greta and I decided to follow him. But we didn't alarm him, since I stayed down below, while Greta went upstairs and stayed fairly far behind him. Then, just as we got closer, he left, which helped to verify that we were picking up on something real."

"Also," Greta added, "I was able to catch up to him, while he was downstairs without him suspecting anything by sucking in my aura. It's like I was camouflaging myself like a normal person, so he wouldn't be aware that I had been trying to reach out to him psychically. So, when I said 'hello,' he didn't think anything was unusual. I was just any ordinary person."

"That was a really good approach," Michael complimented Greta. "And I could feel exactly when she did this," he said to me. "Before that, as we were following the man down the corridor, even though we weren't always together physically, I could reach out and feel Greta ahead of me. There was that psychic link. Then, when she did this, I sensed that her energy had gotten very quiet and I realized what she was doing. She was shielding herself from the psychic eye. Then, for a few minutes, I felt her completely disappear. It was like there was a hole where her energy had previously been."

I sank back in my seat in silence, and for a few minutes, I just watched the flickering lights of the valley below as we sped by on the freeway. I felt like I had been strangely out of it, while this psychic adventure swirled on all around me. To me this thin, fast-moving man in the raincoat with an attaché case seemed like just another ordinary shopper. But like trained spies on an undercover mission, Michael and Greta had picked up something else and like psychic private eyes, they had followed their quarry, while I remained largely oblivious to all this psychic energy shooting back and forth.

Then, I heard Michael's voice breaking in on my thoughts and snapped back to attention.

"So you see," he continued, "what you've seen tonight is an example of the operations of the circuit. We don't usually encounter such strong individuals psychically at the mall. But that man we saw was a sensitive trained adept of another system, and he had achieved a level of sensitivity and personal power equal to our own. And since he was psychically sensitive, he was sensitive to other psychics like us. That's why he did what anyone with good training would do. If you feel touched by another psychic eye looking at you and don't know who it is or what the other person's intention is, you don't stay around. You try to get behind physical objects or disappear.

"You might think of what he was feeling as like being in a jet aircraft and feeling another jet has locked onto you. So you take some quick evasive action to avoid a possible missile."

"But why would he have to do this if your intention wasn't negative, I asked? You were just trying to pick him up psychically to sense his energy, that's all."

"Certainly, that's true. But there were two of us, and he didn't know what we were about, so he feared the potential dangers."

"Like what?" I pressed.

"Like someone throwing an energy dart at him, perhaps sucking away his energy, maybe psychically following him home. Once you are hooked into the psychic circuit, you are aware that there are some black magicians, Satanists, and other individuals out there who might use their bad intentions against you. So it can make sense to evade any unknown psychic energies coming at you, until you have a chance to check them out."

I suddenly wondered about the other people at the mall, both the one's we had focused on seeing or feeling with our energy and the one's we had passed during the psychic chase.

"What did they all see or feel while we were working?" I wanted to know.

"For the most part nothing," Michael replied. "They were like background noise. Oh, you could feel a certain rise in the level of intensity from some of them, while we were involved in the pursuit. It was as if they were aware that something was going on, though they didn't know what. And perhaps a few felt a brief brushing sensation, when we felt their energy. But only that one man reacted with real sensitivity to the energy we were putting out. That's because the other people were basically average, ordinary people, who didn't feel anything. So, no, they weren't really aware of us.

"Sure, some might have seen us moving about and perhaps even thought we might be acting strangely. And certainly, the people did respond to ordinary changes of mood. For example, towards then end of the evening, the crowd was slower moving, more relaxed, and as people individually become calmer, others picked that up, so that feeling wemt from one to the other, and the whole crowd became calmer. But beyond that, no. You have to be psychically aware to pick up the kind of psychic energy we were working with, so they couldn't perceive that."

Michael drove on for a few more minutes, then turned off the freeway onto Mulholland, climbing into the hills. Once again, we all lapsed into silence, and I settled back to enjoy the carpet of lights below. It seemed like the lesson and the excitement for tonight was over.

Then, suddenly, I heard Michael announce, "I can feel him out there."

"Yes, he's trying to see us, while we're up here exposed," Greta said.

I sat up straight, uncertain at first what they were talking about.

Michael stepped on the gas and the car lurched forward.

"He's still trying to follow us. So I'll speed ahead."

Suddenly it became clear. They were talking about the man at the mall.

"He's using that Spy in the Sky technique," Michael explained to me. "Now that he's probably gotten home or to some comfortable location, he's trying to tune in on us to see who we are, what we're about. So now he's trying to watch us, like we were watching him."

I glanced back at the lights of the valley. It seemed so calm, placid. Yet now the car was filled with a prickly, nervous, electric energy, as the psychic chase from the mall continued.

Michael turned off Mulholland onto the windy canyon road that descended down towards Beverly Hills.

"Now we'll be less exposed," Michael said.

"And maybe we could suck in our energy, too, so he can't see us," Greta suggested.

They both breathed in deeply and drove on a few minutes in silence. Then, as we drove through a wooded area, where tall tree branches hung over the road, Michael observed, "Now he's gone. There's too much hill for him to look through."

But as we came into a clearing, Greta commented: "No wait, I can feel him again."

Michael concentrated for a moment. "Yes," he agreed. "I'll put up a wall."

As he drove he focused on raising it. "Anyway, we'll lose him soon," he said. "We're almost down to the bottom of the hill and we're moving very quickly. Besides..." we drove into an even more heavily tree-lined area "...there are all these trees. It's an ideal cover."

Both Greta and Michael sank back more relaxed.

"Now he's finally gone for good," Michael said.

All at once, the electric tension in the car seemed to dissipate. It was like a fog lifting, and now, as if nothing had happened, Michael and Greta once again began trading their stories about eccentric Hollywood stars who lived in the hills.

A few minutes later we pulled into Michael's driveway. Now, in front of this sprawling ranch-house, the psychic world we had just visited seemed very far away.

I gathered up my notebook and tape-recorder and headed towards my car.

"Now remember to practice your exercises," Michael reminded me as I got in my car. "And try reaching out with your energy and seeing haras like we did tonight."

I said I would and started the motor.

"Then, tomorrow we'll talk about how you can use your energy to call on and work with your own familiar," Michael said.

I waved and drove off. I felt like I had been at the fringes of a strange psychic world of which I had only glimmers. The man in the mall had been like an emissary into this other dimension, but I wasn't quite ready to take the step. I wasn't even aware the door was open. But maybe if

I practiced more; maybe if I tried even harder to step into this world, to really see, I could.

Tomorrow, I decided, I would try some experiments on my own, and curious about what my adventures would bring, I drove off into the night.

6

LEARNING ABOUT FAMILIARS

Around 3 p.m., after I finished up my writing for the day, I went out to try some energy experiments, and I decided to go to Venice Beach. It seemed the perfect place -- since there would plenty of people, like the mall we went to last night, with a mixture of wild and crazy people. So I felt I could wander about looking at people and projecting energy without feeling self-conscious. Rather, if I seemed like I was acting strangely, people would think I fit right in.

I put on a heavy sweater, since the day was cooling down and hopped in my car. It was just a short drive from my hotel, near the Santa Monica/Venice border, and in about ten minutes I was there. I found a parking place a few blocks away and walked to the beach.

At once, I felt like a kid walking into a carnival. Hundreds of people walked up and down the broad roadway by the beach, and dozens of shops with T-shirts, stuffed animals, postcards, posters, sunglasses, and other tourist fare spread out on either side of the narrow road by the beach. People excited talked and laughed loudly; they snapped pictures. And on the far side of the road was a side show. A man in red pants and a long red tie bounced back and forth like a bird on roller skates. A small bowl and card at his feet announced, "Your tips are my source of living." Now and then someone walked by and dropped in a coin.

A little further down, a woman at a table read fortunes, and just beyond her, a man in faded jeans with a guitar sang country songs. "I'm an old cowhand," he wailed a little off-key. A few feet beyond him, a man with a long scraggly beard who looked like a 1960s renegade sat beside a large sign that announced offbeat tours for a donation. "Come see the canals and unseen sights of the real Venice," the poster said.

Meanwhile, teenagers on bikes and roller skates came zoomed by on a side path, and a woman with heavy matted hair who looked like she was in a drug daze wandered about asking people for quarters. She zig zagged up and down the boardwalk looking homeless, like she was wearing everything she owned on her back -- a heavy jacket, an oversize vest, jeans, a pair of torn and soiled sneakers, and high rolled socks.

Yes, it seemed like an ideal place for experimenting with feeling people's energy and reading their haras. I started off by simply walking, trying to see the doubles or the haras of the people coming towards me.

At first, I had to squint a little and had a sense of a relentless mob of people coming at me. But then, I began to focus on just one person in turn, and soon I started seeing some images -- a fuzzy ghostly afterimage trailing behind one person; a soft glowing ball in the stomach of another. I thought perhaps I was projecting these visions, creating them by my intense concentration. But then, I remembered what Michael had told me about these images being a symbolic representation of each person, so whether I saw it or created it didn't matter. I should just concentrate on seeing and feeling, and not worry where what I was seeing was coming from. So I pushed my thoughts aside and just watched.

Soon, I was seeing through the people in front of me, like they weren't quite solid, more like energy forms with the outline of a person around them. Then, as I continued to observe, a pattern started to emerge. The younger and more energetic the person, the farther away his double image seemed to be; and the more aggressive the person, the brighter his hara. And if a person seemed especially powerful or self-confident from his walk or dress, the image of his hara seemed to become more pointed and elongated. It was as if I was translating my sense of the person before me into a double or hara, like a shorthand for telling me about the person in images and not in words.

I had no way to test the accuracy of my perceptions, of course. At least I didn't feel I could talk to anyone I saw. But after awhile of forcing these images to come through by my intention, they suddenly began to pop up automatically, each time I passed and focused on someone, as if by a few minutes of repeated practice, I had trained myself to see and didn't have to concentrate on doing this anymore. I could just walk down the boardwalk using automatic looking, and in a flash, I would see an image of the person's essence emerge as a double or hara, or sometimes, if the person walked slowly or stopped to linger somewhere, I might see both. My imagination? Perhaps. Or maybe I was seeing something real. It didn't matter. I was getting an instant reading of the essence of the person, and as I walked along taking quickie snapshots of a series of people, I felt I was suddenly seeing them in a new way.

Then, letting the experience go, I headed back towards my car, soaking in the ambiance of the late afternoon beach. The atmosphere seemed diffuse, languid, filled with a variety of people, each one striving to stand out, to be a character. One was a girl with a New York accent who was directing and singing her own songs in a create your own song concession. She wore a short mini, high black boots, and her long black hair swirled behind her as she sung. Meanwhile, across the boardwalk, three women in heavy black jackets stood holding five large black puffy dogs, who strained against their leashes and barked when anyone passed within a few feet. A little further down, a woman with long red hair hung upside down in gravity boots, while the setting sun went down behind her. Then, as a muscular teenage boy in a jump suit with long blonde hair pumped up and down on one of the bars at the Muscles Beach gym area, a short 50ish woman with graying hair sidled over him. "Does your mother know you do this everyday?" she asked.

It definitely was a very strange energy -- a trying to be different, creative wackiness, and I felt I could tune in on each of these people I focused on for an instant to see the world from their point of view. It was like not only touching but getting inside their energy.

Then, as I passed a strange gray-haired birdlike man sitting in the back of a cafe, he seemed to be sitting alone, looking intently down at a stryrofoam cup he was holding close to the table, I sensed he had built a wall of energy between himself and the people around him. Then, as I looked a little more closely, I noticed he had the fly of his pants open and he was holding his hands around his penis, draining it into a cup. No wonder he was in his own private energy cocoon and the people around him were carefully staying away. At once, I looked away and decided I had been doing enough seeing and it was time to disengage.

So I headed back to my car. As I left, the beach was rapidly graying, and the shop owners were closing their shops. The crowds had thinned out, and I felt a hurried, frenzied energy was settling over the place. Later, I would learn why, because after dark, the tourists left and the beach area was largely taken over by drug dealers and gangs. But for now the beating of seagull wings as they rose in the sky and whirled around seemed like a signal of the darkening energy to come.

Then I was in my car heading back to my hotel in the twilight. I stopped there quickly to change into the black slacks and shirt I wore to most regular meetings at Michaels and drove on. I was eager to tell Michael about my experiments with energy and learn about working with familiars.

When I arrived at Michael's, I joined Greta in the living room, and soon after Paul, who had been studying shamanism for almost 10 years and did some of the teaching with Michael, joined us. He sat down in front of the room besides Michael, a little tired after a long day at the plant where he worked as a manager.

Michael began the lesson after his usual ceremony to create a small magical circle around us and call on the elemental forces and spirits of the four directions to join us and help us. Tonight, as he did this, wearing his usual black ODF uniform, I thought the ceremony particularly apropos, since I would be learning about spirits and how to call on them, so I could have my own personal spirit to help me.

After the ceremony in the dim candlelit room was completed, Michael turned up the lights, stepped besides his blackboard, and began the lesson by pointing out that the tradition of the magician, shaman, or sorcerer working with one or more spiritual helpers was very old.

"The idea of having a magical servant or spirit bound to oneself goes back eons. In the Inquisition, the Inquisitors believed that the witch or magician gained this magical servant, called the 'familiar,' through a pact with the devil, and they thought of this servant as a demon from Hell. But in reality, this tradition of the servant is very old and has nothing to do with demons or infernal spirits. Rather, this special relationship comes about due to a focused act of power that creates a close relationship between the magician and a member of the elemental kingdom. Then, that elemental energy or spirit becomes bonded to the magician, sorcerer, or shaman, and can help him in working his magic."

Michael turned to the board, where he had written the words "fire," "earth," "air," and "water," and went on.

"Commonly these elemental forces or spirits are divided into these four kingdoms or areas of activity, so that certain supernatural entities are thought to correspond to a particular emanation of power. For example, earth elementals are associated with earth; fire elementals with fire; and so on. However, this is really just a convenient way of dividing up the spiritual world, because when you work with these energies in the field, you will find, as we have over many years, that these beings and forces don't fit so neatly in these categories. Rather, they are extremely diverse forms that can readily move about and change their location and form. For example, out in the field we've encountered everything from luminous balls of energy to glowing coyotes to spectral human forms to wraithlike smoky beings.

"It may be easier for us to to think of these beings in particular categories, so in a pseudo-scientific way we make these classifications. For example, we might assign the luminous balls of light to air, the glowing coyotes to the earth, the wraithlike smoky lady to the water. But the beings don't regard themselves as particular elemental beings. They don't classify themselves like we do, though we make these classifications to make sense of the natural world. However, another way to think of these beings is as different vibrations or forms of energy, who occupy but are not limited to particular areas of the natural world. So they can readily move from one place to another. For instance, an energy form we first encounter on the earth and so call an earth elemental might later choose to take up residence in the fire, and become what we might consider a fire elemental. But in essence, we are dealing with the same energy, though transformed and expressed in a different form."

Michael turned away from the blackboard and continued. "Initially when anyone first learns to be aware of and work with these beings, they are just part of the environment or like events. So at first, we may just encounter or see them, find they fascinate or frighten us, or use them as part of our early work. Or they may be only fleeting presences in the distance. But however we experience them, at first there's no personal relationship -- it's just a general relationship like sighting animals in the woods.

"But after awhile, through willed magic, you can seek or develop an ongoing relationship. For example, if you work in the same area again and again, you may see the same spirit and get to know it. That's what happened when Paul and I did a lot of work in Yosemite. We got to know a group of werewolves who kept appearing while we worked. We learned their names through astral inquiry. We became familiar with their specific look and appearance. So soon an ongoing relationship emerged.

"But a magical relationship can be even more than that, because a magician or shaman can use his will to create a special relationship in which a particular being agrees to work with him. And that creates the relationship of the magician and his familiar. In turn, when this relationship is created, the familiar or elemental being becomes bound to the sorcerer to perform certain specific and defined services."

"But wait a minute," Greta cut in. "Being bound -- that sounds a little like slavery; like having a personal slave. And that bothers me," she said with a huff.

"No, no, not at all," Michael soothed her. "There's a voluntary agreement. It's like an understanding, a contract, in which the elemental agrees to enter into a personal relationship with the magician and provide these services. Moreover, some elementals will agree to provide certain services, but they are not interested in doing others. It depends on the spirit as to what they do."

Michael went on to describe the different types of spirits. "There are four basic kinds of services an elemental will perform. It can act as a ward, a messenger or spy, as a soldier, or as a guide. It depends on their capabilities and interests. Often, the elementals tend to do one thing or another, but they can sometimes do a combination of tasks."

Michael wrote the word "ward" on the blackboard.

"Now, the ward is like a protective house spirit, which lives around the house. Its main job is to chase away or consume any negative energies or other entities which aren't positive or don't contribute to the health of the home. It's a little like having a watchdog, and these wards can be used to protect other places, too, like a church or temple. In fact, this idea of having a ward or watcher spirit is very ancient, and you'll find them in most if not all ancient and traditional cultures. In India, China, ancient Egypt, Africa, Central America – the people called on their house and temple gods for protection."

Michael wrote the words "messenger" and "spy" on the blackboard and began to describe them. "These can be especially useful, since you can send them out to find out things and report what they have found. Also, when necessary, they can observe clandestinely, or you can send them out with a message. For example, if I want to contact someone or want him to contact me, and can't do this easily at the moment, say by picking up the telephone, I might send out my familiar as a messenger."

"Like at the mall last night, when you were trying to stay in touch with Greta psychically?" I asked.

"No, last night I was sending out my personal energies," said Michael. "Greta wasn't that far away and she was already receptive. If I wanted to send out my familiar, I would have had to stop for a moment to evoke that elemental, and then I would have sent her. But in this case, there was no point in taking the time to do this, since Greta was so near and tuned into me."

"In other words," Paul put in, "you don't need to ask someone to get you a glass of water, if you can go and get it yourself."

Michael went on. "So mainly I would use a messenger in special circumstances, such as if Greta was far away and there was no way to contact her. Then, I might ask my familiar to get her the message."

Michael went on to the next category, the soldier. "Now this being tends to be very aggressive and somewhat more negative. And generally, the times you might use the soldier, if at all, is in some kind of conflict situation, since these spirits have this negative, aggressive, fighter aspect. However, because of these qualities, these beings can be very hard to control, and a person needs to be a very powerful, trained magician to even establish the agreement in the first place. Then, because of their combative nature, these soldiers may at first even try to attack the magician, because he's already readily accessible, having called them. So the magician may have to first get over that hurdle to work with them. Then, they may reluctantly go ahead and take the desired action. However, because of their reluctance, the magician may still have trouble controlling them. Thus, generally, it's not that good idea to use them."

"Are these evil spirits?" asked Greta.

Michael shook his head. "No, just basically predators that are very aggressive. Such spirits are the closest to what the Inquisitors were worried about, when they came down hard on the witches. They thought the witches were sending out their spirits like attack dogs. But no, they're not evil, just prone to violence. By contrast, other spirits are used for more passive and positive pursuits, so it's best to work with them."

Michael turned to the next category. "Finally, there are the guides, which are usually encountered in a high state of awareness. For example, you might contact an astral guide to show you things or answer questions for you. Or say if you want to go through a gateway, a guide could help to lead you in or show you the terrain. The guide might also introduce you to other beings. And generally, you'll find them very cooperative, more than willing to help."

Michael paused for a moment, and then spoke slowly, thoughtfully, underling the importance of his next words.

"Now, the act of binding a familiar to you involves a ceremonial process. You must properly call it or invoke it, and then work out an understanding or agreement with it in which you in effect create a contract for the terms and conditions for this being's service to you. You want to work out exactly how the familiar will function in your service, and what you will do in return. Then, the familiar will enter an agreement to be bound to you. It's an extremely important agreement. In fact, we consider it so important that we award a grade for this, and when you have been able to do this, you will advance to the next level -- the 6th degree."

"Okay," I nodded. I stopped writing and put down my notebook for a moment, to reflect on what Michael was saying. This would be my next test, the next step I would need to achieve on this path of the shaman.

"However," Michael cautioned, "when you do this ceremony, the binding process is not complete until the being gives you its name. Its name is critical, because this name is very private; it's something special which the being shares with you to show it is now willing to enter your service. Also, the name is the particular vibration this spirit responds to, and it's what you will need to call on it again in the future. In fact, this importance of names has long been recognized in ancient spiritual traditions, so the names of power have often been kept secret and sacred." Michael gave a number of examples from the Judaic, Christian, and Islamic traditions to illustrate. "In any case," he concluded, "when you seek to bind your familiar to you, full control is not possible until the name is known. So you need to do that to fully complete the ceremony."

"Besides the name, what sort of agreement are we supposed to make?" I asked.

"A variety of agreements are reached," Michael said. "Basically, the being will indicate to you the type of service it will provide, such as being a messenger or a guide, and you will specify what exactly you will do for it. For example, it may ask for specific gifts of energy, such as I'll do this service for you, but I want you to give me some energy before or after I do this. Or some familiars may be willing to do a service for you, because by calling them into your service, you have drawn them through a gateway from another dimension so they can exist on this plane. And they appreciate being here, because this plane offers them additional opportunities."

"Like what?" I asked.

"Just opportunities to see and do new things," Michael said, glancing at me with some impatience, as if I was asking too many questions again and pulling him off track. "It's like you opened up another world to them. And in effect you did this by opening up the doorway of a gateway to bring them here, and they couldn't open up that doorway themselves."

"Oh, I see," I said, and I remembered my own experience of cutting a gateway and stepping into another reality (described in SECRETS OF THE SHAMAN). While I had only seen a foggy area at the time, Michael, Paul, and Greta later reported that they had seen all sorts of beings suddenly come through my gateway. And Paul and Greta had even run about, trying to chase them back in, while I was returning to everyday reality, totally oblivious to these beings.

Michael went on. "Now, there are a number of ways in which to relate to these spirits once they are bound to you. Some spirits will hover nearby in an adjacent reality on the other side of a gateway, and then they can come when called. Or sometimes these spirits may stay near the shaman at all times, ready to come into service, when requested. For example, many Mezo-American Indian shamans have their spirits near them, and often these spirits are visible to other shamans. Still another common way of bonding is for the spirit to occupy an object, like moving into a house. Then, the spirit stays there and can be evoked from this object in a time of need."

"What kind of object?" Greta asked.

"Some common objects are a mask, a statue, a stone, and a shrine in the house, though there are many possibilities."

Michael gave an example from his own experience when an elemental he had just encountered took up residence in his house.

"It was my first familiar, and it happened many years ago, when I was doing some work with some earth elementals. I had been working with them for several years, calling on them from time to time, and this time, when I was doing a ceremony to call on them in my house, I suddenly became aware that these earth elementals were gathered around watching me like an audience. They were standing nearby my circle, and when I reached out to them with my energy, they explained that because of my work with them over the years, they wanted to present me with one of their own as a gift to work as a servant to me for a limited time."

"How did they say this?" I asked.

"Telepathically, astrally," Michael said. "I could feel them at the limits of my circle on the astral level. Visually they were invisible, but I sensed them there. In any case, since I had already worked with them and was familiar and comfortable with them, I opened my circle and let them send in this being who was willing to serve me. Then, this being appeared in my circle like a small, concentrated puff of black smoke. It glided in and stopped right before me.

"At first, I wasn't sure to do with this fellow. But then, I remembered my training, and I asked this being what he wanted. When he told me, astrally again, that he wanted someplace appropriate to stay, I grabbed a small clay statuette of an elflike spirit that was nearby on the mantle. Then, I ritually cleaned it and brought it to the center of the circle. Finally, I asked this being if he wanted to take up residence in this statue to act as a ward for the house, and after he agreed, I inscribed his name on the statue in a magical script in a little ceremony to ritually sanctify the statue and indicate that this was now the being's home. After that, the being had a regular place on my altar for as long as he served me, for several years, and when I wanted, I could call on this being for help in taking care of and protecting the house. At other times, I knew he was there, watching over and protecting things generally. So it worked out to be a nice and mutually satisfying arrangement."

"What sort of things did this spirit do to provide this protection?" I wondered.

"Well, a number of times when I felt negative energies around the house, I would call up the being by name, and then I sent him out to deal with the problem. Generally, he appeared in the form of black smoke coming out of the statue, and then he would assume a misty human-like form which was a larger version of the statue. Then, he went to the door, filtered through the keyhole and dealt with the problem, so the negative energy was gone. The atmosphere felt lighter, less oppressive. After that, the being returned to the statue, and the puff of black smoke was gone."

"Is he still there?" Greta asked, and when Michael nodded, she wanted to know "How long is he staying?"

Michael looked at her puzzled. "I really can't say how long this relationship will continue. Like any relationship with a familiar, it depends on use. The more I use and work with the familiar, the more it will be there for me. But if I forget it, it may wander off."

Then Paul broke in to describe his own experience with familiars. "I use familiars in several ways, as do all shamans," Paul said. "One way is as a teaching aid. For example, I use it to give the students a focus. To do so, I call on this one being who becomes luminous – an aqua-green to amethyst color, and I found the being's appearance a good aid in the development of seeing. This vaporous apparition is more visible than the average aura, so this helps with the initial stages of seeing."

"How does it appear?" Greta asked.

"Outside of my own aura," Paul replied. "Normally, it's not good to work with these beings too close to your own aura or energy fibers, because you want that separate space, unless you have a reason to touch it, such as to call on it for an energy healing. So usually, when I call on this being, I set up a triangle of manifestation, using my vision to imagine this, and I have him appear in this spot. Then, I'll ask my familiar to do various tasks."

Paul went on to describe them. "Sometimes I use my familiar to emanate power or take in power. Sometimes I ask it to call on other beings or take astral trips. Or when a person is first starting on this work and I take him out to be by himself on a solo, I'll call on my familiar to help protect this person from any unnecessary interruptions on their trip. It's not that I want the familiar to inhibit things or make anything happen. Rather, it's there to keep an outside magical energy from interfering. Also, I use my familiar to report to me when the solo is done, so I can make a recovery to get the person and bring him back."

"You'll also find that each of these familiars have their own personality," Michael observed. "Not only can they do different tasks, but they have their own way of doing it. For example, I have another being I work with, who's very independent and feisty, a really independent entity. I met her one night, when I was working in the moonlight behind the house, and I saw her suddenly appear as this little silver being. After she said she was interested in serving me, she began naming the things she wouldn't do, such as be a soldier or a ward, and she told me what she wanted – some regular gifts of energy. Then, when I sent her out on her first assignment, she said no, she wouldn't do it, so at first I thought she was very obstinate. But later, I realized she was right, the assignment could be fairly dangerous, so she was just being independent, and I came to appreciate her for that. Now we have a really good ongoing relationship, and she's an excellent spy and messenger."

"What was so dangerous about the first mission?" I asked.

"Oh, I wanted her to contact another magician who was doing things to disturb me, like sending me bad dreams to interfere with my sleep. I also wanted her to see what he was doing, so I could better stop him. But he was a person with very formidable defenses, and you have to be careful when you send out your familiar to do something, because they can get hurt."

"In what ways?" I wondered.

"They could get hit with a charge of negative energy," Michael replied. "They're own energy could be repelled and disrupted. They could even be trapped or captured and taken over by someone else. So you have to be careful about potentially hazardous assignments, and realize that you are responsible for the being that's bound into your service. If they get hurt, injured, or captured, they won't come back. It's like owning a pet. You have a responsibility to see that any familiar in your service is properly cared for; it's like having a karmic obligation.

"Then, too, you have to take into consideration the abilities of the being, because beings with different temperaments or capabilities are better suited to different services, just like people. For instance, you can send some beings through a gateway or a mirror to see things for you, but others might get lost, because they're not as intelligent or knowing. And some might have more difficult getting through or maneuvering, because they are much more dense. For example, earth spirits tend to be this way. Then, sometimes you may encounter spirits that are not very bright, while others are very intelligent spirits.

"So you can get a very wide range of beings, and you need to honor these differences in working with these spirits, because you're not just dealing with some mechanical-like robots. Rather, these are living beings of energy that have a sense of their own existence. They have a self, a soul, a spirit, and even though their body is different than our own, they are still alive, with varying temperaments and levels of intelligence. In fact, some are not only very intelligent, but can be quite devious. So you have to take into consideration who you are dealing with and respect them, just like when you are dealing with another person with different desires, abilities, and interests."

"Or think of it this way," suggested Paul. "You are dealing with beings which have a life force or spirit and are interested in acting as an apprentice to a magician, and they have offered themselves to you."

"As long as they're satisfied with the arrangement," added Michael, "they'll continue to work with you in a spirit of voluntary service. Which is one reason there's such a problem if you try to get a being to do any negative or hazardous work. If a magician tries to do this, the being will do all it can to get out of the arrangement and even turn against the magician. It's much like the situation with soldiers. A being asked to take on a negative assignment will try to get the magician to give them as much as possible for their service. Or they may try to get changes in the original agreement. For instance, they may ask for more freedom or more gifts of energy from the magician. Or they might decide they would like to live in his house when the original agreement was to live outside.

"In short, these beings asked to engage in negative tasks can easily start pushing for more and more, as they look for weaknesses in the magician they are working with. So they can easily get out of control, though a good magician will be able to control them. Yet they'll keep pushing, and it's a continual struggle to keep them in line. Which is why it's a good idea to avoid such spirits, as I certainly do. You don't want to work with all that negativity and the risks it involves."

Then, pulling out a drawing pad, Michael changed the subject.

"Now, once your spirit is bound to you, it's useful to draw a picture of your being with its name. The reason for this is that the more precise your description of the being, the better you can summon it next time and control it, and the more specific you can be in focusing your intent on what you would like it to do."

Michael flipped open his drawing pad to show some sketches of some of the familiars he worked with. One looked like a hulking blue human-like form with spiky projections from its head. Another looked like a small female fairy, a little like Tinkerbelle. A third looked like a grayish bat.

"These are just some of my familiars," he said. "For there's really no limit on how many you can have, although you only want to work with as many as you really have the time and energy for. Otherwise, some of your familiars might feel neglected and start to wander away, or not feel motivated to continue to help you. But as with friends, if you feel the mutual benefit is over or you're drifting apart, you can simply say goodbye, until it makes sense to renew the relationship again."

Michael next passed around a sketch of a circle with a dozen symbols and strange-looking letters, like hieroglyphs, from the magical alphabet he used called Fermese. "It's a seal or energy design I created, and it contains the essence of an energy being, which can take various forms. In some forms, such as this, you can take your familiar with you, so if you wish, you can call on your familiar on an everyday basis if you need some help, say to get an answer to a question."

"It sounds like carrying a credit card," commented Greta with a sly grin.

"Perhaps a little," observed Michael. "He pulled out his wallet to show a small version of the seal, which he inserted in a pocket behind his money. "I keep the picture as a reminder. And if you have an image in color, that's even better. The more vivid the image, the more connected you can feel to it and the more power and energy you can feel."

He snapped the wallet shut and put it away. "Anyway, the point to emphasize is you can work with these beings who take a variety of forms in many different ways. Sometimes they may come to you to volunteer their help; at other times, you can actively create them. For instance, I created the seal you just saw and as I did the familiar emerged from it. But many other familiars I've worked with just showed up and offered to help and work with me. Or in some cases I actively called them and they appeared."

Michael looked thoughtful for a moment. "I guess at this point I've worked with thousands of spirits, and at one time or another, a few dozen have become familiars. However, there are some who offered their services, though I turned them away."

"Why?" I asked.

"Because you don't have to work with everyone who offers," Michael said. "As you'll find out, you need to be selective with your time and energy. Sometimes you may not feel a rapport with a particular spirit or you may not trust it. It's like choosing your friends, employees, or co-workers. The arrangement has to be mutual and feel comfortable on both sides for it to work.

"Anyway," said Michael, turning to the board, "you'll find all this out for yourself, when you've learned to work with your own familiar starting Friday night. Now I'll show you what you need to do to begin this contact."

I felt a sudden rush of excitement, as Michael began describing the plans for a field trip to do this. We would be going to a wilderness area about an hour north of Los Angeles, since this setting would help to open up the doors to another dimension, and thereby facilitate contact.

"The first thing you will do is make a circle for yourself," said Michael. "Then, you'll make a triangle of manifestation for the spirit."

He pointed to the diagram on the board which featured a small circle connected to a nearby triangle by a dotted line. "After you have drawn these images with your willed intention, you will put out a general call for an elemental spirit to come into your service as a familiar and be bound to you for a certain time. Then, hopefully, a spirit will respond to your call and show up visually in your triangle."

"What will it look like?" I asked.

"It could take any number of forms, anything from a vapory apparition or smoky form to a more concrete animal or human-like appearance. One purpose of all the sensitivity exercises you have been doing is to be able to see with your heart and senses as well as your eyes, so you should be aware of your feelings, too. Thus, your full description of this being won't only be visual, but you should be able to really feel its signature and get an impression of its personality, just like you do in tuning into people."

"You mean like we did the other night at the mall?" I asked, and then briefly described my experience in seeing and feeling the people's haras and auras at the beach.

"Yes, exactly that," said Michael. "You want to feel for the spirit's essence, just as you do with people. For these beings have an underlying soul or spiritual energy, too, even though they may not have a physical form like us. So when you reach out to this being, you want to use both your seeing and feeling, and pick up what this being is like both visually and based on what you feel with your heart."

Michael glanced over a list of questions and continued. "Now, the next step, assuming this being appears, is to ask some basic questions to find out who this being is and work out a basic agreement. First, you want to know what kind of being this is. For example, ask what element it is associated with, although it doesn't necessarily have to have this connection. Secondly, note its appearance. Is it humanoid in appearance or not? Thirdly, notice the sex of this being. Even if it isn't in a human or an animal form, you still should sense whether it has primarily male or female energy, or is it neuter.

"Fourth, try to get something of its background. For instance, ask where did it come from? Was it from a nearby dimension, or did it come from far away? Maybe ask something about its environment. Is it from a place that's much like our own, or is it from a spiritual level of being?"

"Fifth, ask what it requires from you. In particular, you might ask if it requires a gift of energy to feed its own energy or is this unnecessary, since its existence on this plane is good enough. Another key question is does it require a home, such as a statute to house it. Or is there some activity you might need to do, such as a ceremony, to contact it in the future?

It's important to clarify these things, and if it specifies something and you refuse, it will leave your service. So you must be willing to offer such things, and you must be honest in making these promises so you carry through. In other words, whatever you offer and agree to, you must be ethical, just as you must be in dealing with people, to keep the familiar's ongoing loyalty and willingness to serve."

"But how do I get all this information?" I asked. I suddenly felt strange, uncertain about this idea of talking to this formless being I imagined or felt.

Michael gave me one of his "oh-another-dumb-question" look. "You just use your intuition," he replied. "Since these beings are from another dimension, most don't speak English. So your communication will be on a psychic or telepathic level. You'll be doing spirit to spirit communication. They'll talk to your inner spirit.

"For example, my familiar who appears like a silver woman communicates as a wave of energy. I suck in the energy, and I interpret what she is saying as a series of images which translate into words. Then, I communicate back in return. My words become images and then energy so we can speak to each other.

"It's like the process that happens in a computer. You have this program language which humans understand, and it gets translated into source language and finally into operating language which corresponds to the binary bits that talks to the machine. Then, after the machine gets through with its operations, its operating language gets translated back to the program language. So sometimes, your communication with a spirit can be like that. In other cases, you might have direct thought to thought transfer or the communication might be by touch, in which the being reaches out and touches you with a tendril of energy. Or maybe you might even see or feel an actual limb, as if the being is actually shaking hands with you. So just like the beings can appear in many different ways, your communication with them can take many different forms.

"Also," Michael continued, "some of these beings will want to come into your circle to communicate. You have to decide if you want to let them in."

"Why wouldn't you want to?" I asked.

"Because when you let the being in, you open yourself up to it. So you need to be careful and know what you are doing. You want to be sure this is a friendly, positive, helpful being you can trust. You have to go by your intuition. It all comes down to what you feel."

Michael went on with the other guidelines needed for binding the familiar to me.

"Sixth, you must work out the specific terms of your agreement with your familiar. In particular, you must not only find out about its energy requirements -- the kind of energy it requires from you, but its length of service, and most importantly, it's type of service. It must fit within one of these four categories we discussed. If it's not clear what type of service it is offering to you that's not enough. It must agree to do something specific for you.

"Generally, the way this usually works is for you to make a proposal for what you would like this being to do. Then the being can choose to accept if this is agreeable. At the moment, it's probably best to ask the being to be either a guide, which can be especially helpful at this stage of your training or a messenger. You have no need now for a ward or a soldier, and such beings can be more complicated to deal with, even potentially dangerous like the soldier, so guides and messengers are best.

"Additionally, you need to ask and the being must willingly give you its name, so you can call it into service. Generally, this name will be in the being's language, so you must come as close as you can in expressing this name in English. In fact, when you ask for a name, you may sometimes only see colors or lights, expressing its name non-verbally. If so, come up with some English equivalent you can use to call it. In any case, it will usually be a fairly exotic name, which feels very powerful, because this is a special relationship."

"So if the being tells you its name is Fred or George," put in Paul, "it's probably a mistake. Or it's just kidding you. These are beings from another dimension. So you can expect it to have an unusual name of power."

"Anyway," added Michael, "once this agreement has been made and the being has given you it's name, if there is a requirement from you, such as a gift of energy, which is generally the case, you want to give it. Then, the being will leave, and you can call it back at another time.

"However, " Michael cautioned, "you generally don't want to call these beings unless you first make your circle and triangle, unless you are very adept, and even then it requires quite a bit of focus to call on them. Rather, you should consider this process of calling on your familiar as a formal ceremony, and do this ceremony each time you seek to make contact. Then, you can specify what you want and ask them to do it."

"What sorts of things might I have them do?" I asked.

"Well, say you are working with a messenger or courier. You might send the being to find something out or contact a person. When you do, ask the being to come back and tell you it did the job and what it found. That's what I do," Michael said.

"How long will this take?" Greta wondered.

"That depends on the errand. It depends where they are going and the difficulties they might encounter in getting the information. However, when they come back, you don't need the formal circle. Rather, the being will just return with the information. For example, when I send out my silver lady as a messenger and she comes back, I get a definite sense of her presence nearby, and I experience a burst of energy with the results. Or if Gratha, the being in my statue returns, I may not see him come back and enter it. But I'll see a shadow passing through the room which is very distinctly his presence."

I glanced at the small wooden statue on the mantle that Michael referred to as Gratha's home. It was made of a reddish wood, with a kind of gargoyle-like face, reminiscent of a Polynesian deity.

"And now?" I asked.

"He's there, of course," said Michael. "He's just waiting for me to send him out on his next errand."

Michael had a few last reminders about proper ethics. "It's really important to treat these beings with respect," he said. "You have to be ethical. It can be very easy to develop an imperious attitude towards these spirits, since they aren't substantial, just ethereal creatures. So it can be easy to abuse the relationship or try to take advantage of the spirit willing to serve you. But you must be responsible. It's like owning a pet or being a responsible employer. Or like being a friend.

"So don't just look at this relationship in terms of your own benefit, which could lead you to be selfish and create an uneven relationship. Rather, you should seek for a harmonious relationship with benefit for all concerned. For example, remember to give the spirit the attention or gifts of energy it needs; treat it with honor and kindness. Otherwise, the relationship can sour, and it can become a negative relationship if you abuse the spirit. So then it may play tricks on you, try to deceive you, or leave."

"Okay, I'll be careful," I agreed.

Michael picked up a sword from the table in front of him, held it aloft, and continued.

"Now, one of the simplest types of familiars exists in a power object. This is a spirit that has been fused into the object, such as this sword, which is one of the most powerful tools of ceremonial magic."

Michael laid the sword back on the table and invited Greta and me to look at it. It shimmered slightly in the flickering candlelight, and I noticed some strange letters and symbols along one side.

"Those are runes," Michael explained. "A ceremonial or magical sword must be properly constructed, and that includes inscribing it with runes. In this case, these are Norse runes, although the particular type of runes doesn't matter. But all magical swords must be inscribed with something, and the specific combination of letters or symbols is important, because unless the sword is inscribed properly, it can't function to its full power potential."

"Why not?" I asked.

"Because," said Michael, "the runes draw the energy to and through the object in a specific focused way, depending on the combination of the runes. It's like having a formula that directs power to the object for a particular purpose. In the ancient traditions, such as in the times of the Vikings or the Middle Ages, the magical swords were usually inscribed to focus power towards a specific objective, such as the evocation of a particular magical being, which might reside in that sword. However, if you're going to be doing a variety of work, as we do, it's better to inscribe a sword with runes that provide for a more general power that can be used in all operations.

"In fact," Michael picked up the sword, "you might think of a proper runic inscription like an electronic circuit. Unless the pathways are laid out correctly, the board won't function well. Likewise, unless the correct runes are used or are in the proper sequence, the sword won't function well."

Michael pointed to a series of symbols near the tip of the blade. "One side of the sword should be inscribed with your magical name -- like this is my name in runic writing. In turn, it's important to give some careful thought to this name, because it's the name that personifies you as a magician or shaman. It's a name you give yourself, just as the spirits you work with have a name. So it's not just your everyday name. Rather it's a special name, something you're not called normally. In fact, it must be a carefully guarded name, since these names have power, and this secrecy helps to maintain that. Also, this name will generally be in another language, because it is so special."

Michael held up the sword in front of himself and drew it close. Then, gazing at it, he continued. "The purpose of inscribing your name into a ritual tool, such as a sword, is that it binds and personalizes the object to you, so it's more efficient in responding to you and better able to help you achieve your goals in a ceremony. That's because the inscription of your name puts it in contact with you and your energies. It's like you have given it your personal combination."

Michael lay down the sword to show the other side, which was also inscribed with runes near the tip. "So your name is on one side. On the other side, it's important to have runes designed to empower the object with your goal or purpose for the object. For example, I use the traditional magical phrase: ' By my will,' plus some additional runes in the proper numerical sequence to give it some extra energy and at the same time provide the proper balance."

"Based on your intuition or feelings?" I asked.

"No, not only that in this case," Michael said. "To work with runes, you have to study them, say from a book on Norse runes. But for now, you just need to understand that runes have individual power and a combination of runes bring about certain forces. So it's important to balance them out numerically to get the appropriate vibration of energy."

Again, Michael picked up the sword and now he moved it back and forth firmly in front of himself. The room had an electric, charged feeling, as he did so.

"Wow, I can feel the energy and power around it," exclaimed Greta.

"That's because this is a very powerful object," said Michael. "For I given it my name, the intention I have in a phrase, and have added additional runes, so this object functions for a specific purpose and has a very strong focus as energy is channeled through it. Once I inscribed it, this object showed increase power and energy, and as soon as I pick it up, the contact with my skin gets the energy flowing strongly through it. So this isn't just a common power object which I built. Rather this is a customized precision power instrument, in which the energy is brought into a very fine and tight focus."

"So what would you use it for, rather than a regular power object?" I asked.

"Well, I would use it in works that require greater energy and precision. For example, I prefer to use this rather than my staff when I'm doing any work of great importance."

"Like what?" I pressed.

"Well, it's not for the more everyday sort of work, like calling your familiar, doing an invocation of an elemental, or going out on a solo."

Paul cut in. "You have to understand. This is a really sophisticated tool, and we just want to introduce you to it, since Michael will be using it shortly, when he shows you how to make a good circle. But this kind of tool is put together by a person who has already done a great deal of work, so he or she has already achieved a high level of magical development, and he needs a very specific tool for an act requiring a very high focus."

"Like what?" I still was unclear what Michael and Paul meant.

"Well, some of these things are unexplainable," said Paul "because they are of such a high degree of power. Or then again, some things are better left unsaid, because it takes the power away from them."

I still looked puzzled. I felt like a child left out of the conversation by the talk of grown-ups. "But what sorts of things? Just give me a general example so I can understand."

Michael and Paul fell silent for a few moments. Greta and I watched them breathlessly, waiting, as if hoping to hear about this special secret.

"Well," said Michael finally, "one example might be work with the elemental kings, which we'll talk about later. They're highly sophisticated beings, and a great amount of energy is required to work with them. So a sword can be useful in evoking and working with them. Or you might use a sword to ordain someone who has advanced to a high level of magical or shamanic power. Then, through that act, he advances to an even higher level as the power flows into him from the sword."

And that was all Michael or Paul would say about that.

Michael quickly changed the topic to tell me how to make a proper magical circle, since I would need to make one to successfully call on and work with my familiar.

He drew a circle on the board to illustrate, with four small circles located at each of the four directions. It looked something like this:

"You can make a variety of magical circles," he commented. "But this is the most common one we use in most of our workings. The practitioner draws a central circle, usually with a staff or other power object. Then, standing in that circle, he invokes the elements of the four quarters, and invokes each one separately as a specific and focused act.

"When you do this..." Michael looked directly at me, "you want to invoke each of these elements separately in order to focus your consciousness on knowing that being, and at the same time feel and pay attention to this feeling of their presence. Thus, don't draw the circle casually, but create a strong circle by putting your concentrated energy into evoking these beings, so you feel the element was really called and truly manifested itself. In short, you have to put out a lot of energy, particularly when you are first starting to do this, to make a good circle.

"Additionally..." Michael sketched a second medium-sized circle to the right with the image of a triangle inside it, "...you need to draw a triangle of manifestation with the intention that this is a temporary spot or housing to contain the spirit you are calling forth. The spirit doesn't just come from an open door or gateway into this other reality. Rather, triangle in the circle is the place where the spirit materializes, interacts with you, and is bound until it is banished or asked to leave.

"It's important that you maintain that focus or intention, because if you lose that, the triangle will no longer act as a binding tool, and the spirit may tend to wander out. In fact, a spirit may tend to do this as soon as you let go of your focus, because spirits don't like being bound in this triangle, since it's like a cage, and just like any animal, no spirit likes walking into a cage. So you may have to exert some will to convince the spirit to reside there temporarily."

"How far away should you draw this triangle?" I asked.

"You can draw this triangle at any working distance you are comfortable with, Michael replied, "though I usually draw it about 20-30 feet away. I find this a nice, comfortable, safe distance for dealing with the being, when it first arrives and we're getting acquainted. Also, I can readily see into the area and see what's going on. On the other hand, if you are making this circle in a smaller working area, you may need to make your triangle of manifestation much closer. I've known people who have created these up to hundreds of feet away and sometimes within a few feet. So any distance that feels good for you is probably fine."

Michael paused for a moment, while I hurried to catch up with my notes, and then continued.

"Now another important point to keep in mind in dealing with this spirit is that you must keep a specific focus on your circle while you are doing everything else. You can't let your visualization of the circle and the strength of this visualization waiver or fade from view. If it does or if you doubt the presence of the circle, it can collapse. So you have to continue to visualize your circle around you in full strength at all times. You can't take it for granted.

"It's like building a house. You must carefully visualize and construct your circle in the beginning, step by step, and do this slowly, with close attention to detail, so you properly visualize it and maintain that visualization. Otherwise, if you hurry through it, you will generally find areas that are patchy or missing, so you must build it carefully and slowly to build a solid, strong wall."

Michael walked around in a circle, and to further reinforce what he had just said, added:

"So, the circle you create in the center must have your intention of being your circle of focus and intent. Then, when you invoke the elementals, you must draw each invoking pentagram in mid-air with the definite intent of drawing that element to stand guard to help protect your circle and focus its energy.

"Moreover..." Michael reached out and made a pushing motion, like a bricklayer laying a brick, "you must carefully draw your triangle of manifestation with similar attention, so it's very clear where you want this temporary housing or area of confinement for your spirit to be. Then, it will be very certain where you want this spirit to manifest, and you don't have to guess where it has appeared. Then, you can feel free to talk to it until you are ready to ask it to leave."

"What if it wants to leave before then?" I asked, noting Michael's earlier comments about the spirits not wanting to be confined in this cage-like area or sometimes being capricious.

"Then, you have to work on persuading it to stay with your will. That's the whole point of developing your power, intention, and focus. You want to exercise that control. So if you experience any resistance, work on trying to persuade the spirit a little harder.

"On the other hand," said Michael, drawing a dotted line between the large circle and triangle of manifestation, "if you feel it's appropriate and feel comfortable with this spirit, you can invite it into your own circle. The time to do this is when you feel the spirit is friendly and cooperative. To do this, make a bridge from the triangle to your circle. Draw it with your power object or visualize it; then ask the spirit to come across until you want it to return to its triangle.

"However...." Michael paused and looked very serious. "Be quite careful when you do this. Because once you create the bridge, you open the triangle of manifestation and let the spirit into your circle. So you should only do this if you feel it's a good risk to do so. You have to feel you can trust the being to come in."

Michael picked up the Polynesian-style statue with the gargoyle face from the table.

"Now, another point," he said. "Later, after you have bound your familiar to you, you can use your triangle of manifestation to call your familiar to come out of the object where it has taken up residence. For example, that's what I do with Gertha, who is housed in this statue.

"The way to do this is to step out of your circle and put the object there, where you are visualizing the triangle of manifestation. Or first create the triangle around the object. In either case, once the triangle is created and the object is within it, you can call that being to come out and respond to you.

I personally prefer to begin with the object outside of the triangle, and after I create the triangle, I step outside my circle, get the object, and place it inside. But you can do it either way. The important point is to clearly visualize both your triangle and your circle and invest them both with your focus and power. Then, you can better get the spirit to manifest and bind itself to you or do your bidding, once it is bound."

I had one last question. "Do I have to draw all these circles and triangles with a power object? Or can I just visualize them in my mind?"

Michael glanced at me with some impatience. "Look, there are many other ways to make a circle or manifest beings. Some people paint their circles on the ground; some draw them in the form of a square or in a star; there are all sorts of working areas. We use the circle because it is very basic, and we find it especially powerful. Also, we use the circle around both the protective pentagrams and the triangle of manifestation to serve as a focus for the energy. And yes, you should use your power object to draw the spirits in, at least in the beginning when you need a very strong focus for your visualization and intent to make anything happen.

"So yes, you must go through the actual gestures, and you must visualize the energy coming out and describing or inscribing the object in the ether. If not, your circle will be weak, and you may have trouble manifesting a being. Later, when you are more adept at this, you may be able to quickly experience a circle around yourself or call a being forth without all these procedures, because the power is on tap whenever you want to draw on it. But that's later. This is now. Don't try to move ahead too fast or nothing will happen now."

Then, with that admonition, we went outside, since Michael wanted me to practice making a really good strong circle. "You need to do this,"

Michael said, "if you are to succeed in calling your familiar when we go out in the field Friday night."

I put on my black jacket, got my staff from the car, and joined Michael, Paul, and Greta at the patio, where they had gathered.

"Now I'll demonstrate contacting a guide familiar first," said Paul.

He went to the center of the lawn, about 20 feet away to demonstrate. It was dark, with just the hint of a moon hidden behind the clouds, and he looked like a shadowy figure, who nearly blended in with the bushes behind him.

We stood quietly for a few minutes, as Paul shifted and turned in the darkness. It looked like he was turning, making a circle, when a smoky, grayish area began to extend in front of him like a line, almost like he was projecting some energy from his body. Then, he walked along this line to an area about 20 feet ahead of him and bent down, as if he was having a conversation with something small in front of him. Afterwards, he came back and stood facing this area where he had been breathing deeply for several minutes. As he breathed in, the smoky, grayish line seemed to gradually become smaller and thinner, as if he was pulling it to him, and then it was gone. Shortly after this, Paul turned about and walked back to us on the patio.

"What did you see?" he asked me, and I reported my observations.

Paul seemed pleased. "Good, you're becoming more observant," he exclaimed, and he explained that after creating his personal circle, he had reached out with luminous fibers from his solar plexus rather than drawing a line between his circle and the triangle of manifestation.

"So that's what you perceived as a bridge," he said.

Then he described how he had gone out to meet his familiar halfway between his circle and the triangle.

"After we met there, we talked, and I got what I wanted, he got what I wanted, and I came back, and the guide went away."

"But I couldn't see the guide," Greta complained. "Though I saw everything else."

"That's because it was a guide," Paul explained. "Often guides don't let themselves be seen by other people, so they can't be followed.

A person who sees them can keep that image of them and call them up by that image. So sometimes guides may seem invisible to observers."

Then Michael announced he wanted to demonstrate the circle I would do.

"I'll go through the steps using my sword to make a working circle with a triangle of manifestation."

"Why a sword?" I asked, since I would only be using my staff, and usually Michael used his staff, too.

"So the circle will be especially strong and visible, so you can see what I'm doing," Michael said.

Then, he stepped out on the lawn. Like Paul, he looked very shadowy in the dim moonlight, and as he moved about in the darkness, he explained what he was doing, so I could repeat these motions later.

At first, he stood there quietly, facing away from the moon towards the road.

"The first thing I'm doing," he began, "is selecting a direction in which to work. I like to start in the East, since that's the direction of the rising sun. But you can start wherever you want.

However, for consistency, it's a good idea to always start in the same place."

Holding out his sword towards the ground at a 45 degree angle, Michael continued. "Now I start by projecting energy out of my sword towards the ground to create the circle."

Slowly, surely, he turned in a clockwise direction with his sword outstretched.

"Now, as I draw the circle, I'm visualizing it as a sold ball of energy. And I move slowly, carefully, and then..." Michael gradually lifted the sword as he spoke. ".I'm slowly raising it up in a spiraling motion to make the circle into a cone. Then, I visualize that cone rising up above me."

Meanwhile, as Michael worked, a misty haze gathered around him, so he faded further into the dark bushes. Then, making some forward slashing motions with his sword, Michael continued.

"Now I'm making the protective pentagram in the air, starting in the East, to invoke the elemental of air associated with the East and bring it here to guard the circle. I make a circle first, and then the pentagram."

I could barely see what Michael was doing in the darkness, but I watched intently, straining my eyes to see. After he turned, facing away from us and made a few more slashing motions, he continued. "Now I make the pentagram and circle for fire, associated with the South."

He turned again. "Now, I do the same at the quadrant for water."

I noticed that Michael was now facing us in the direction of the ocean to the West.

"Finally earth," he announced, turning another quarter turn to the North. "So now I have invoked all of the elemental forces, and each of these pentagrams and circles I made is a gateway for a specific elemental to enter into the circle, and contribute it's energy and protection."

For about a minute, Michael stood silently, motionless, concentrating. Afterwards, slashing his sword up and down and moving it in a circular motion, he announced: "Lastly, I make the pentagrams above and below me to fully protect and seal the circle. And next I make the triangle of manifestation."

This time, Michael extended his sword outward with some broad reaching strokes. "First I make the circle around it, then the triangle itself. Then I charge it."

He thrust his sword forward, and at once I noticed a slight fogginess where he was pointing. Was it my imagination or the triangle of manifestation, I wondered? Meanwhile, Greta and Paul near me watched in rapt silence.

Then, I heard Michael's voice from far away, and I snapped back to attention.

"Now I'm going to call the familiar I work with into the triangle," Michael said.

I saw a slight sparkle of light, perhaps 6"-8" high, as he spoke, and after making a few more slashing motions with his sword, Michael announced: "Now I'll invite her to join me, because I feel comfortable with her nearby, and here she comes very close."

Stepping out of his circle, Michael went towards the sparkles of light, and for a few minutes, he knelt down half-way between his circle and the triangle, apparently talking to something. Finally, getting up, he announced: "Well, now I'm finished, and I'll let her depart. Then, I will banish the triangle of manifestation and take down the circle."

Again I saw Michael move around in his circle making thrusting and slashing motions with his sword, moving in a counterclockwise direction. Finally, the triangle and circle removed, he returned to our group on the patio. Like Paul, he wanted to know what I saw, and I described how I saw him make the circle and triangle and walk out to it.

"But what did you see in the triangle?" He wanted to know exactly how I perceived his familiar. He wanted specifics, and he questioned me like a lawyer cross-examining a witness.

"I saw sparkles," I began.

"How big?"

" About 6-8" ."

"What color?"

"Bluish and yellow?"

"Did that change?"

"It seemed to get a little warmer red after a while?"

The questions went on and on, since this was Michael's way of validating my ability to see. But was I correct?

"Was any of that consistent with what you were doing?" I finally asked.

"Yes," Michael nodded. "But what you're seeing is what's important. You need that ability to make your own circle and call your familiar successfully."

After Michael described some details of what he had been doing ("I placed an object in her triangle for her to do some psychometry work on"), and asked if I noticed how she had left ("She drifted up into the air as usually with a fairly vivid display"), he asked me to go out and make a circle.

"And be sure to do it in the exact and careful fashion I just did," he cautioned. "You want to feel it, experience it, and really see the energies as you go. You want to come up with a really good circle. I'll be testing you to make sure you can do it."

"Okay," I said quietly, and went to the center of the lawn.

I felt suddenly self-conscious, standing there, with all eyes looking at me. Then, taking a deep breath, I began as I had seen Michael do, drawing the circle with my staff. Next, I moved my staff up to make the cone, and after that to make the circles and pentagrams to call in the four elementals from each of the directions. I walked slowly, thoughtfully, as Michael had done, and I concentrated on sending out a radius of energy in the form of light around me, which gradually spread up as I made the cone. Then, as I stabbed ahead with my staff to create the protective pentagrams, I imagined four spots of energy, like searchlights spreading out around me. As I did, my awareness of the people on the patio watching me gradually slipped away.

Then, as I stood, feeling the circle around me, I heard Michael's voice from far away calling to me.

"Now remember to put the pentagrams above and below you to seal the circle."

I nodded and made the proper motions, suddenly feeling a little insecure about everything I had to remember to make a circle, and I wondered if I could remember the many things I would have to do to make a triangle and call a familiar as well.

"Now concentrate on your circle," Michael called out again, as if he could read my thoughts. "You want to really feel it as a totally self-contained ball of energy around you."

I sank back into visualizing the energy again. It seemed to feel comfortable, protective, like I was shutting out the world outside.

Just then, I heard Michael's voice calling to me again. "What do you feel?" he said, as he moved slowly around my circle.

"A little sense of pressure, I guess," I said.

"Well, good," Michael replied. "I was just checking out your circle at each of the four directions to see if it was solid. I was sending some energy to it, and it bounced off, which is good. Now just concentrate on what you experienced again."

Again, I focused on experiencing the energy of the circle around me, as Michael moved about in the darkness, and I felt his presence shifting about me like a cat.

"What did you feel?" Michael exclaimed.

I suddenly noticed a slight tingling and reported this.

"Well, I just cut a slight hole in your circle with my magical sword," Michael said. "So what are you going to do about this?"

I stared down at the ground for a moment wondering what I was supposed to do.

"Close it up," Michael said. "Use your staff or visualization to project out energy to seal it up."

I made a few motions to do so, and started to go back into my trance-like concentration, imagining that the circle felt solid again. Then, once more, I heard Michael's voice, almost laughing at me.

"What do you feel now?" Michael said.

I tried to sense around me. What should I notice? What was there? I felt that Michael had done something to play a trick on me. But what? Was there another hole he had created? I couldn't feel any differences in the energy ball around me.

"Look at your feet," Michael finally said.

I looked down, and the ground seemed dark and misty.

"Well, I just sent in a being into your circle," said Michael.

I looked up surprised and then back at the ground.

"Well, it's gone now," Michael said. "I just called it back. So what that shows you have to be quick. You have to keep your circle closed and tight, and if it should weaken at any point, you have to shut it up again and make sure nothing gets in. Or if it does, you have to send it out."

I made another circuit, reinforcing my circle by moving my staff around and visualizing another burst of energy strengthening the ball of energy around me.

"Good, that's much stronger now," said Michael.

Then, satisfied, he asked me to make the triangle of manifestation. "But don't call up any beings," he said. "Just create the triangle for now."

I reached out as Michael had done, moving my staff around to create the circle and the triangle within it. I visualized the circle and triangle forming as I did.

"Now what do you see?" Michael asked.

"Just some sparkling of light in the area," I replied.

"Anything else?" Michael asked. I felt he was testing me and looked more closely.

"No, nothing" I said.

"Well, I just sent another being into your triangle," Michael said with a laugh. "And there..." he looked up into the air, "...she goes. You're not supposed to be able to project your own energy and beings into somebody else's circle like this, but as you've seen, you can. If you have sufficient power, you can use another person's magical diagrams."

I glanced up into the air to see if I could see anything, but I just saw the dark sky, with wispy grayish boundaries around the clouds which now hid the moon. I felt a little like I did as a little kid watching a magician pull out cards from thin air and then make them disappear again. Or maybe I was more like the unsuspecting stranger left out of the joke everyone else knows.

"But I didn't see anything," I finally managed weakly.

"Well, you've got to learn to be quicker, more aware. Now that you know some of the things that are possible, that will help you be more alert."

"I'll try," I said.

Since we were finished, Michael asked me to take down my triangle and circle.

"Do everything in the reverse order. Imagine the energy dispersing from the triangle and pentagrams, and draw in your energy from the circle."

I turned and began to do so. Meanwhile, I heard Michael coaching me from the sidelines. "Yes, that's right... Use a thrusting, banishing motion with your staff to get rid of the energy from the triangle... Then do the same with the pentagrams around your circle... But slowly, take each one in turn. Take it down in a reverse direction. Draw a backwards circle, now a backwards pentagram...Then push, thrust, send the energy back to take it down ... Now, as you take down the circle, start with the spiral ...Move around counterclockwise carefully, slowly... That's right, turn, drawing your staff down slowly, seeing the circle collapse in on itself...Now finally, retrace the boundaries of the circle on the ground, drawing it all in."

As Michael spoke, I moved slowly, deliberately, gradually letting go of the sensation of the circle around me. Finally I felt it was down.

"Now clean up those last bits of energy lingering there," Michael instructed.

I glanced around, trying to see something in the inky black carpet of darkness around me. Finally, as if I must be stupid or blind, Michael pointed towards the spot of grass where the triangle had been. It seemed to shimmer a little, and I noticed that the moon had just popped out from behind a cloud.

"Right there," he said. "Some of the energy from the triangle is still there."

When I didn't respond quickly enough, he strode over and gave a few flicks with his sword.

"There, it's gone," he said.

Since we were finished, Michael motioned for me to follow him to the patio and rejoin the others.

"So now you know how to make a proper circle," he said. " The whole objective of this demonstration was to show you what a really strong circle should be like and for you to get a sense of what it might be like when you call a being to enter your triangle. That's why I caused one to come in and then leave, so you would be aware of the presence of a being and then its absence. The point is that when you are calling in your familiar these other beings may come in and appear like sparkles or wisps of energy, as well as assuming human or other forms. So you need to be prepared and ready."

"Other beings?" I gave a slight gasp of surprise. I was starting to feel a little overwhelmed and confused again.

"Don't worry," said Michael. "Just be aware of what you can. And if other beings do appear, try to send them away. But don't worry if you can't. We'll be around, so you'll have help."

Before I could say anything else, Michael turned and headed back into the house, and we followed him inside. I gathered up my tape recorder and notebook and got ready to leave.

"Now the next time we get together," Michael announced, "we'll go out in the field so you can meet and work with your familiar."

He pointed to the diagram of the circle and triangle on the board which he had discussed earlier.

"Now be sure to review your notes on the processes for creating the circle and triangle. You want to be sure you can go out there and create them that without anyone there to coach you. Afterwards, if you can call and work with your familiar successfully, we'll discuss what you saw and what your familiar is going to do for you."

If you can. If you can. The words repeated themselves over and over in my mind like a record or a call from a bird in the dark night. They were another reminder that soon, in only two days, on Friday night, I would be tested again. I felt a twinge of nervousness as Michael walked me to my car.

We stopped by my car door.

"Now, it's very important," Michael emphasized, "that you are very clear of the steps to do this and that you will come away with a clear idea of the being you meet and your relationship, since you will be working with this being for the rest of your training here."

"Yes, I understand," I said somberly, and I got in my car and closed the door.

Michael tapped on the window. "Now be sure to bring a notebook to write down the appearance of this being and whatever else you learn about this being."

I said I would and started the car. As I drove off back to my hotel, I felt very small and alone. I had a sense of encountering all sorts of forces and energies I didn't fully understand. Yet I was trying to call on them, communicate with them, ask them to do things. At the same time I was still asking whether they were really out there, and whether they would respond to me, and whether I would carry out the proper procedures. Could I do it? Would I do it? Would I get a response? And what did I need to do to make it happen?

My mind was a jumble of impressions and thoughts tumbling all over one another, like clothes in a washing machine or dryer. Meanwhile, the cars on the freeway rushed past me, their lights like beacons of ordinary reality in the night.

So slowly, carefully, I imagined a circle of energy around me to keep the cars out. Then, feeling a protective circle around me, I drove on in the night. There was so much to do, so much to think about, and I was eager to take the next step. Just two more nights. Two more nights.

7

MEETING MY OWN FAMILIAR

The next two days collapsed into a collage of ordinary activities -- writing up my notes in the morning, going to the beach in the afternoon, seeing a movie in the evening, doing more reading and writing, practicing a few exercises. It was as if I was looking to these day to day activities as an anchor into the everyday, mundane world before venturing out again into unknown and mystical territories at night.

What would happen? I thought as I looked over my notes about making my circle and creating the triangle of manifestation for this new being I would be calling forth from another dimension later that night. Paradoxically, the procedures I would follow were very mechanical and specified, like going through a military drill. It felt like a very ordered, structured way of taming this contact with the other world to make it more manageable.

Even so, despite all these trappings of management and order, there was still that quality of the unpredictable, the unknown, like going out to sea. One could do all one could in advance to be fully prepared and have a smooth, well-controlled, charted voyage. One could stock the ship, train the crew, use maps to plan the route, review weather reports, have radar, and the like. But once at sea, there could always be the unexpected -- the high wave, the unseen rock, the unpredictable storm.

I felt that my upcoming encounter with this familiar I was going to call on might be a little like that. Michael had given me a formal structure for calling it; yet what happened after I used these procedures would be completely unexpected and unknown. Though Michael called this being a "familiar," I thought of the irony of its name as I headed to my car to drive towards Michael's. The being was supposed to be bound to me and become my "familiar." But to make this connection, I would have to reach into the unpredictable, the unexpected, and the unknown.

I pulled onto the freeway thinking of all these ironies and possibilities, and a little after 5 p.m. as the night's darkness was settling in, I arrived at Michael's. Greta was already there, and like me, both of them were wearing their black ODF uniforms.

Michael led us out to his car, and after we were on our way, he explained that we would be going to a usually deserted wilderness area near Chatsworth, about an hour's drive North of Los Angeles. But first we would stop at Paul's in the Valley, so that Paul and his girlfriend Sara could join us.

"They both want to be along for this special occasion," Michael explained. "It's like an initiation, a rite of passage, if you can connect with your familiar, and they want to be there for this event."

I felt pleased at their interest, yet nervous too. Now there would be four people watching me, and I felt I had a deep responsibility to perform and complete this act successfully. For now, more than ever, I realized the success of this trip depended on me. The only purpose of this long journey -- the drive to Paul's, the drive to Chatsworth, the hike to the location, the time we would spend there, the hike and drive back -- was for me to make the circle and call my familiar. And the four people with me would be watching and waiting. So what if I failed? I fingered the staff in my lap nervously as we drove along. What if I failed?

As we drove along Mulholland, with the lights of the valley sparkling below, I felt like we were truly embarking on this long uncharted voyage, and in a little while I would briefly be given the rudder of the ship. Then, I would need to steer it through this unknown passageway and bring it safely back. I felt this heavy weight of responsibility as we drove along.

Then, we were in the Valley at Paul's. We went in briefly, while Paul and Sara gathered their gear and got into the cab of his truck. Then, Paul led the way to the wilderness area. Michael, Greta and I followed on the freeway after him, plunging in and out of the traffic, until Paul turned off on the road towards Chatsworth, and soon we wound along a road past a few last houses of a development. They stood in the moonlit darkness like the lonely outpost at the edges of civilized society, before the wilderness and wildness of the unknown took over.

Then, we were bouncing along a rocky dirt road that led upwards into the foothills, and the loose dirt and open fields had the smell of the wildness around us. There was a sharp nip to the clear night air, and the hills gleamed in the moonlight like silent beacons urging us on to a new adventure.

"This is near the old Paramount ranch," Michael commented, as we pulled up where the road dead-ended in a narrow cul-de-sac. "They used it for Wild West movie sets. Maybe they even still do, before the developers take over."

"And this is where the Manson group used to hang out before they committed all the murders," said Paul.

I felt a shiver run through me as we got out of the car. Even their comments contributed to the nervousness I felt at going into the unknown and leaving the world of everyday, ordinary reality behind. The cul-de-sac where we parked did, too. It was as if the houses of the development down the hill behind us stood like symbols of the standardized, sanitized, ordered society we were leaving. But ahead was this vast wilderness that stretched beyond us like a Wild West plain surrounded by hills and canyons, and for a moment I thought of these mysterious beings and spirits out there like Hollywood Indians, waiting and watching, perhaps treacherous, perhaps not, and we were the settlers and cowboys venturing into this unexplored land.

"Now we'll cross over the bridge," said Michael interrupting my thoughts. He pointed to the cement road across the freeway that was pitted and covered with dust. "The developers are building a road into the area, but they haven't done it yet. So it's still largely unexplored and wild."

Slowly, quietly, we started our journey across the road. Michael and Paul led the way; Greta, Sara, and I walked slightly behind. A few cars roared past on the freeway that was fading into the distance, their lights flashing like further reminders of the ordinary world we were leaving behind.

Soon the cement road gave way to dirt, and after we walked up a slight rise, the place we were going to gaped before us like a vast crater. It looked eerie, almost forbidding in the silvery moonlight. Around the edge of the crater, the hills stood like dark silhouettes against the sky. Dark clumps of bushes and brambles flecked the plains. And here and there darker lines and fissures looked like openings into the earth, surrounded by the hulking shapes of rocks and trees.

"Now we'll go down," said Michael.

He stepped over the lip of the crater, and strode quickly down the rutted road, Paul right behind him. Meanwhile, as Greta and Sara followed quickly after them, I slowly picked my way down the steep rocky grade into the valley, afraid of tripping or sliding down the hill. It was one more reminder of this journey from the everyday world to the non-ordinary unpredictable unknown world that lay beyond.

"Do you need some help," Michael called to me.

When I said no, I could manage if I took it slowly, he hovered near the bottom of the hill waiting for me to get down safely. Once I got to the bottom, the road spread out like a broad brushstroke on a canvas, and we walked along briskly.

"We want to find the right place with the right kind of feeling," Michael said as we walked.

On and on we went, and I marveled at the vastness of the area, as each step led us further and further from civilization. We passed lone trees, rocks, gullies, all like sentinels marking our way in the inky darkness. Finally, near the center of the vast crater, Michael and Paul stopped.

"Wait here a minute," Michael said, and he and Paul went off to confer.

"This seems fine," I said, when they returned.

"We'll tell you when the area is fine," said Paul.

Michael motioned for us to continue on.

We hiked along for another five minutes or so in silence. Then, as the road narrowed and wound into a grove of trees before beginning a steep incline into the hills, Michael held out his hand for us to stop.

Again, as we waited quietly, Michael and Paul walked ahead to discuss the matter. A few minutes later, as Michael stood about 30 yards from us, Paul went along the road like a scout.

After he came back, followed by another brief conference, Michael and Paul agreed. We would return to the open area where we had stopped earlier, and we headed back.

After 10 more minutes, we were there. The dirt was a little wet, almost marshy, from the rains of the past few days, and brittle wild grasses and twigs crunched under our feet. As Paul, Greta, and Sara spread out on the nearby slopes 20 to 30 yards away, Michael came over to me.

"Now pick out a place that feels right to you to make your circle and call forth your spirit. You can choose any direction."

I shifted around, noticed that I was in the center of a kind of a gentle sloping gulley with a tree at one end near the road, and I started to position myself facing towards that.

But Michael stopped me. "You don't want to face the tree to make your circle, because you might call up the tree spirits, and you don't want to do that. Though near the tree is fine."

I turned about 90 degrees, so I faced a low open area parallel to the road, just below the slope where Paul, Greta, and Sara were standing watching me.

"That's fine now," said Michael. Then, he reviewed the procedures for making a circle and triangle, which I had learned two nights before.

"I just want to be sure you'll remember everything you need to do," he said.

After telling me I was facing north, he strode off, and stopped about 30 feet away.

"Okay, anytime you're ready you can start," he called out to me.

Start! I suddenly became very aware of all the eyes watching me, and drew a deep breath to concentrate on sending the watching eyes away. As I did, I began to feel very alone, like it was just me in the middle of this wasteland, and everything depended on me. It was like being a fulcrum. On the one hand, I felt a sense of power, a surge of energy pouring into me, as a result of feeling I was in the center and everything around revolved around me. But on the other hand, I felt a heaviness, a feeling of nervous responsibility, for now I had to muster my forces to achieve this breakthrough into another dimension now everything depended on me.

So slowly, cautiously, I reached out my staff to begin my circle, visualizing the energy coming out of me to form it. But suddenly, my staff hit a root, and like paper, my visualization crumpled, and I felt the energy drain away. This wasn't starting very well, I thought nervously, and I retracted my staff.

"There's a root," I called out softly to Michael, by way of explanation. "I have to move."

I walked ahead several feet to a more open area. The tree was no longer to my right between me and the road, serving like a protective barrier, and I felt even more vulnerable for now I was standing in the open with the hills of the crater around me, like a huge open circle.

"Whenever you're ready," said Michael, and I began again.

This time I moved around in a preliminary circle, not trying to visualize, just trying to test out the area to make sure it was flat and comfortable. When I scratched a few roots, I shifted ahead a few feet, repeated the process, until finally, I felt the area was clear.

"Okay," I nodded. "I'll start now."

Once again I focused, trying to remember. First the circle. Next the pentagrams. The instructions began to well up in my mind like a chant. Then, as if a faraway voice was commanding me, I began to make my circle. Meanwhile, I visualized the energy coming out of me, pouring through my staff into the ground, and gradually rising up, as I raised my staff, to make the cone. Finally, it felt like the energy covered me in a ball of glowing whiteness, though I was vaguely aware of the presence of Michael and the others watching me, as I tried to keep them out. But even as I felt the ball growing around me, I kept wondering: "Am I doing this correctly? Can they really see it? Is my circle all right?"

Then, trying to ignore these questions, I proceeded to make the protective pentagrams. Slowly, carefully, I drew them in the air, as Michael had taught me, imagining each one as a glowing protective spot dotting my circle. After that was done, I began drawing the triangle, though I suddenly realized I had forgotten the pentagrams on the top and the bottom of my circle.

For a moment, I hesitated. Should I go back and redraw them? Would I fail the test for not making a proper circle, as Michael had stressed? Would Michael even notice? How important was this really? I wasn't sure what to do. But then, the circle felt complete, even without the pentagrams, since it seemed to fully surround me and contain me. So fearing that going back would be worse and more disruptive than proceeding on I plunged ahead, forgetting about the missing pentagrams, and finished the triangle.

Then, I stood waiting, gazing at the space where I had created the triangle, hoping that something would appear.

After a few minutes, I saw a slight sparkling in front of me. Was this my imagination or my familiar? I continued to gaze at the misty sparkly area, wondering if I would get a reply to my questions, and finally began asking them: "Who are you? Are you here to serve me? What do you want to do? What do you want me to do for you? Where are you from? What's it like there?" Slowly, I asked, or perhaps more accurately, thought my questions and waited for the reply.

Then, slowly, more like a thought in my mind, the answers came. "I'm a female being. I'm from another dimension. I'll be your guide. You can ask me questions, and I'll give you answers. You must acknowledge and honor me each night."

Then, I sensed a small being or presence in the lights, who was about 6" tall, and I thought of Tinkerbelle from *Peter Pan*. Finally, I asked her name, and some strange syllables that sounded like "Elynuria" popped into my head.

I stood quietly for several minutes watching this glowing space in front of me. Now what, I wondered? Was this all? Had I actually met my familiar? Was I just imagining this communication, perhaps creating it in my mind to meet the test? Could Michael or the others see what was going on? Had I passed the test or not? Should something else happen?

I kept wondering if I should expect something dramatic to occur as a symbol that something extraordinary had happened. But no. I just saw the faint sparkles of light and had a vague feeling that something was out there.

I still wasn't sure I had accomplished the process successfully, though I felt any communication completed. So I said a brief thank you towards the sparkling lights, bid the presence I felt there goodbye, and took down the triangle of manifestation with a few sweeps of my staff. With a few more passes, I took down my circle, using reverse sweeping motions to erase the pentagrams and the circle, while I imagined the energy dispersing.

Finally, it was over. The triangle, the circle were gone, and I was standing alone in the crisp, clear darkness of the moonlit meadow.

Michael came over to me. "Well, what did you experience?" he said.

I described what had just happened, indicating how I had drawn the circle and triangle and describing the answers I had gotten.

"But I forgot the two pentagrams," I added.

"That doesn't matter. A small detail," said Michael. "You had a good strong circle. I saw it. The others saw it. What's important now is did you get a name?"

"Yes," I nodded.

"Well, don't tell it to me. That's between you and her," Michael said. "But now you have a name you can use to call her in the future. And it shows she is ready to serve you. She gave you her name."

Then, Greta, Sara, and Paul came over from their perches on the hill.

"So did I pass?" I asked Michael uncertainly.

I felt like so little had happened that I hadn't done enough.

"Why of course," Michael said off-handedly, as if tonight's events had gone like clockwork. "You made a good circle; you called on the being; she appeared in the triangle; we saw the sparkling, too; you spoke for awhile; and she gave you her name. That's all we expect. Now that you have met her, you will learn more about how to work with her over the next few days. But for now, you have done enough."

"I have?" I said, surprised that Michael hadn't expected more, or that more hadn't happened.

"Of course," Michael repeated again.

Since the purpose of our journey was now finished, Michael motioned for us to start back. On the way, Paul, walking beside me, commented that he had seen another being hovering around me while I was creating my circle.

"It was pretty large," he said, "a big hulking form, and it looked like he was considering coming into your circle. But then he didn't."

"I didn't see anything like that," I replied.

"Of course not," he said. "You were concentrating on the triangle. Then, when your spirit appeared in the circle, you were surrounded by a foggy mass of energy, which probably prevented you from seeing. But that also prevented us from seeing in. So we didn't see much of what you were experiencing. However, this meeting with the familiar is usually a more personal encounter, so the observers don't expect to see much. The person meeting with the familiar should see much more."

"I see," I nodded, relieved that Paul had seen what Michael did.

Suddenly, Paul cried out "Wait," and bounded off. He stopped by a small sandy area about 100 yards from the spot where I had called the familiar. There was a lone rock about the size of a volleyball in the center of the area, and Paul bent down and held his hands over it. He seemed to be breathing it in, though it was hard to see, since he was just a shadowy form in the dim moonlight.

"Shhhh," Michael told me before I could ask anything, and we watched silently.

Paul now picked up the rock, placed it on the ground nearby, and bent down even closer to it, as if he was holding his ear to the ground, listening for something. Then, Paul motioned for us to join him by the rock one at a time.

For a few minutes, each of us in turn bent down at the rock, listening, feeling, breathing. When it was my turn, I came over hesitantly, not sure about what was going on.

"Just come look," Paul said. "Look closely. Then, feel and breathe."

I noticed an open hole, about 12" across and 6" wide where the rock had been.

"Now put your hands over it," Paul said.

As I held my hands above the rock, Paul asked: "What do you feel?"

I wasn't sure. My hands felt a little tingly and I felt a slight pressure, like the area was pulsing with energy, as I told Paul.

"Yes, it is," said Paul. "Now try dipping your hand a little inside."

Slowly, I reached down with my right hand. The hole seemed dark, forbidding, and I dipped my hand in hesitantly, as if this was a pit filled with unknown creatures that might snap up and grab my hand.
Then, as I dipped my hand in further, I noticed a misty fog that seemed to well up out of the pit, and I felt my hand grow colder with every few inches.

"What is this?" I asked as I withdraw my hand and described what I experienced.

"It's a natural gateway," Paul explained. "It's like a hole into another dimension, and that's what you were feeling and seeing. So, yes, you would expect it to be cold and misty. Other dimensions are usually like that. For example, I saw this strange mist rising up while you were working with your familiar."

I glanced back at the hole, which looked much darker than the blackness surrounding it.

"It's like every once in a while, nature shares its special mysteries with us," Paul continued. "It's another reminder of this world that exists around us and beyond us, yet so few of us see."

I returned to the group, and after Greta had a chance to experience the hole, Paul closed it up with the rock, and we moved on.

Just as we passed a large clump of trees, that looked like the gathering of a dark army, Paul bounded off into the clump of trees. Greta started to follow, but Michael stood at the edge of the road stopping her.

"No, keep going," he said.

Then, he disappeared into the clump of trees after Paul. Meanwhile, Greta, Sara, and I continued on the road for about a hundred yards, and stopped, waiting. After about ten minutes, Paul emerged on the road again, followed by Michael, and in a few minutes had caught up with our group.

Again, we walked on, although now it felt like the magic was over. The mistiness that made the crater shimmer in the moonlight, like some magical, mystical wilderness, was gone, and now the stars seemed to shine crisply overhead, and the moon had a steady, solid glow. And now walking up the hill to the lip of the crater seemed easy, in contrast to my struggling to get down.   We strode along quickly, and we were soon back on the main dirt road near the freeway.

A few yards before the concrete bridge over the freeway, Paul asked us to stop. He had an important message to tell us.

"It's a lesson for tonight," he said as we gathered around closely. "When I left the path earlier to go into the trees, you weren't to follow. The point is that sometimes a shaman is suddenly called to do something, and he must follow that call. There may not be time to explain to others, but when the call comes, he must respond right away, because he must take care of something important. So when that happens, you shouldn't try to follow. You should just wait patiently or continue on, and not interfere with his special calling."

"Oh, I'm sorry," Greta started to apologize.

"No, you didn't know," said Paul. "Just keep this in mind for the future."

"What sort of important things might be happening?" I asked.

"Maybe he might have to do something to take care of a spirit, maybe something to restore the harmony of a particular place. The particular thing doesn't matter. What's important is that you need to respect this call when a shaman hears it and let him do what he needs to do without trying to interfere. It's like respecting the magic and mystery of the other dimension, as you saw at the hole. You don't have to understand everything. There are many things you can't know right now. The important thing is to honor the way of the shaman, which can include many things you don't understand."

I said I would and we headed back over the freeway. The lights and horns of the cars below were one more reminder that we were back in the modern everyday world.

* * * * * *

Back at Paul's house, Sara brought us some apple juice and cookies, and we sat in the den discussing the experience. I was glad for the more detailed feedback on what had happened.

Paul began with a more elaborate description of the beings had seen around me.

"There was a dazzling array of all the energy in the area gathered around you, as we watched from the hill. All these beings seemed to be really enticed by what you were doing. As you set up your circle, some beings first appeared around the sidelines, curious to see what would happen. They appeared like bright flashing lights, sparkles of energy, and a few were almost human in shape, though smoky in form.

"Then, I saw one of these beings come up to you, and as I moved in closer to check it out, he took off like a flash of energy whizzing off. But he probably wouldn't have been a good selection as a familiar, since usually the first being to step forward and volunteer is not the one you want."

"Why not?" I asked.

"Because, it could be too eager, and sometimes these more aggressive spirits can be troublemakers. In any event, the being probably took off, because it didn't want to take any chances with my intervening, since you didn't notice it. Then, another being moved in, and you took over. As soon as that happened, the two of you were covered in a cloud of sparkles and energy particles, so I couldn't see anything anymore. However, this initial meeting with the familiar is generally a very personal act, so that can be expected. You want to be alone."

I glanced around the room at Michael, Greta, and Sara with a questioning look, my question unspoken, though it was the same one I often had. Were these visions from the imagination, or were they something real? Did other people share them?

As if he already knew my question, Michael cut in. "What happened tonight is real. We all saw exactly the same thing. Everyone saw the bright whitish being appear the first time. Then, we saw it go towards the triangle and make a circuit around your circle. I got the feeling it was trying to get inside to mess with you. Then, it reluctantly went back to the area around the triangle, saw Paul, and left. It was frightened by Paul's power, since it had a negative intent."

"Why should it be frightened? What could Paul do?" I wondered.

"It could have rightly feared it would be physically attacked and dispersed. So it split. It's much the same thing that happened when one of my students was perched on a cliff during a solo and some negative forces tried to lure her off, as you may recall when you first started your training three years before. As soon as I walked up, they saw me, and I scared them off. Likewise, Paul's presence scared this one away."

"I wasn't aware of it at all," I acknowledged. "I was so focused on the triangle. I thought about looking around for a moment, but I felt if I did, I might have broken my concentration."

"Well, if you feel your concentration will be broken, it will. So probably you did the right thing," said Michael. "But in time, you should feel free to look around to be more aware of what's around you, not just what's directly ahead, and still stay in that altered state. In other words, the whole process should be like driving. You're driving along, focused ahead, but from time to time, you can check your mirrors and glance around to see what's happening on your side. Similarly, you should be able to maintain the visualization of what you are doing, but you can look around, too.

"It can be hard when you are first starting. Many years ago when I did, I needed a tight focus, too, and at first I couldn't pay attention to other things. But you have to learn to balance both staying focused while aware of what else is going on around you, and in time it will come."

"That's right," chimed in Paul. "And the key is exercise and practice. So just exercise, exercise, exercise."

Then, like a winding river, the conversation shifted course, and everyone began to talk about the rock and the hole Paul had discovered.

"It was amazing," Paul observed. "While you were doing the exercise, I saw this rock that seemed to be vibrating with energy, and I felt strongly drawn to it. Then, when I rolled it over, I saw not just a hole in the ground, but a hole in the universe. It was one of these natural gateways that are always there. You don't create them, and it's important not to disturb them, because that would be like disturbing the natural order. But you can use them as long as you don't alter them. They're there for a reason -- to keep a balance."

"But why? How?" I was puzzled.

"It's like the process of balancing the polarities or reconciling the opposites to create a sense of harmony in nature. Think of it this way. For every foreground, there must be a background. For every inside, there must be an outside. For every void, there must be a presence. Likewise, for the reality to exist here as we know it, there must be a non-ordinary or spiritual reality, another side of the wall, if you will.

"Well, that hole was like a link between these two realities. It was a gateway to the underworld or lower world, which is a mysterious alternative dimension of darkness. Yet, it's not evil or bad; just different and very powerful. For example, if I wanted to, I could put my face at the opening to this other dimension and breathe in whatever is there, and use that for healing or other shamanic work."

"Healing?" I asked.

"Certainly," Paul said. "I could breathe in whatever is there into the patient, and suck out from them whatever is bad or negative within them. Many shamans do this. It's part of the process on drawing on the energy of that other dimension to resolve an imbalance in this. Or if you are experiencing your own psychic difficulties here, drawing on the nectars of this other reality could help you balance. Plus you have to expel what's bad. Then, whatever you suck out of yourself or someone else, you should put it back in the hole, for give and take is part of the process of achieving balance. You have to take in and give out in equal measure."

"But how..." I began.

Paul stopped me. "Anyway, you don't want to attempt any of this now yourself, because any work with the underworld regions involves a great deal of focus and awareness, because there could be great dangers, since the beings there have a different, dark nature. So only someone who is advanced should try to work with these beings."

"What about that smokiness we all saw coming out of the hole?" Greta wanted to know.

"It's like a veil or membrane appearing in the ether," Michael explained. "It's part of the semi-permeable membrane between the two worlds. It lets you see that the other world is there, but you can't see into it. You can only see when you're in it."

"That's what happens when someone steps into a gateway," said Paul. "They can see what's there, but the people watching generally can only see them disappearing or stepping into a smoky mist."

Sara wanted to know about the temperature and other differences she felt when she put her hand into the hole.

"I felt this immediate warmth," she said. "I also felt I was dipping my hand into something not of our world. It felt like my hand was going into water and coming out, because the air felt heavier, denser, yet it didn't feel wet. Then, when I looked into the hole, it looked like I could see very deep within it, like the edges were giving way to something else; and there were sparkles on the other side."

"You were seeing and feeling the energy," said Michael. "In fact, if you felt it closely, you might have noticed the air in the center was much warmer, but the air around the edges and at the surface was much cooler."

I nodded to indicate that the hole had felt colder to me.

"That's because at the edges and surface you are feeling the draft of the air going into the other world and mixing with the warmer air from the center, so there's this breeze going between the worlds."

Sara and Greta described their experience reaching into the hole.

"I saw a glittery blue aura around my hand," said Sara.

"And mine felt warm and tingly," said Greta. "I felt like I had just pulled my hand out of a sparkling, bubbling cauldron."

Michael and Paul smiled broadly. "Yes, that sounds perfectly natural," said Michael. "It's another indication that you have reached into a gateway." And Paul agreed.

"And so," said Michael, concluding the discussion about holes and gateways, "you see that the underworld is like another gateway. We've worked with gateways in the air before. But there are gateways into the earth, as well, though they have a darker, more mysterious quality, and can be harder, more dangerous to work with, because of this darker, heavier energy.

"So for some people, it can be a little frightening, when these gateways first open up. That's why you only had a small taste of this energy. But as you become more familiar with this underworld energy, you may find it very warm, comforting, and friendly to work with; at least I do. That's because you are drawing on the energy of the nurturing earth, and it has this nurturing womb-like quality. So you may feel a sense of uncertainty because you are reaching out into the unknown, which is like stepping into and submerging into a void. But once within, you can draw on this warm, protective energy, which has the solidness and heaviness of earth."

"It's like a whole other realm, very different from working with gateways in the ether," observed Paul. "It's deeper, more mysterious, like exploring the caverns and hidden places of your mind."

"That's what you'll find yourself, as you go further with this," added Michael. "There's much you can't talk about or explain, and much you won't want to, because this private work can become very personal, if you use it, as many shamans do, to develop a special relationship between you and spiritual power.

"Initially, what may draw many people to this work is the ability to use it for practical purposes -- for answering questions, getting information, and healing. Also, many people may be intrigued by the fascination of the phenomenon, as you have seen, which occurs when you start working with power, such as manifesting beings and ESP. But as you go further..." Michael spoke very slowly, seriously, "you'll find a feeling of humility in the face of all this power. It's like you recognize both the vast possibilities and the responsibilities that go with that access to power. It's like you are putting on that karmic mantle and assuming the karmic debt that comes with it. Otherwise, like a king or any ruler who misuses his power and gets toppled from his throne as a result, you can suddenly find yourself losing your power too. Think of this power like a gift which comes with the shaman's calling; then he or she must use that power well or lose that gift.

"But if you do use it well, many realms of power will open up. Take your experience of contacting your familiar tonight -- that can open up many new worlds on your journey."

I said I would try to use the power well, and Michael had a few last cautions.

"Now, the next step in using your power is to find your own path and magical personality. You want to be able to move from not only using the power, but feeling and being the power. It's like shifting from experiencing yourself doing magic to having a vision of yourself as a magician or shaman. It's like stepping into another life or persona, where you move on to another or higher realization of the truth and can call on the energies of nature as they become part of your being. You become different -- larger, more powerful, like you are living another life.

"Doing your own private and personal work can help you do this, because as you go off and get into yourself, you discover your own path, and that's where you start gaining real personal power. That's because at that point, the power gives you gifts that are specific to you. Then, once you have experienced this feeling, you can tap into it or recreate it again through various means, such as ritual, deep meditation, or being in a setting conducive to an intense spiritual experience."

Michael sank back into a reverie for a few moments. Then, remembering, he recounted one of his own experiences of this magical transformation.

"It was one of those times when I felt this very powerful energy calling me to do something, much like Paul felt tonight. In this case, I was out on a field trip with Paul and with Serge, a second-degree student, and I felt this call to do something to reaffirm my links with the universe. So I started to breathe in the underworld and earth energy from the hills, and I felt myself undergoing this transformation as I did so. I felt I got taller; I felt my hands grow longer and get claws; and I felt I was becoming an earth elemental myself."

"In your imagination?" I asked.

"No, no," Michael said firmly. "I began to breathe more heavily, and others could see the change happening as well. For example, Serge looked like he was ready to run in terror and Paul looked alarmed."

I glanced at Paul, seeking verification, and Paul jumped in with his confirmation. "That's right. I felt you had contacted someone else in the forest and had switched. So I didn't think it was you there any longer. You had become someone else."

"Then, another time," said Michael, "that same power caused me to take on another very different form. In this case, I felt uplifted, and as the power welled up inside me, I experienced myself levitating, and as I did, others could see this beautiful vibrant aura around me.

"So you see, this power has the power to transform you in multiple ways -- from the depths to the heights of experience. At the same time, you are still you. For example, in both these cases, I was still myself, but my power inside caused me to do as my heart dictated, and it was like becoming another person. Yet it wasn't really another person inside me. Rather, it was like a higher, more powerful aspect of myself that had moved forward into consciousness, and that specialized state of mind led me to act differently than I would in a conventional state of mind.

"So, because of this transformative power of magical power, it's important to have a sense of your magical self and even a name to identify it. Because when you reach this state of being, you have become a unique individual with your own signature reflecting your level of power and your psychic being. For we all have different natures, and your nature becomes apparent as you work -- both to yourself and to others sensitive enough to see this. For example, that's what Paul and I sensed about that magician we saw at the mall. Externally he looked to you like a very ordinary person; but inside he had this magical persona, and that's what Greta and I were picking up."

I flashed back to our chase in the mall and remembered how Michael had seemed so aware of the man's presence following us as we drove and he tried to get away. Now Michael's earlier explanation made a lot more sense.

"Anyway," Michael continued, "the purpose of all these exercises and experiences for the past few weeks has been to help you develop your own magical persona. Then, once you become a person of power, there's no way to tell what kind of person you will become, for then you take your own path. Ideally, this path will lead you to release and explore your higher self in a positive productive manner, with a positive, good intent. But there are no guarantees what this sorcerer or shaman within will become. The power released is always neutral -- so the result could be good, bad, or indifferent."

I looked a little uncertain, and Paul cut in. "Yes, that's so. In the world of the shaman or sorcerer, the power just is. So some things a shaman might do could seem very scary, such as the transformation Michael underwent into a kind of werewolf. Or some things might seem very comforting and gentle, such as when a sorcerer is called to heal. But the point is that as long as whatever is done is done by pure intent, in response to the call of power, it's an act of shamanic mastery, and it's neither good nor bad. But for that to happen, the person must be acting from their power, not ego. They must be acting purely from the heart.

"And from that perspective, nothing can be wrong. The ordinary, everyday rules don't exist. Rather, at that point, the shaman becomes a being of power, and power comes up through him and manifests in a certain way. So that means some sorcerers can be really scary people, while others can be very nice. Or they can be scary and nice at different times. You just don't know. For there's no such thing as good and bad in the world of the shaman -- just pure power coming from the heart."

"But what about karma?" said Greta.

"And what about ethics?" I said.

"Perhaps look at it this way," said Michael. "There are only actions from the heart and neither good nor bad, because the shaman or sorcerer perceives the world as a thing of balances infused by power. You haven't reached this stage yet, but you get a superhuman feeling when this power is running through you, so you feel like a different person. You're not different in actuality. But you and anyone with you can feel the differences, for they way you are as a powerful being at the height of a ritual and the way you are when you walk down the street is like the difference between night and day. It's like you have two opposite parts of yourself -- you the magician and you the ordinary person. It's the difference between thinking and working from your heart and working from your head and mind."

"Or look at it this way," said Paul, jumping in again. "If you react from the heart, you are more likely to react from power. When you act from your head, you are more likely to act as you have been told. So, say I see a red light as I'm walking down the street. If I stop, that is more than likely be an act of my mind and the world telling me that I should stop when a red light appears.

But if I just stop at the light regardless of what color it is, it may be that my heart is telling me I need to stand in this particular place for a moment. Or I may suddenly walk across the street or do any number of unexpected or erratic things. But the point is that such spontaneous acts are more likely to spring from the heart. And that's the way of the shaman -- responding to power, like jumping up in response to a jolt of electric current from the socket, and then acting from the heart."

Michael got up, signaling to me and Greta that it was time to go. "So the point of all this," he said, "is to recognize these two sides of your being and to realize there can be these great contrasts within you, as well as between you as your magical self and the magical self of other people.

"For example, some people who are very warm and bubbly outside, can have this dark, somber side in magic, while others may be much lighter. And some people have this magical self that is like sunshine, regardless of what they are like when you relate to them as people. But whatever you experience, you need to respect that magical being and realize that there's no such thing as right and wrong if you truly act from the heart -- just responding to and merging with pure power.

"When you do that, your own magical essence or power will become more defined. You'll find your own level of resonance. You'll have your own magical signature, your own level of command, and the spiritual forces out there will acknowledge and respect that, just as happened tonight when you were doing your ritual. This being was about to interfere in your circle when Paul intervened, and then the spirit suddenly left, like it was stepping out of his way out of this recognition and respect. As you work with this power more and more, you'll experience this sense of power and assurance, too; you'll have a greater sense of who you are in this other magical world."

We walked through the kitchen, and as we stood there in the hallway, Michael asked us to wait. He had a few last important points to share about spiritual mastery.

"So the whole point of grades is to give you a sense of markers and guidelines to follow along the way. But after you have done your gateway, discovered your familiar, signified by grades five and six in our system, you are already starting to define what you want from power and what power wants from you. Plus you are now starting to discover your own magical style, as well as your own attitude, level of interest, and commitment in working with power.

"And you are also discovering how very real this shamanic world can be when you learn from and respond to the feelings that come from your heart. I found this myself when I did my first gateway. I spent several weeks in preparation, using mental, physical, and spiritual exercises, because that's what my heart told me to do. Then, when I did this gateway, it was different from anything else I had done. It was so tangible and real. As I walked through it, I smelt, felt, tasted, and experienced everything.

"Then, as I was gathering information, I let go of all limiting questions, such as 'What will I do with this?' or 'Am I really doing this?' Instead, I had a sense of complete wonder and amazement. I kept thinking to myself, 'This is amazing,' and 'I'm going to absorb as much as I can.' At the end, when I asked 'Why am I doing this?' I got a sense of purpose about my work. Also, I was reminded of the need for silence and patience, because you need to shut off your thoughts and preconceptions to learn. You need to just listen and receive. Likewise, you should start clarifying your own sense of magical purpose."

I started to interrupt with a question, but Michael pressed on.

"You've been taught philosophical principles about magic to shape your outer self. You've worked with exercises to develop your will. Finally, your magical self has been shaped by the whole experience. As you grow up in levels, your magical self and your real self will become more and more defined, and therefore your own magical purpose will become clearer and clearer, until you reach this stage of full definition, where you truly know what you are about magically, and so are fully grown."

"When does that happen?" I asked.

"At the tenth degree in our system. At other levels in other system. The key to reaching this point is that you have passed a barrier. You've gotten all your basic skills, and your magical self has come into full focus, so now, magically, you can do what you want. It's like being knighted. For after years of study and preparation, you can paint your own symbol on your shield and go off on your own personal quest. It's like you have gone through a rite of passage in which you have become spiritually and psychically fully adult.

"You start off like a magical child with a lack of knowledge or confidence in your abilities. You aren't sure what you are doing and can barely walk. From there, you go up the levels to adolescence, the older teenager, and finally to the adult, which is about where you are now. But as a new adult, you are still very young, and you have to go through a period of seasoning based on your work, experience, and how well you learn your lessons. Then, the results can readily be seen in your improved focus and control, as you move up from level to level.

Anyone who is sensitive magically can sense this. It's like your signature as a magician or shaman becomes more and more clearly defined."

We walked towards the door, ready to leave now.

"So, your goal now," Michael told me, "should be to become fully defined. Think about who you are magically and where you want to go, since the first major step towards full spiritual adulthood is to have a clear sense of purpose and identity. So ask yourself 'Who am I and what is my magical purpose?'"

With that, Michael opened the door and we said goodbye. Then, as Greta and I got in the car and drove back to Michael's, I had much to think about. Who am I? What am I doing? Where am I going?

Just then, Greta turned on a pop rock station, and the sounds of "A whole lot of shaking going on" vibrated through the car and seemed very apropos to all the things I had to think about. I felt like each step of the way had been shaking up my world. So yes, there was "a whole lot of shaking going on." And I listened to the song, lost in thought, as we drove through the night.

8

LEARNING TO WORK WITH FAMILIARS

The next day, Saturday, I had little time to reflect on what I had experienced, since I spent most of the day writing and doing errands. But it felt stabilizing and grounding to feel this real world connection, like the night before had been a dream. Besides, I still needed to learn the techniques for working with the familiar I had called, which Michael planned for that night.

I dressed quickly in my black uniform, and this time I took along my mirror to use it in working with my familiar. It was wrapped in the flowered pillowcase Michael had given to me to keep the surface away from the light to protect its magical properties.

On the elevator, I noticed a tall man with graying hair and a starched blue suit gazing at me, as I held my mirror in my arms like cradling a small child. He looked at me strangely, with raised quizzical eyebrows, as if he was trying to make sense of this flowery swaddled form I held tight against my heavy black jacket, and when he looked intently at my black furry Russian hat, I imagined he must be thinking Satanic cults, mysterious baby rituals, sacrifices, and I held my mirror even tighter and stared back.

Finally, after what seemed like a long 30-second eternity, the elevator thumped to a halt in the lobby. The man gave me a last curious look and stepped off. Then, I walked in the opposite direction towards my car in the hotel back lot. The encounter had lasted less than a minute, yet I felt the man's questioning presence follow me, and his questions cut through the growing early evening darkness like a knife. "What are you doing? Why are you doing it? How can you do it?"

What? Why? How? It was like the consciousness of the everyday world questioning the reality and purpose of the mystic world on the other side -- questions I kept asking myself, though with an open mind. What? Why? How? The questions kept coming at me like little knives, trying to shred the fabric of this other world.

Finally, arriving at my car, I opened the door quickly and got in. Then, holding my mirror in its flowered case, I imagined a glowing circle of light around it, spreading outward, enclosing me and the rest of the car. Finally, like knives or arrows hitting a solid barrier, the man's questions dropped away.

Then, I started the car and drove on to Michael's, though as I drove, I sensed the questions lingering outside, following me, and I glanced at my mirror on the seat beside me from time to time, as if to keep them away.

About a half hour later, I was at Michael's, and the smoke of the incense and the magical circle he draw around us helped me to feel I was stepping back into this other world. Tonight, since the others were busy, it was just Michael and me.

First, Michael wanted to go over my experience with the familiar from the night before. Did I still have a very clear idea of this being? Did I recall her background, what she was going to do for me, what she wanted me to do for her in return, and her name? Had I written down these things to help me remember?

In response, I began describing what I had seen the night before.

"After I made my circle and the triangle, I saw this smoky energy appear, and I started talking to it a little bit. I got the communication telepathically, like the answers just appeared in my mind. I asked what this being wanted me to do, and it said I needed to honor and recognize it each night. It indicated it was a feminine energy and it would be a guide for me, and I could ask it questions and it would help me get answers. Then, I asked it where it came from, and it talked about coming from another dimension through a gateway. And I got a name."

"What about any limitations? Anything it wouldn't do?"

"Just that it mainly wanted to be a guide," I said

"Then what happened," Michael pressed.

I described how I said goodbye and it went back to its triangle and I took down the circle. "Well, what did it look like?"

I described how it was about 4-6" high and how I perceived it as a female.

Michael still had more questions.

"If you had to describe this general shape, what would it look like?"

I mentioned my image of Tinkerbell. "But it wasn't really that form. It was more just a feeling of a female entity being there. I felt it was human, but beyond that it wasn't that clear."

"Was it a generally positive or negative feeling?"

"Generally positive," I said. "So I would feel comfortable opening up my circle to it."

"Very good," said Michael, leaning back against his chair.

As he paused after all his questions, I felt a little drained, like I had just been cross-examined. Then, Michael continued.

"It's important to recall all these details, because now you want to start right away to honor your contract, which is to acknowledge the reality of the being and lend it reality, since it's from another place, so you can give it a firmer basis in this dimension."

"So what should I do?" I asked.

"Well, I would suggest you make a drawing to reflect as best you can the vision you saw or how this being appears in your mind's eye. Make it as close to what you saw and felt, though the image you saw in your mind's eye is most important?"

"What's the difference?" I wondered.

"Your vision is the original smoky image you saw in the physical world, while the picture in your mind's eye is the image the experience or feeling of this vision evokes -- such as the image of the small fairy-like Tinkerbelle you saw. You want to use the mind's eye image, because it's clearer, more vivid, and your way of translating your initial perception into a more meaningful, tangible form, so you have a more personal, intimate relationship with this being.

"Then, too," Michael continued, "it's important to use your familiar as much and as soon as possible. For instance, since it's a guide, ask it questions, send it out on errands. A guide is not just limited to passively showing you things. It can also go off and find things. But the key is to start using it now for whatever purpose, while the relationship is still new and fresh, because now you have opened up this connection. Otherwise, if you don't take some action, your familiar can be very apt to wander away. Or your experience of calling up the familiar will seem less real."

For a moment, I thought of the man in the elevator and his questions. Then, I pushed the thought away.

"So what you want to do now," Michael went on, "is to take some action to reaffirm your connections with your familiar to make this other dimension more real."

I said I would and Michael went on with the lesson.

"Now the first step to working with your familiar is calling it. It doesn't matter if your familiar inhabits some object in your house or not. You can simply call it."

Michael circled around the room as he spoke, a little like a panther in his black uniform.

"One of the most basic ways to call it is by using your conscious projection exercise. During your astral travels, you can call upon the being by name and have it visit you in your vision and carry out its function. For example, since your familiar is a guide, once it appears you can have it guide your astral projection from that point on. Also, have some questions or some goal or destination in mind before you begin your exercise. Then, your guide can help you get those answers or reach that goal or destination."

I mentioned that I had already done some shamanic journeying with other teachers where I had traveled to the upper and lower worlds of shamanic reality.

"Is it appropriate to incorporate these destinations when I use my guide?" I asked.

"Of course," Michael said. "It doesn't matter what other teachings you have experienced. You can use any destinations you want; the difference now, though, is you have a guide to accompany you and help lead you when you get there.

"Then, whatever destination you choose or whatever questions you want answered, leave some openness in your visualization, since you are relying on your guide's talent to show you things."

Then, Michael wanted to know if I got any sense of how long the relationship might last.

"Over the next few months," I said.

"Fine, then you can work within those limits," Michael said. "It's helpful to know this in thinking about how you want to work with your guide. It's like having an informed friend from out of town on a visit. If you know how long he or she is going to stay, you can better decide where to go, what to do, and what to ask your visiting friend.

"In any case, whether you know or not, you must treat your guide or any other being as a valued visitor and use and honor the relationship, or you may find the relationship strained or impossible."

Michael eyed me closely, and I felt like he was observing me like a hawk.

"Yes, I understand," I said, though I was concerned that my agreement had been somewhat vague and unclear.

"So if you're not sure of the agreement you've made," said Michael, as if he could read my thoughts, "work that out more precisely when you next call your familiar."

"Yes, I will," I agreed.

Then, Michael pulled out his mirror covered in its black velvet case and put it on the chair beside him.

"Now what we'll be talking about tonight," he began, "is one way you can work with your familiar. It's called 'riding the familiar' and you can use a mirror to help you do this."

He pointed to his mirror, and I put my own mirror in its flowed case on the coffee table.

"Riding the familiar," Michael went on "is a visualization experience. It involves going into a conscious projection or trance state, and in this state, you summon up your familiar and place your consciousness within the consciousness of your familiar. The reason for doing this is that your familiar can transport you to whatever location you desire.

"However..." Michael paused for a few seconds, as he usually did before telling me an important caution, "...you may not be able to accomplish this process right away, because it may take some bonding with your familiar, before you can achieve this intimacy with your new servant or assistant. Tthi time to develop the relationship may be necessary, because you have to feel completely comfortable with this being, since you are placing your consciousness with it.

"In turn, your familiar needs to be receptive to this, so some time may be necessary before this sense of mutual comfort and acceptance develops. Or in other cases, this sense of rapport can happen right away. It's like with people. Sometimes you can feel this connection with someone immediately and quickly establish a close communication; with others it can take time to feel comfortable and open up with each other. It's like that with familiars, too."

I wrote hurriedly in my notebook, and Michael continued.

"This work with familiars is a very old custom. For example, traditional witches did this by sending out their cats as familiars. Essentially, they used their familiars as a receptor for their consciousness and will. Then their familiars transported this consciousness or will to whatever location the witch selected. So they helped to transport, focus, and direct her will."

Michael turned to the mirror again.

"One good way to do this projection is using the mirror. You use the mirror to help you link up with your familiar. Then, the mirror helps to guide the astral or conscious projection.

"However, when you do this, you have to take into consideration your responsibility to the familiar. Although the familiar may be able to take you all sorts of places, you have to be careful where you want it to go, because each familiar has its limits, and you can run into dangers out there, which could hurt you or your familiar. So it's a good idea to take all this slow. Just like in everyday life, even if you have someone to help show you the way, you don't want to go into dangerous places like some backstreet alley or a garage with explosives. You or your companion could get hurt.

"This can happen on the psychic level, too. For example, if a witch or magician had a fight with another, he or she might try to harm the other's familiar, based on the belief that if you harmed the witch's familiar, you could also harm the witch, because when the witch sent out the familiar, the two became as one.

"That kind of connection is possible, but there are different levels of connection. And initially, this connection may be rather poor, because you haven't yet developed that bond. So while you want to avoid the dangers that can occur when you forge this very close bond and send out your familiar, you want to establish this strong connection to make it easier and more productive to work together.

"The best way to do this is to start gradually. Try experimenting with ways to work with your familiar slowly, until you feel more comfortable with the situation, rather than trying to jump in right away and expect fantastic results."

So that's why, Michael explained, he would teach me a series of successive exercises using guided visualizations, so I could gradually get to know my familiar and do more.

"Basically, what you'll do," he said, "is to call your familiar to meet in some spot. Then, after you place your consciousness within your familiar, you will see through her eyes and act through her body, as you go off on whatever adventures or errands you have in mind. But it's not an overnight process. You'll have to practice on your own over the months you work together. Tonight will just open the door to show you what to do to begin this work."

Michael then described two methods I could use to ride the familiar.

"One way," he said "is to picture yourself riding on the familiar's back and let it transport you. Another way is to imagine yourself within the familiar looking out at the world through the familiar's eyes. But if you use this latter process, you have to be really careful, since the force of your consciousness might be too powerful for the familiar and overwhelm its consciousness. And you don't want to hurt your familiar. So usually it's best to see yourself riding on the familiar's back. Then, you can travel wherever you want and your familiar will take you."

"But why can't I just go myself?" I asked. "Why can't I project my own consciousness to the same place and not use the familiar?"

"Because," said Michael, "your familiar might be better able to go into unchartered territory or take more risks. Or your familiar might have some knowledge about the place where it's going which you don't, at least in your conscious state. Then, too, if you are involved in a conflict with someone, your familiar can act as a liaison to help you see what's going on without getting more involved yourself. Or in some cases, people use their familiars to help them interfere with someone they have a conflict with, rather than risking their own involvement, although I don't recommend this kind of action generally, since you can get hurt."

Michael gave an example from his experience where someone had sent out a familiar against him, though he was able to successfully counter its efforts.

"I was much younger at the time," Michael began, "about 20, and I got into a series of difficulties with a pair of witches. It was a small difference of opinion we had about something, and they were angry and expressed this by sending me a series of bad dreams. Then, they sent out their familiar, which took the form of the classic black cat.

"I encountered it one time when I left my house and walked down the street on a foggy night, and the fog is very conducive to gateways and magical workings. As I passed this alley between two houses, this black cat suddenly came running out of the alley, and it began running up my leg, clawing me, and trying to climb up to attack my face."

"So how do you know it was their cat?" I asked.

"For one thing, this was a very unusual thing for an alley cat to attack like this, and as it clawed me, I felt the connection. I just knew, and later confirmed in conversation with these witches about what they had been doing.

"In any event, a very curious magical thing suddenly happened, which I've experienced at times before when I felt under stress. My magical self suddenly emerged, and I felt it rising up and through me, and I did an act of power. In an instant, I was able literally to teleport myself from one place to another, so I was standing about 6 to 10 feet away from the cat. The cat looked at me very strangely, like it was transfixed or bewitched, because humans aren't supposed to be able to do such things. Then, in a few more moments, I snapped back to where I had been, like a rubber band, except now, the cat had retreated a few feet, and it looked at me terrified, it's eyes wide with horror. Then, still in this state of magical consciousness, I stamped my feet and yelled at the cat. The cat panicked and ran, and that was the last time I was bothered by those witches. So that's an example of someone using a familiar in a conflict situation. The witches sent their familiar out to assault me, although it didn't work very well."

"Was this a real animal?" I asked, suddenly confused. "I thought these familiars were just energies or spirits from another dimension."

"No, they can be real animals, too, though this is much less common, because it takes a lot of focus, and it's difficult to work with animals."

"But how..." I struggled with formulating my question, and Michael explained.

"You see, the binding of an animal involves more than the binding of a regular familiar. You can't just go out and buy a pet and think it will do this. Rather, to send the animal forth as a familiar, it has to be willing to respond to your telepathic request and carry out the act or deliver your message. And compared to ordinary familiars, animals can often be more willful, since they can have a more active will of their own. Yet it is possible, though difficult, to train a real animal to assume this familiar role. In fact, historically, cats have been trained to do this -- to seek out other individuals at the request of the magician and act in response to the magician's will."

To illustrate, Michael pointed out that the European witches and Aztec priests had trained their animals to do this.

"What does it take to bind an animal to be a familiar?" I asked.

"The same kind of ceremony as in binding a spirit or elemental form," said Michael. "Like any familiar, the animal has to be willing to serve you, and the ceremony is designed to seal the agreement and express this relationship. For example, Paul has a cat he has bound to him, although he doesn't send her forth on any special missions, though he could."

I flashed back on my own cat, which I had on a child. I remembered it as a wily, tawny creature, with a will of its own. Some of the dogs in the neighborhood even used to run in terror down the street from this creature. Could such a free spirited animal ever be bound as a familiar, I wondered? As I tried to imagine what it might be like, I suddenly became aware of Michael's voice continuing to talk about the consciousness of animals, and I snapped back to attention.

"Now sometimes people may believe that animals don't have souls or a consciousness like humans," Michael was saying. "But they definitely do. They do have a consciousness; they can feel real emotional love. Anyone with a dog can tell this. Therefore, when you seek to bind a pet as a familiar, it's necessary to work out an agreement or deal, just like you do with any spiritual being, about what that animal is willing or not willing to do. Many animals will not be interested at all. But if they are, like any bonding, the relationship must be regularly reaffirmed."

Just then, Michael's dog Queenie wandered into the room wagging her tail. She was a large black spaniel, with long hanging fur, floppy ears, and long splotches of white slashing across her. As she waddled over to Michael, he petted her and continued.

"Now, another thing about animals," he remarked glancing at Queenie, "is they are capable of astral projection. Perhaps they can't do it in the more sophisticated way we can for many purposes and destinations. But they can move and transport themselves in other than normal physical ways."

"For example?" I asked.

"One of the most common is when you lock up your pet in a room and it gets out. You seal up all the doors and windows so it won't get out, and soon you hear your pet scratching and crying, but then it stops, so you forget about it. But an hour or two later, out comes your pet. Then, you take it back and find the door is still locked. So either your pet is very good at opening doors and locking it again, or something else is going on. I've experienced that kind of thing with this dog and some other dogs we've had again and again, and I know many others who've had this experience."

"So what do you think is happening?" I asked.

"I think it's teleportation," Michael replied. "I think somehow the animals are projecting themselves outside of the room."

He looked at Queenie parked by his feet, as if to get a confirmation.

"And another thing," Michael went on, "all animals can see. In fact, animals are more psychic than humans. I saw this myself after I first learned about making energy balls from another shaman. When I returned from making these balls, I saw Queenie standing there in the backyard, and I visualized throwing an energy ball at her. Then, she looked at me with this strange panicky look in her eyes, and she ducked, and the energy passed over her. Then, she stood looking at me with these wide eyes, shaking. If she hadn't been able to see, she wouldn't have ducked."

"Could you have moved your hands or done anything else to suggest what you were doing?" I wondered.

"No, no. Nothing. I was standing perfectly still; I wasn't even looking directly at her," said Michael. "What she suddenly sensed was this wave of energy coming at her, and so she ducked. She didn't know what it was, but she didn't like it.

"And at other times, I found she could see at well. For example, several years ago, I used to conduct experiments in telepathy with her. I used to think about her, while she was in one part of the house and I was in another. I wouldn't make any noise. I would just think "come here," and then a few minutes later, she would appear with this what-do-you-want look on her face. Each time I called her telepathically and she came, I gave her a cookie to train her, and after awhile, almost consistently, every time I called her she would come.

"So you see," Michael concluded, "animals are psychic. In fact, there are many cases of them being able to sense ghosts, negative energies, and poltergeist activity. So, by extension, it's perfectly logical that it should be possible to involve an animal in working with magic and call on an animal to serve as a familiar, if it is willing to do so.

"Also, if you look back in history, you can see how this practice developed, and why it makes perfect sense. Living so close to the animals in prehistoric times, the people soon became aware that their animals had this powerful awareness, and they sought ways their animals could help them. So the Aztec sorcerers and European witches are part of a long line of people who developed this special relationship with animals as psychic helpers. At the same time, these peoples recognized that a sorcerer could be harmed if his familiar was, since much of his energy was traveling with the familiar. So this is one reason you have to be careful what you send your familiar into. For example, when those witches sent their cat out after me, it wasn't a good idea, since the cat could have gotten hurt, instead of my just giving it a good scare."

Just then, Queenie stirred at Michael's feet and stood up. "Now one final point about animals," Michael added. "Sorcerers working with animals generally believe that bonding with the pet should occur at a very early age and very early in the relationship between the pet and the shaman. They use a variety of spells and rituals to create this bonding. But the key is the pet must be willing..." Now Queenie shook herself a little and trotted off. "Which is why the results are not guaranteed, because the pet may not be interested. So the easier way to work with familiars is to work with entities or spirits. The bonding is much simpler, the communication is easier, and the results are more guaranteed."

I glanced over at Queenie, who was now watching us from the far corner of the room. Suddenly, she gave me a quizzical look, barked with a soft yelp, and flounced away.

"So there...a case in point," exclaimed Michael pointing at Queenie, Then, he turned back to the use of spirit familiars.

"So now," he said, "to facilitate your ability to ride the familiar, visualize some situation where you get together. Then, you are transported by your familiar to where you want to go. The reason for using your familiar, not doing it yourself, is because your familiar has greater abilities for travel and movement than you do, even on the astral level. For example, your familiar can pass through realities easier than you can and will take you to more places.

"So it's an alternative to the regular process of conscious projection or astral travel. It's easier to ride your familiar through to other dimensions, like you might ride a horse. Using a series of guided exercises, you call on your familiar in your mind's eye or in a trance state, sit down together either on or in your familiar, and then send yourself out on a trip."

"How is this travel so different from a regular astral trip?" I asked. "Why is it so different if I project my consciousness out myself or if I project it on or through another being?"

"You'll feel what it's like when you take the trip. The trip with the familiar feels different because there's more power when you are linked up with an additional entity. You may find you go faster or go more smoothly. And if you're feeling through the familiar, it may have senses you don't have, or they may be more finely developed, so you will feel and experience more.

"However..." Michael sensed my impatience, "...you have to develop the feel for doing this. It's like riding a horse. It takes some time to develop this skill, and you have to ride it a few times before you get the ability to do this well. Then, you can go much faster than depending on your own abilities to walk or run alone. You want to start off by flying in your local area. Just call up your familiar in your trance, link up, and take a short flight. I'll show you how very shortly."

"Do I need to use the circle of manifestation to call it?" I asked, recalling the long procedure I had gone through the previous night in the hills.

"No, but it's a good idea to be thorough in the beginning, until you feel this solid connection and bonding with your familiar. So, yes, at first, go through the process of creating your circle and drawing the triangle of manifestation, before you call and project your consciousness into your familiar and take off. It's a step by step process. Then, after you've done it a few times the classic way, you can use the more abbreviated form and simply connect here or in space somewhere. But first you need the formal relationship, the sense of bonding. So it's generally easier to start with the basics and work your way into the more advanced and abbreviated versions."

"Can I do this anywhere?" I wondered, again thinking about last night's long journey.

"Certainly," said Michael. "You don't need an open field. You can do it in your hotel room, wherever you want. Just physically stand up, cut the lights or use a candle, go through the process, and the familiar will manifest. It doesn't matter where you make the circle and the triangle, and you must do it right.

"Then, after you project your consciousness out and your familiar agrees, you should find yourself looking back at your own body from the triangle of manifestation. So you establish that close relationship. Then, you take off. It should be as simple as that.

"However..." again Michael spoke carefully, cautiously, "if you can't get your familiar to go where you want that shows there's a problem in the basic relationship. So you may need to either work on resolving that or you may need a new familiar. That's another reason why it's important to create your circle in the beginning to protect your own physical body. After all, this is a new being you're dealing with on a very intimate level, and you don't know what will happen. So take it slow."

"Okay, I will," I said, and Michael told me to practice riding with the familiar.

"It'll be your homework for tonight," he said. "Tomorrow we can evaluate the results. Remember, you want to do everything from the perspective of the familiar. You're either on the back of the being or within it, so you experience the trip from that perspective. But if you sense any resistance or hesitation, you should detach and return back, and we can talk about this later. In any case, it's good to find out if there are any problems now, so you can deal with them early in the relationship. Or start a new one."

Michael recommended a short trip near my hotel, perhaps to the beach.

"Wherever you do this, put as much intensity into the process as you can," he advised. "The more you work at this, the stronger your visualization, the more satisfying your trip will be."

I said I would and eagerly looked forward to trying these techniques out. But first Michael wanted to show me some additional techniques I could use with mirrors -- sending my familiar through the mirror to get some information for me.

"Then you'll have plenty of time to go home and practice," Michael said.

9

LEARNING TO WORK WITH MIRRORS AND FAMILIARS

After a brief break, Michael began his lesson on working with mirrors and familiars. By now, Greta had arrived, and she joined us in the living room.

"I'll start by setting up my mirror," Michael announced. He propped it up in a chair to one side of the room, took off its black velvet cover, and stood before it with his hands outstretched.

"This mirror already has a nice little glowing aura," he remarked. "It's like it knows it's going to be turned on, as soon as I remove the cover."

Then, standing in front of the coffee table by the couch, Michael picked up a large rose crystal, about the size of a small rock.

"Another tip in working with familiars before we start," he said. "You can have your familiar leave some of its energy for you in an object, so it's easier to call up your familiar and visualize."

Michael turned the crystal around in his hands. "Like the other night when I called up my familiar. I had her place her signature into this crystal, so I could later call her up in my mind's eye and visualize her more strongly. The crystal isn't crucial. You can use a mirror, anything. The point is that I had her leave an image of herself in the form of energy to act as an aid in calling her up."

Michael passed around the crystal. It felt warm and tingly, and I handed it back to Michael.

"But you don't need the crystal," Michael pointed out. "You just need to visualize your familiar clearly. This is one more aid that helps. It's like using a photograph of Grand Canyon, to help you remember the scene. Except in this case, the image is made up of her energy, and I was able to persuade her to leave a bit of her energy, so I could do this.

"Now anyone can leave a trace of themselves in a receptive object, such as a crystal, to be called up later by another person. In fact, some people might give another person a crystal to hold to create a link with that person they can later use. But it's not appropriate to do this without the person's permission. It's not an honest act. But in this case the familiar has agreed to do this, so it's easier to call her up."

Michael walked back to the mirror again. "Anyway, however you call up your familiar, the important thing for tonight is how to use the mirror."

Michael motioned for me and Greta to come over and stand beside him. As we stood gazing into the mirror, he continued.

"I'm going to start with a demonstration, and then you can try. I'll call up my familiar, and then I'll have her travel into the mirror, and I'll send her someplace and then have her come back. It'll be just a short trip, such as to another spot in the Valley. After you watch the operation, we'll go to the yard and you can try."

"Why not in here?" I asked. I noticed that the wind was whipping up, and it was cold and blustery outside.

"Because I don't want this new familiar in our circle. You're still establishing the relationship, and you don't know what will happen. But with my familiar, the relationship is already established, and I trust her. I know what she's going to do."

With that, Michael blew out the candles and pulled the drapes to begin the demonstration. At once, the room became almost pitch black, and I could barely make out Michael's and Greta's shadowy forms by the mirror.

"Now use your seeing exercises," Michael reminded me, "and I'll cut my gateway in the mirror."

Michael breathed in deeply, and using a small knife, he projected his energy through it and into the mirror. He made a few slashing motions, and then stepped back, letting his hand drop to his side.

"Now the gateway goes from here to a point in space just above the house," Michael said. "You can feel it like an opening up there."

I turned my attention upward, and noticed Greta nodding her head in agreement.

"Next I'll go ahead and manifest my familiar here on the table," Michael announced.

He turned slightly and made a few more slashing motions in the direction of the coffee table to draw the triangle of manifestation.

"Now it's drawn," he announced, "right around the spot where I placed the rose crystal earlier. Now I'm going to evoke her from that crystal with her signature, and then I'll work with her from there."

Again, Michael moved about with his knife, sucking in his breath, as he focused on his familiar appearing in this spot. I gazed closely, trying to see in the inky blackness. Then, I saw a few sparkles of light and a slightly smoky haze.

"There she is!" Michael announced proudly. Turning to me, he asked: "Well, do you see this?"

Again, I felt Michael testing me.

"A little," I said and describe the sparkly and smoky forms.

"Anything else?" pressed Michael.

"No," I acknowledged.

Then, Greta said she saw or felt a small feminine form. "Maybe a foot high."

"Okay, now," said Michael, moving on, "I'm going to draw a line of energy from the triangle of manifestation out to the gateway. That way she has a clear line to the gateway."

Again, he waved his knife about.

"Now I will direct her to enter the gateway. And there she goes."

The mirror looked a little smoky, like a dark cloud was in front of it.

"Now she just popped outside. I just felt her on the roof," Michael said.

"Yeah, she's there," Greta agreed quietly.

"And now I will reach out through the gateway with my energy and call her back," Michael announced.

A few moments he declared: "And here she is. I'll direct her back now to the triangle."

Again I saw the smokiness and sparkles, though now they seemed more translucent and dimmer against the pitch black background.

"It looks like she's weaker, after all her travels," said Michael. "She needs some energy."

He rubbed his hand together to create an energy ball and threw it at her. "Now she's getting better. You can see her image more strongly."

Greta picked up a styrofoam cup from the table and handed it to Michael. As he held it, he breathed in deeply, focusing intently on the table.

"Now she's even stronger," he announced.

I wasn't sure what happened, and Greta explained. "I gave Michael some energy to help out. However, I gave it to Michael and not to his familiar directly, since it's Michael's familiar. So I did that to show respect. Normally, you shouldn't directly contact someone else's familiar yourself. You should go through the familiar's owner first."

Then, satisfied his familiar was sufficiently energized again, Michael said a quick thank you to her.

"Now I'll cut her out of the circle, and she can go."

Again, a few slashing motions in the air.

"And there she goes."

Then, turning back to the mirror, Michael announced. "And now I close the gateway."

His knife shone briefly from the reflected glow through the curtains.

Then it was over, and Michael relit the candles and turned on the lights. After he did, I had a few more questions.

"Why did Greta give you the energy to help out?" I wondered.

"Because," Michael explained, "it takes a lot of energy to go through the mirror. Even if you aren't going through yourself, you are still sending your familiar, and you need to replenish the familiar's energy afterwards."

"That's why Michael gave me some extra energy to hold for him while he was doing this," Greta added. "It's helpful to have a reserve when you come out. So Michael infused the crystal in this cup with some energy before he sent his familiar in, and I added some of my energy."

"What if Greta wasn't here?" I asked Michael.

"Then I would have drawn on the reserve I created myself. The point is that going through a mirror gateway like any gateway is very strenuous, because it involves going into another dimension, and the mirror gateway is even more difficult, because the mirror makes it more intense. And it can be even more strenuous for a familiar, since it's going through completely, whereas you are only standing outside or projecting part of you through. So afterwards, that extra charge of energy is important. It's like an athlete needs energy after completing a race. You can use breathing, crystals, any method -- just something that recharges the energy of you or your familiar after either of you come back."

The demonstration over, we went outside, so I could try the process myself. We put on our heavy coats, and I gathered up my mirror and long black staff for working with my familiar.

"Now what I'd like you to do," said Michael as we assembled on the patio, "is to first cut a gateway in your mirror. Then, you'll draw your circle and triangle of manifestation. Then, you'll call up your familiar by envisioning her, thinking, or whispering her name,. After you see her appear in your triangle, you can tell her that you want her to go through the mirror, turn around, and come back to the triangle."

I tried to imagine the process as Michael spoke, though it was hard to keep it all the details in mind. Meanwhile, Michael continued.

"Now the next step is to leave your circle by cutting yourself out. Seal your circle behind you, so nothing you don't want in there gets in, and go over to the triangle. Now, standing there, draw a line of energy from the triangle to the mirror to create a pathway for the familiar to the mirror. You may need a few trips to do this, to make a nice firm line.

"Next, go back to your circle, cut your way back in, seal it up again, and direct your familiar to make the trip and come back. Then, watch the familiar go in, wait, and summon the familiar to come back through the mirror and reappear again in the triangle."

"Okay," I nodded, trying to take it all in. Would I remember all this? I expressed my concern to Michael.

"Don't worry," he said. "Just take it step by step, and I'll help guide you through it. Just a few simple steps."

A few simple steps. I felt like I was being given instructions on how to guide a missile.

Michael went on. "Now when your familiar comes back, sever that energy line between it and the mirror, so it has no reason to go back. You can use your power object to do that, and maybe put a banishing pentagram out at the mirror to seal it temporarily. Then, ask your familiar what it experienced going into the mirror, and after you get your information, give your familiar some of your energy, and send your familiar off."

I nodded blankly. I felt like I was spacing off.

Michael continued: "Then, take down your circle, seal up the mirror permanently, and you are done."

I went to the center of the backyard, put my mirror on a lawn chair, and stood before it, gazing into it, my staff pointed at it.

"That's right, start with the gateway," I heard Michael coaching me.

I moved my staff up and down a few times with a few thrusting motions, as I heard Michael's voice in the distance like an instruction video tape. "Now, into the glass gently... Slowly... Widen it... Try to center it a little more... Really get a sense of the gateway penetrating the glass; feel it penetrating down through the mirror into the other dimension. "

I noticed the glass seemed to fuzz over, vibrating a little in the moonlight.

Michael's voice continued. "Now you can see it shimmering ... Now start to widen it some more... Gently... Imagine you are reaching inside a pocket and widening and opening it up... Feel it deepening, going down through the glass into that other dimension."

Finally, Michael seemed satisfied. "Now you can create your circle and triangle and summon your familiar."

Slowly, I walked across the lawn to where I had previously made some circles. It felt comfortable, familiar to be there. I went through the familiar motions of making the circle around me and found it reassuring, like the act of creating the circle helped me step into this altered reality, where all things became possible and real. Then, the circle completed, I made the triangle at a distance and called my familiar. Soon, I saw the familiar fuzzy smoky area and sparkles.

"I can see her too," Michael reassured me. "Now you can explain what it is you want her to do."

As Michael had instructed, I told her to go into the mirror and return, while I cut my way out of my circle and stood by the triangle, imagining my energy going out in a line to the gateway in the mirror.

Soon, I felt I could see a slight wispy line, and I heard Michael coaching me again.

"No, make it more solid, so she has a clear pathway to follow."

I tried focusing and projecting my energy again.

"Now a few more passes to strengthen the line," Michael called out. "Have your familiar wait while you do this. Don't let her out of the triangle until you are back in your circle. That way you have more protection and control."

Again, I concentrated, radiating energy from all of my body into this line.

"Now do another nice firm pathway," Michael urged. "You don't want your familiar to get lost on the way."

Finally, Michael seemed to think the path was firm enough.

"Okay, you can go back to your circle now and direct your familiar into the glass."

After I had done that by imagining the little sparkle of energies of my familiar traveling along the path, Michael exclaimed: "Good, I saw her go in. Now when you're ready, have her return back along the path."

After she was back, he reminded me about the final steps.

"Now cut yourself out of the circle... Sever the line from the triangle to the mirror ... Seal the triangle so she stays there... Be gentle... Seal the mirror. You don't want to leave any open gateways open ... And go back to your circle."

I felt grateful for Michael's suggestions as I went through the motions; there was so much to remember, so much to think about. So I felt I had to practice at least several times to make the process part of me, so I didn't have to think and could easily step into this other reality that transcended thought.

Finally, it was time to send the familiar back.

"But first give her some energy ," Michael cautioned. "She just went through the mirror for you, and she'll be really low in energy. That took a lot of work. As you notice, she's not as bright as she was."

I glanced at the triangle, feeling drained of energy after all the concentration, and I noticed the sparkles were no longer there.

"Send her lots of energy," Michael urged. "Don't send her away until she looks as bright as she was when she first showed up. You want to get a feeling of vitality and health from her. You don't want to feel she's depleted."

Again my attention snapped back into focus, and I concentrated on sending out a stream of energy. Soon the bright sparkles were back.

"Now thank her and send her back," Michael said.

I did so, imagining her disappearing into the black night air by the bushes. I started to reach out with my staff to take down my circle, but Michael's voice stopped me.

"Wait until you're sure she's gone. So double, triple check. You want to make sure she's out of the circle. Otherwise, if she's still there, she could linger around and get hurt, since she's trapped in another dimension. You want to be sure she goes home."

"Okay," I agreed, and concentrated again on her presence dissipating and disappearing.

"Good," Michael finally said. "She's gone. Now you can take down your circle."

I felt tired and moved quickly, trying to complete the motions as rapidly as I could. But Michael seemed to sense my lack of energy and broke in:

"I know it may seem picky, but you have to do this take-down carefully. You don't want to leave any of your energy out there. So take your circle down carefully. One way to do this is to suck it all back in. Just draw in that energy with your visualization and your breath."

When I had finally done this correctly, Michael asked me to go to the mirror, and he followed right behind me.

"Now close it down fully," he reminded me. "There's still some energy here. You can see it and feel it."

I looked closely and saw a slight shimmer, like a faint aura surrounding it.

"This thing is still activated," Michael went on. "So do a few more banishing pentagrams to close it down."

Finally, after I moved my staff about in the air several times, Michael agreed the circle was closed.

"That'll work. So wrap it up."

So it was done. I breathed a sigh of relief, feeling like I had come through one more test, though it had been a practice walk-through of Michael's demonstration, so I could send my familiar through the mirror on my own. Yet, I felt drained, like I did after taking an exam. Or was it because I had sent my energy through the mirror along with the familiar?

Thoughtfully, I wrapped my mirror in its flowery pillowcase, then followed Michael and Greta inside, so we could talk about the experience and other ways I might work with my familiar in the future.

First, I wanted to know about the need to make a circle. "Why can't I just visualize and send my familiar through a mirror without going through that whole process?" I asked.

"Because" Michael explained, "the circle helps you focus and gives you more power to continue to make a careful energy construction. Later you may not need this circle, because you've built up the power and can focus more quickly and intensely. But now you do need it. In fact, this technique with familiars has required you to call on a number of tools, which together help build up the power -- seeing, projecting your energy, working with mirrors, creating a circle, working with spirits, using power objects. So there's a whole set of skills involved, which is why this is an advanced technique."

"Then, what's the advantage of sending my familiar in, rather than going myself and visualizing myself traveling?"

"So you don't go yourself. By using your mirror as a tool and visualizing the gateway, you can send your familiar through space and time, even great distances, to any location. Also, it's a very focused process, so you can guarantee they get there and come back. Meanwhile, you can watch the proceedings by gazing into the mirror, so you can see your familiar go in, do its work and return. So using the mirror is a very important skill."

"What about riding the familiar?" I asked.

Michael looked thoughtful. "Well, you can gain even more information that way. And the mirror makes the process much more controlled. Your focus is tighter than just doing astral project, so the results are better by riding the familiar and going with it through the mirror. But that's more advanced. So you should first learn to ride the familiar well, and then you can try riding it through the mirror. Then, this should be easy to do, since you've already done astral projection through the mirror yourself. So you'll combine the two skills together -- riding the familiar and astral projection through the mirror.

"But," Michael cautioned, "try practicing them separately first. Also get used to working with the familiar. You can already give it commands. Then, when you feel comfortable with both these skills, you can combine them together."

I said I would start practicing that very night, and Michael looked pleased.

"But a few cautions," he warned, "since you'll be using a lot of energy. First, if you feel your familiar is losing energy, send it some of your own, since you're right there with it if you're riding it. Or pull in energy from the other energy sources around you, and feed it to yourself or your familiar. For example, if you're flying around and feel drained, you can draw in some energy from the sun or moon to energize yourself or your familiar."

"And what if you're here and have sent your familiar through the mirror? Can you still send out this energy?"

Michael shook his head. "No, that's hard to do. If you send your energy out to your familiar in the mirror, the energy can get lost along the way, and sometimes you can't get the energy to your familiar because of intervening factors, such as if your familiar is very far away, some geographical barriers, like mountains, are in the way. So the process is not very reliable. Thus, it's much better to go with your familiar to send any energy.

"And another caution," Michael said. "If you send your familiar out to do something for you, especially if it's going through the mirror or doing something strenuous, give it a little extra energy in advance. It's like packing lunch for a kid. Then, when your familiar comes back, give it more energy, too, since it's done something energetic for you, and it needs nore energy and strength."

"But I didn't give my familiar any energy before I sent it out in the yard," I suddenly remembered.

"No, that's fine. It's a different situation. You were only sending your familiar out on a short trip, and it came right back. So this didn't take much energy. But if your familiar is going to do something for you, it generally needs a boost when it goes in and comes out.

"Then, too, if you send your familiar to some places which are hard to travel through astrally, it will need some extra energy to retain its focus and shape on the journey."

"What kind of places?" I asked.

"You'll find out when you do this, or you may feel this intuitively before you send out your familiar. For example, this could be a place that's especially dangerous."

I had one last question. "Can my familiar do additional things? For example, my familiar is a guide. Can I also ask her to take messages?"

"Yes, if it's willing, you can ask it to do more, and asking a guide to take messages is certainly reasonable. You just have to see what your own familiar is open to doing. As you'll discover, the relationship can deepen and change as it goes on, and your familiar may offer to do other things, though these beings don't tend to do this, but they may. More generally, a shaman or sorcerer works with a lot of different spirits, because each one has its own limitations. But if your familiar is willing, go for it. Let each relationship develop as it will, on its own terms."

After Michael reminded me again about practicing, I packed up to go, and Michael walked me to the back door. Once outside, I looked down the path towards the backyard where the gateway I made in the mirror had been, and I had another question.

"When you send a being through a gateway to somewhere else, does it go into everyday reality?"

"Of course," said Michael, "if that's where you are sending the being. But you have to create that opening to the other side, as well as the opening here. The being can't create it.

On the other hand, you can work with gateways that are already there, which can make things even easier. You have less work to do yourself."

Michael pointed up towards the roof of the house. "For example, there are already several gateways up there and around the backyard. Some we've created, while some are natural, such as natural weak spots in current reality. In either case, you still have to visualize the opening at both ends. Otherwise, your familiar may either not get in or may end up wandering around in this null space or mirror world, which is like a cold, foggy world between dimensions. The already created gateways just make it easier to into and beyond this space. It's like having a door you can open, rather than also having to create that door. But you still have to push the door open or take off the lock. Your familiar can't do this. He or she can just only go through already open doors."

I glanced around the lawn and above the house, looking for these gateways Michael spoke about. But the house and grounds just seemed shrouded in a curtain of darkness, and I asked Michael about this.

"Of course you can't see them now. The doors are closed, since I locked them up. So they're very hard to see. You need to do your seeing exercises or be in an altered trance–like state to actually see or feel them. But they're there."

Michael walked me towards the car. "Now remember," Michael told me, "whenever you make a gateway to send something through, whether you use a door that's already created or not, you must envision the other side. You can't just open a single gateway and send your familiar out, or it will get lost. You must have both an entrance and an exit, and you must clearly visualize them both, which is why making a gateway is so difficult."

I opened the door and got in.

"That's why," Michael continued, "when you first start working with gateways, it's best to pick something familiar which you can visualize as an exit, so you have a firm location to go to, such as a bathroom mirror. But when you get good at making gateways, you can project your consciousness to create a gateway anywhere. However, for now, until you get really good, you need a specific focus of where you are going, which has to be clear and well-defined, with plenty of detail, so you end up sending your familiar or your own consciousness where you intend to be, and not someplace else."

I started the car, and while the motor was purring, Michael had a few last words.

"Now as you work more with gateways, you'll find there are many types of gateways."

He reminded me of the one in the ground we had seen with Paul when I first called my familiar.

"That type of gateway is very advanced, because it leads into the underworld dimension.

And gateways into other planes of being beyond the everyday world are even more advanced. But once you can send your familiar through an ordinary gateway, that prepares the way for more advanced work.

"So now, you are ready to go on, and you will learn more about both familiars and gateways from your actual experience. But..." he cautioned me again, "you must be very careful to take all this work a step at a time. Also, be very gentle with your familiar. For example, don't use her for dangerous messages or assignments, and realize that she may be good at some things, not at others, and you may want to start calling on other familiars for other tasks."

"What about when I practice tonight?" I asked Michael. "Do you have any suggestions?"

Michael left me with a few ideas to think about.

"My own familiar is very good as a messenger. So generally I send her out to contact people for me, and after that, the person will generally call me or contact me in another way. Also, she's good at finding out information and transmitting messages. And I've used her for more esoteric studies, such as finding out information about other dimensions and the names of spirits. So I've used her for everything from the most mundane to the most advanced tasks. Likewise, you can try out different possibilities. Think about what you would like to do and try them out with your familiar. Learn what she is good at and what she likes to do. Then, you can plan your tasks for her accordingly. And if you want, ask for another spirit to manifest in your triangle, and develop a relationship with another being, too.

"The point is that there are many possibilities, and the only limits are your own imagination. And of course..." Michael leaned over to my window and whispered quietly, "...the limits of the familiars you work with."

Then, pushing away from my car, he said goodbye, waved, and walked back into the house. As I drove away, I noticed it had become foggy, almost like I was plunging into a gateway myself. So thinking about familiars and gateways, I drove off into the night.

What would I practice tonight at my hotel? Go step by step, Michael had told me. But I felt impatient; I wanted to try more. I can just imagine whatever I want, I told myself, as I drove on in the darkness.

10

TRAVELING WITH THE FAMILIAR

B ack at my hotel room, I decided to try to ride my familiar and see if I could travel with her through the mirror. Since I had already tried astral projection and riding the familiar, I thought it would be fairly easy to combine the two methods as Michael suggested. I recalled his warnings -- take it step by step; don't move ahead too fast -- but I was impatient. I had only a few more days left to work with Michael in L.A. and then had to go home. So I wanted to go as fast as I could.

I began by lighting a candle and turning out the main lights. I shut the drapes, and I lit a small stick of incense. Meanwhile, outside I heard the hum of traffic across from the beach.

As Michael had instructed, I made my circle in a small space about 5' square between my bed and the hallway alcove. It felt cramped, restricted, unlike the lawn, where it was possible to reach out and project energy across large distances. Even so, I concentrated on visualizing and worked slowly, firming up the image of the circle in my mind. After I made the triangle of manifestation near my bed, I saw the small sparkling I associated with my familiar. I imagined an energy bridge between my circle and the triangle, and I invited her into my triangle.

In minutes, I felt like I had mounted the familiar, and we were soaring out of my hotel room window, out into the street, down along the beach, and into Venice, where I had explored several days before.

But now, instead of bustling crowds of people, the beach was quiet. Darkness hung over it like a cloak, and here and there, I saw sad hulking forms curled up like embryos under overcoats or tattered blankets, and I realized I was gazing at the underbelly of the city at night. These were not the happy tourists of the day but sad homeless creatures who had turned the beach into their home. Then, down the beach, near a small campfire, I saw a fight break out, as two men, sitting beside each other and sharing a bottle, began pushing and shoving, and I felt the anger boil up from them, as if I was there.

I wanted to stay and watch, but my familiar jerked away and went flying down the beach in the other direction. I glanced back, watching the hulking forms recede, and I suddenly wondered: Who's in control, my familiar or me? Then, scared by the potential danger of the drinking and fighting homeless men, I fled towards the open beach by the ocean that felt safe.

Once there, we stopped by the water's edge, and I watched the steady lap of the waves against the shore. It was calming after the rising terror I felt at being around the two homeless derelicts, and I felt uplifted, like I could cut the darkness out of my mind. So for awhile, I sat on the beach relaxing, feeling my familiar like a point of consciousness on my back, as glimmers of moonlight skipped across the waves, like small water insects shimmering in the light.

After about 20 minutes of what seemed like a very long time, I became aware of my familiar stirring beneath me, like a horse wanting to go home.

"Okay," I thought, "let's go, and in a few moments, I felt like I was on my familiar, who was galloping back across the beach, while I felt the wind rush by.

A few moments later, we were back in my hotel room and I was back in my circle. For a moment, I wondered if the two derelicts were still fighting, but pushed the thought out of my mind. It was time to be back and not wonder about other, uncertain realities.

As I looked down at my feet in my circle, I saw a faint sparkling of light that seemed to be waiting, like it was expecting me to do something. Then I remembered what Michael had said about giving the familiar some energy and sending it back.

"Thank you," I said finally to the sparkling light.

Then, concentrating, I projected a bolt of energy, like a sudden spark from a wire, and almost instantly, the luminous flickering mass at my feet seemed to expand and become brighter.

As I waved my staff at it, the sparkling form seemed to retreat along the glowing bridge of energy I had created and headed back to its triangle. Then, after I concentrated for a few moments on its going back to its home, the flashing stopped, and I felt the energy form was gone.

Using reverse motions, I closed the triangle and my own circle, and collapsed on my bed for a few moments to rest.

The whole experience had felt tiring, and I wanted to relax briefly before trying my next experiment -- riding the familiar through the mirror. So what could happen if I did? After all, you're in control of your own visualization, I told you want. You can do what you want. But could I? I felt confident and cocksure I could do anything and could deal with anything no matter what came up. I tried not to think about what could happen if things went wrong, as I relaxed on the bed, feeling an odd glowing power that seemed to pour out of me and surround me.

A little later, feeling rested, I set up my mirror in a chair alongside my bed near where I had made my circle before. It glowed slightly in the dim candle-lit room, and I noticed my reflection in the distance became a fuzzy haze, as I made my circle and did my seeing exercises to see beyond everyday reality. After I mate the triangle again and the white sparkles associated with my familiar appeared, I suddenly remembered I had forgotten to make the gateway in the mirror.

I hesitated. Should I start again, press on, or not do it? I glanced back and forth between the sparkling image in the triangle and mirror, not sure what to do. Finally, I remembered how Michael had told me that it wasn't that important that I had forgotten to make the top or bottom of my circle; what mattered was my visualization and concentration; so I decided to press on.

Turning back to the mirror, slowly, carefully, I brought my staff up and down, creating the opening, and then widening it with my hands to create what appeared to be a fuzzy white slit in the fog in the mirror. Then, I turned towards the triangle, created the energy bridge to my circle, and the fuzzy white sparkly form came over towards me.

Now, to ride my familiar, I projected my consciousness as a beam of light at it. Then, when I felt myself perched on its back, I directed it to head through the mirror.

However, suddenly, I felt some resistance. It was as if I was urging my familiar to go through, like a rider on a horse; but now my horse was holding back, as if scared of what might lie ahead.

"Go on, go on," I persisted.

Again, still imagining myself on the familiar's back, I sent my consciousness ahead. But this time, after a few paces forward, I felt a wall of jagged energy, like a barrier blocking my way, and ahead I saw a dark smoky line hanging in the center of the mirror, which looked like the edges of a tornado. That's ridiculous I thought, and pushed on. But instead, I felt a puff of smoke coming out from the mirror, pushing me back.

What's going on, I wondered? Then, thinking I needed to make the opening wider and deeper, I raised my staff and made a few more deep slits in the smoky cloud in front of me. As I did, a clear firm line appeared and opened up in the cloud, which hung there like an ominous warning. But at least the hole was wide enough and deep enough, so I urged my familiar to ride in. At first, I felt some resistance and pulling back, like my familiar didn't want to go in. But then as if it was finally giving in to the power of my will, I felt the resistance surrender, and moments later, I saw a quick flash and I crossed through the opening. I was in.

Inside it seemed very dark, like a void, and as I traveled about, the darkness seemed endless, like riding back and forth along a flat dark plane. I wasn't sure where to go next. I kept coming up against what felt like a wall of dark, forbidding energy; and then I would turn, and ride on. I began to feel a little anxious, as if trapped in a dead end freeway late at night. As a way of calming and reassuring myself that everything still was normal, I began asking the familiar questions about everyday ordinary things: Would I work with a toy manufacturer to bring out some dolls? Would I move to L.A.? Would my book be published?

At first, I got a few answers. Telepathically I heard a "yes" to my questions, and I felt reassured, both at the answers and at the way I was getting these answers – very clear, intense, certain -- like powerful, sure messages sent to me from the heart of hyperspace.

But as if my familiar didn't want to answer more questions and was tired of my guiding her on this endless ride through some dark nowhere, she started bucking up and down and twisting about. At first, I felt she was being playful, like a bucking bronco in a rodeo, who wasn't bucking hard enough to throw me off, just give me an exciting ride. So fine. I went with it, and soon felt the bounces radiating through me like waves. I felt enlivened, exhilarated, and I felt a soft breeze blow through my hair.

But then the bouncing got wilder. I felt my familiar leaping and jerking under me, and I held on tightly, like a rider on a bucking horse. Then, I notice the wind whipping up, turning into raging whirlwind, and I felt like I was being whirled back and forth, and I was suddenly afraid. What would happen if I let go? I dug my hands in even tighter, until I felt inside my familiar's sparkly white form. Yet still I continued to whirl about, now like I was in a tumbling drum in a whirling current, which was spiraling down -- down. But where? It was so dark around me - and the raging wind pushed the barrel back and forth. I gripped on tightly.

Suddenly, I felt a crash, as if the barrel had caught on a jagged rock, and a moment later, an explosion sent the pieces of the barrel hurling outward, and I felt myself falling... falling. Then, almost miraculously, I was standing in front of the mirror, gazing in, and seeing the reflection of my black shirt shimmering in the dim candle light.

So what had happened? I felt a little uncertain, confused, and bruised, as if I had just been thrown off a horse. As I glanced around the room to feel more anchored again in everyday reality, I noticed a bright sparkling in the mirror in front of my reflection, like a display of firecrackers in the night, and I suddenly felt it was my familiar laughing at me. The flashes were like cackle of laughter coming out of the mirror in waves towards me, and I felt very foolish.

Then, pushing that feeling aside, determined to complete the exercise of riding the familiar through the mirror, I projected my consciousness back in like a beam o light. In moments, I was back on my familiar holding onto one of the sparkles radiating out from her.

"Now, no more of that," I thought firmly. "Just a brief ride through the darkness, and we'll corn back," and with that, I felt I was astride again, fully in control. And now the strange breeze I had felt was quiet, too.

I urged the familiar on, and this time felt no resistance. Instead, we looped briefly around the dark plane, which felt calm and silent now, a little like I imagined a mortuary or cemetery at night to be.

Then, as I started asking questions again -- What books should I work on next? Wwould I get together with someone I hoped to see? -- I felt my familiar drift with me in and out of the mirror for several minutes. First, we would be in the void, then flying around my hotel room or out on the street, and then back to the blackness again.

After awhile, feeling tired, yet complete, I was ready to go back. I sent out that thought to my familiar, and in an instant, I felt her stop, turn, and like a horse eager to return home, I felt a zip in her movements. We seemed to whiz back, as if she was relieved to return.

A few moments later we were back in my circle. I got off by withdrawing my consciousness, thanked the sparkly form before me, directed her to return to her triangle, and breathed some energy to her. The sparkly form grew bigger as I did. Finally, I said goodbye, waving my staff in the air. My familiar hesitated for a few moments at the edge of the triangle. Then, like a puff of smoke, she seemed to dissipate in the air, and I felt her presence was gone.

I finished the exercise by taking down the triangle and my circle. Then, I closed up the mirror and the gateway within it, using a few slashing motions with my staff. Afterwards, I lay down on my bed, feeling very tired and drained. What had really happened on the other side of the mirror, I wondered, as I drifted off to sleep?

* * * * * *

The next evening, Sunday, when I went to visit Michael for the last lesson, the first thing he wanted to know about was my experiences with the familiar. Paul, Sara, and Greta, who sat around me in the living room, listened closely as I described the ride out of the hotel and down the beach, and then my ride in and out of the mirror.

"It was so strange," I concluded, "and then I felt so tired."

Michael grimaced. "No wonder," he said. "You got stuck in the void. You're supposed to have a clear destination, not travel around in there. And your familiar didn't like it. No wonder she was bucking, and you kept drifting in and out. Besides, all those questions helped to scatter your focus. I told you to practice. But do just one thing at a time, until you know what you're doing. Riding the familiar, going through the mirror, and having a conversation with your familiar are three separate activities. And you're new at doing all this. No wonder you lost focus and felt anxious and tired. You were trying to do too much without knowing what you were doing or where you were going. You're lucky you and your familiar got back at all, or that your familiar wasn't permanently hurt."

"Oh," I said, suddenly feeling very dejected and foolish. "I'm sorry...1 didn't realize," I said helplessly. I felt Paul, Sara, and Greta's eyes piercing deeply into me, like my jury and judge.

"Well, you're just learning," Michael said reassuringly. "You just have to learn to take it slow."

I felt like I had just been given a reprieve, and sank back with a sigh on the couch.

"So now, let's backtrack for a few minutes, let's review," Michael said, "and then we can go on."

I turned on my tape recorder and flipped open my notebook again, ready to listen.

"First of all," said Michael, getting up and pacing about as he spoke, "since your spirit is a guide, she can be helpful in going on extended astral projections and in taking you places. But as you have seen very clearly, you need a sense of where you are going first. She can help you decide on the final destination, since she may know better than you the advantages and disadvantages of particular locations.

But initially she needs some input from you, or she can end up wandering or getting lost."

I nodded, remembering my experience with the mirror.

"Then, too, a guide can be helpful with vision questing," Michael continued. "As we'll talk about tonight, the guide can help you explore and see your vision.. It's like being able to drive instead of going on foot."

"Can you clarify the difference between normal conscious projection and working with a spirit?" I asked. "I'm still not sure I can tell the difference?"

"Well, for one thing," snapped Michael, "you're in the presence of another being. It's more vivid than regular conscious or astral projection, and when you use a mirror to focus, which contributes to a more intense, clearer experience, using a familiar will up the power even more. So individually, using mirrors and familiars are powerful advanced techniques. And together, it's an even more powerful combination, but only if you know what you're doing. Otherwise, the power can work against you."

I nodded quietly, feeling the power of the lesson digging in, and Michael continued.

"In any case, the familiar is probably easier to work with than the mirror, since you have this immediate direction and control over your spirit once you complete the bonding process. After the initial agreement, it helps to reinforce this bonding by taking some time to work with your familiar. It's like solidifying a relationship with a friend. Then, as that firms up, you're in a better position to ask your familiar to do more."

"Like going through a mirror with me?" I commented quietly.

"Yeah, like doing that," Michael said. "As you'll find, that sort of thing is much easier after the two of you have had some time to get more acquainted.

"In any event, once you do have this solid relationship, your familiar can give you a vehicle you can use to transport yourself, and it can take you to places you may not know of yourself, which is one reason to use a guide. Then, too, if you're seeking a vision or going on a magical journey, you can ask your familiar to help you have a specific vision. Or it can help you cut through any barriers or obstacles, so you get there. It's like having your own personal genie to show you the way.

"In addition, since this being is more directly in touch with power than you, it can sometimes better select the location to go to, because it may have a better sense of your needs and what you need to know than you do. Also, it's more adept at traveling through other dimensions, since you're not a very experienced flyer. For one thing, it has a better knowledge of the hazards and dangers out there, and it can sense them before you do."

"What kind of dangers?" I asked. "We only traveled around the street and beach on my first trip. Then, on my second, we were mostly in the mirror, and otherwise didn't go very far."

"That doesn't matter," said Michael. "Even if you take a short hop along the street, you are still out on the circuit when you fly. And you could encounter all sorts of things -- odd feelings, other sorcerers, unexpected energy fluxes, strange vortexes -- and that's only in our own dimension. When you travel to other worlds, you can encounter unpredictable happenings. So an advantage of your familiar as a guide is that she or he can help to get you through. "

Paul cut in. "And the reason guides can help you do this is that they are better at sensing these dangers and alien presences than you are. Humans are more apt to pick up something and analyze whether it's true or not. But a spirit or familiar is more apt to respond out of pure gut instinct, so they can better protect you on these travels, at least until you are better able to recognize these dangers for yourself."

"Then, too," Michael added, "your familiar might help you avoid going some place you want to go, if you might run into problems there, because it can often recognize something you can't see. The reason it can do this is you are using basic human senses, which have certain limitations. But this being isn't human, and it sees the world with other senses. For example, perhaps it can perceive higher frequency light energies, X-rays, different colors, or other qualities, so it is aware of different disturbances you should avoid. So, for all these reasons, your familiar can be a very powerful tool."

Michael made a circuit around the room, as if to underline the importance of his message, and stopped in front of me.

"So my suggestion to use this tool properly is to continue talking to and riding your familiar. Start out in your local area, like around your hotel or around your house when you get home. Then you can get more exotic and go as far as you wish. You can go to other dimensions, other planets."

"Should I go through the mirror?' I asked.

"Certainly, can after you are comfortable with this ordinary riding process. But you don't have to do so. The mirror will give you more focus, and it's more powerful. However, it's best to first work with your familiar in the local environment without the mirror, since the mirror can be very taxing to work with, as you have found. But as you grow in personal power, you'll reach that point where you can work with the mirror successfully and powerfully focus you towards your objective.

"However, as you have seen," Michael cautioned, "if your gateway through the mirror is not focused on your intended direction, you could have trouble getting back, because you can get lost. Perhaps your familiar might help, but it can get lost too. If you get lost in that middle space, you can end up losing a lot of energy very fast. Like you did."

I cringed. Would Michael never step reminding me about my trip through the mirror. His words were like a litany of what not to do.

"So," Michael went on, "it's helpful to use a parallel approach. On the one hand, you can work with riding the familiar, and on the other, you can work on creating and projecting your consciousness through mirror gateways, until you have both skills developed. Then, you can do both. Maybe you send your familiar through on occasion as a test now. But as far as the two of you going through together, that requires a great deal of focus, and it's easy to get confused or lost if that's not there. So it would be better to wait until your abilities are more developed "

"Okay," I agreed, hoping Michael would change the subject and get on with the rest of the lesson. But then he ripped into my questions.

"Now another thing," he began, "there's nothing wrong with asking your familiar questions. But if you ask your familiar to give you suggestions and make predictions about your future, while you're flying in and out of gateways, that's a recipe for disaster. The problem is you get too preoccupied with the questions and not with what you're doing. If you want to call your familiar or get in a circle together and talk, that's perfectly fine. But if you're flying through a gateway, which could be dangerous, your focus should be on flying through the gateway. Otherwise, you risk all sorts of psychic harms if you don't have the proper focus.

"Also, bouncing back and forth between the middle world and the street is not a good idea."

I nodded, remembering how this too had happened on my trip.

"Either settle on the middle world or go to the street," said Michael. "You don't want to drift in and out. And probably your preoccupation with questions led to this drifting, since this could easily distract you from your focus. So you get lost, which could be dangerous and certainly wasn't productive.

"In short, your trip into the mirror should be a single action with no interruptions. Otherwise, if your focus is bad, you can end up in limbo, which can harm your familiar and you."

"What kind of problems?" I wondered.

Paul jumped in with an answer. "There could be all sorts of problems. Say health problems, because you feel drained of energy. There could be focus problems in daily life, because you are involved in too many projects at one time, and you feel scattered. There could be energy leaks, where you drift in and out between worlds and don't bring all your energy back, so you might feel tired and distracted.

"So the key is to focus, as I found when I first got involved in astral projection work. I had zillions of questions, and at first I got lots of answers. But gradually, the answers stopped coming, until I realized this key. It's like the situation of the parent and the child. If the child asks too many questions, the parent can get tired of answering them and after awhile, may stop.

"Likewise, as with any discipline, including sex, art, sports, and religion -- the key to success is focus and doing one thing at a time. For example, yogis expound on the value of having only one thought in your mind; sports people visualize catching the ball. So stay focused on whatever you are doing.

"And remember you don't always need to use these advanced techniques. For example, if you want your familiar to be a counselor to you, do an exercise specifically for that rather than going through a gateway which could be very dangerous. Or you might use more standard methods of divination, such as the Tarot, without involving your familiar.

"Then, when you do go through a gateway, focus on that, whatever the particular reason, Then, once you know what you are doing in a gateway and have a good working relationship with your familiar, including riding it, you can go on. For then you'll truly be ready to ride your familiar through the gateway into other dimensions and spheres, as well as our own. And your familiar will go willingly. You'll see. It'll be a much better ride."

I nodded, and for a moment, I imagined a Hollywood ending -- riding off in the mirror with my familiar into the sunset. But then Michael's voice broke into my fantasy -- he was ready to talk about what would happen next – what I could do with all the skills I had learned.

11

THINKING ABOUT THE FUTURE

"The next thing to think about," said Michael, "is where to go next. The important thing is to have a larger purpose. That's why the next phase of this work involves a vision quest to seek information for your personal spiritual growth. Because now you need to understand what you are using your personal power for. And the vision quest is designed to do that -- to help you discover your purpose and destiny."

Paul spoke of the many Indian tribes and other groups that used vision quests. "After the child or young person on one of these quests comes back, he returns with some insights, some sense of direction. He might be inspired by recognizing some talent, some new ideas. Whatever it is, he can take this thought form which he has been given on his quest back to ordinary life and try to make sense of it or apply it. It's like he has been in touch with this higher truth. Then, that truth helps him guide his life."

So now, Michael explained, in the ODF system, the 7th and 8th degrees, would involve my pursuing this quest.

"It will help you discover and align yourself with your path," he said. "Every shaman of true power needs to do that."

Michael then described his own experience from many years before. "It happened at dawn after I was out all night. I had been concentrating and praying, and I asked for the divine essence to show itself to me. Then, I saw this brilliant vision of a woman surrounded by the purist white light. She literally glowed and radiated light, and I felt bathed and enfolded in this myself. After that I had a very intense sense of what my own magical path would be from then on, as well as a feeling I was charged with power. So it was a very powerful, life-changing experience. I felt I had an immediate experience of the divine.

"In turn, this realization of the essence of the divine was part of a long process lasting several months, which involved a lot of thought and self-study. Then, after this essence touched me, I thought about what this vision meant and how to put this purpose into practice."

Michael paused, and walked around slowly, thoughtfully. Speaking very softly, profoundly, he continued.

"So you see, to be a shaman, as I recognized intensely myself, there's a need for a religious focus, some spiritual or religious view. You need a sense of the divine, for if you can't feel some essence of the god or goddess within, you have no guiding star to steer your destiny. You can't be a powerful shaman and be an atheist. Certainly, some people have been able to work with shamanic techniques and develop some ordinary psychic abilities. But without this central belief, it's impossible to achieve any great power. For real power doesn't come until you have this vision of the divine, which gives you a feeling of connection to divinity. Then, you can interpret this connection in a personal light to shape your own spiritual and magical path."

"What's this divine essence like?" I asked.

"For each individual shaman, the face or image of this divinity may be expressed in many ways. It could be a Christian image, a Pagan image, a vision involving American Indian images, whatever. It doesn't matter, because the sense of the divine draws upon your personal religious symbols, whatever has been meaningful to you in the past, or what you feel most comfortable with now. These symbols act like a mediator to link you to the divine essence or ultimate power. You need these images or links, because this ultimate essence is so powerful

-- so you can't normally contact it directly. It's like reaching out to the energy of the sun. You need some shields or filters to protect you from the tremendous power of that light. But you still want to reach out for that light as a source of sustenance and life."

Michael paused, circled around the room, then continued.

"So it would be good for you to think now about what you believe in -- a god, a goddess, a divine energy, whatever -- to give yourself the beginnings of a framework for seeking out your divine vision. For that's the real dividing line between the ordinary occultist or metaphysician and the real master shaman -- seeking out and getting the divine vision."

As Michael explained, this is what I should do next in working towards my 7th and 8th degree. "Once this vision is granted," Michael went on, "you can follow this path to working closer with and feeling more unity with this divine essence through the act of magic. For now, you have gone beyond doing magical and psychic acts for their own sake. Instead, you have set out on a more holy, spiritual path."

"What about day to day life?' I asked. I suddenly had visions of Michael talking about some mystical spiritual path that involved withdrawal from the everyday world.

Michael quickly made it clear that wasn't the case. "This spiritual path I'm talking about is very much in the world. For example, these skills you have learned can readily be used on a daily basis to help you lead a smoother life. Then, as things move along more smoothly, you can have the time and ability to seeker greater visions. For ultimately, this search will help you gain much greater personal enlightenment, and that is part of our own group's mission -- to help you achieve that recognition."

"Also," Paul added, "when you get in touch with that essence, it will give you a greater respect and meaning for everything you do, which will give you a greater sense of fulfillment. For example, when a saint or monk does a very menial task, he recognizes the quality of the divine even there and experiences that as part of his enlightenment and personal fulfillment. It's as if every thing he does, feeding his body, tilling a garden, they're all ways of furthering the works of his maker and so divine. Thus, when you do an act of magic, interact with others, whatever you do, you might see it as an aspect of the divine, which will give you a higher sense of mission and purpose. Often, we tend to take the things we do, the food we eat, the activities of everyday life for granted. But if we recognize the divine essence around us and within us, we'll experience life so much more fully."

"So, you see," said Michael, "the whole point of the training you have gone through from the beginning to your present degree is not just to showcase the psychic talents you can develop. Also it has been designed to open your consciousness in an orderly way to make you more sensitive, so eventually you can encounter this divine essence we've been talking about; so eventually the light of the divine can find its way into your heart."

Michael paused for a few moments, and as I glanced around the room, I felt a profound silence. Paul, Sara, Greta sat almost motionless in a semi-circle around me, and it felt like there was a sense of this divine presence Michael spoke of in the room, connecting us, focusing us as he spoke. I felt strangely awed, moved, and perhaps energized by a little power, too.

Michael continued. "So, the next step is to go beyond the basic psychic skills to get in touch with this divine purpose. It has been necessary to learn these basic skills first, so your training has involved learning all sorts of psychic and magical acts, such as projecting your energy, working with energy darts, reading auras and haras, and opening up gateways to other dimensions. It's like building the foundations of a house first or going to school. You've got to learn the fundamentals like reading, writing, and addition first, so you start with kindergarten and first grade and then go step by step before you can go to college.

"It's like that in working with more advanced levels of magic and shamanic initiation. You've gotten the foundations. Now you can go on less concerned about mundane things, because you take them for granted. So, now, the major thrust of your working will be seeking out and finding more and more powerful levels of initiation, based on realizing your own purpose and this divine essence in your everyda1 life."

"So there's a major shift now," added Paul. "And a key reason for this shift is our own development as a species, which the shaman is a part of. For we have evolved to a point where we are more intelligent and spiritually aware as a species due to natural selection or our own conscious efforts over the years. Many modern shamans have become aware of this and are actively pursuing the evolution of the human race by gathering spiritual knowledge and enlightenment and giving it back to the people, so we can use this knowledge to evolve further into even more intelligent, spiritually aware beings. So as you work on your own spiritual development through this contact with the divine essence, you can contribute to this larger process of development, too."

Michael walked slowly and quietly around the room.

"So now, let's discuss your process from here," he said. He described how the next stages, the 7th and 8th, were like a new beginning, but at an advanced level, and they involved going out on solo, much like my first solo when I began studying with the group three years before. Yet, as Michael pointed out, this would be much different.

"In your first solo, you were just opening yourself out to the universe saying 'Here I am.' It was your first act of showing yourself as a magical being. But now, in this solo you are seeking visions granted by the divine and then going back to the world with these answers to your visions, so you can interpret and applying them in your personal and your magical life. So this is really a much more advanced procedure.

"Then," Michael spoke slowly and thoughtfully, "this prepares you for the next phase of feeling a sense of total connection or unity with the divinity, and then being able to work with the higher principles of nature, which we call the elemental kings."

To show me how the personal vision quest would prepare me for this more advanced work, Michael began describing what was necessary to experience the unification with the divinity, for once having the experience of unity, one could better deal with ordinary situations, such as work, taking care of one's family, and relationships with others.

"Basically, it's a six month or longer process, which involves a serious commitment, coupled with regular prayer and meditation. You don't have to go out in the desert or isolate yourself like some ancient mystics have done. But you have to have work towards this experience of unity regularly with a divine focus, and going on this vision quest first is important, since you'll obtain an image of the divine you can relate to. You need this picture to have something to pray to or to focus on in your meditations, since you can't pray to an abstract power alone. You need a specific focus to relate to. Then, that will begin your special connection with the divine which can last you the rest of your life."

"What kind of image of the divine?" I asked.

"Anything," Paul cut in. "It doesn't matter what particular system this divine being comes from, and your views can change over time. For example, it could be Christian, Jewish, Pagan, or it could be drawn from some ancient religion, even something that comes to you in your astral travels. What's important is that if you pray for something, you must expect an answer, so you need to relate to something that can respond to you. An image of the divine from a traditional religion can be especially powerful, since collectively people have poured so much energy into recognizing and honoring that being. But you can use any image you can relate to, as long as you believe in it; that's what counts."

"In any case," said Michael, "you will find your vision of this when you go on your vision quest for the 7th degree. Then, you will make that part of your life by discovering or creating your own code of ethics based on that vision. The idea is to prepare yourself for experiencing this unity by living your life in accord with the ethical demands of your vision of the divine."

"It sounds like quite a commitment,' I said.

"Yes, it is. But it's worth it," said Michael. "For it gives your whole life a sense of unity and purpose. It's like working out your whole living script, in which all parts hang together, because now it is unified as a whole, and it's infused with this tremendous vitality, because it has been touched by the force of the divine."

"What exactly does this involve?" I asked.

"First, you plan on spending about six months or longer doing this, and you frame a prayer to the divine as you have worshipped it. In this prayer, you ask for knowledge of the divinity through an agency or aspect of that divinity, since it's presumptions to call down the ultimate deity. So you relate to an aspect of it. For example, in many traditions, spiritual teachers or angels are considered aspects or messengers of the divine. Whatever tradition you respond most to, the message you are seeking it to gain a knowledge or understanding of the divine as a life force through some sort of divine messenger.

"Secondly, you need to offer a vow or promise to commit yourself to achieving this goal. Then, once you make this commitment to gain this objective, there can be no return if you are to achieve it. Along the way, you may encounter many temptations to set aside the work or experience many distractions. But one of the keys to completing the work is perseverance and patience."

"What kind of temptations and distractions?" I asked.

"Almost anything ," said Michael. "There could be everyday things like phone calls, unexpected visitors, people who pull on your time and commitment. Or there could be more spiritual and psychic questions, such as renewed thoughts about 'Why am I doing this?' or 'Can I really do it?' which can test your faith. But as such issues come up, you must keep doing this concentrated work for at least six months or maybe more, whereby you continue to act out of your dedication and desire for this wisdom. In other words, you need to put this quest for knowledge first in your life, and even though you do many other day-to-day things, you must keep this quest in focus. You must remind yourself during your meditations or daily life activities that you are guiding yourself towards this purpose of unification with the divine."

Michael gave an example from his own experience about a decade before.

"When I did this," he said, "I came up with two prayers I said regularly, and I also got a red sash which I charged and wore when meditating as a symbol of my bonding and dedication to my goal. Each day when I got up in the morning, the first thing I did in my room was to put on my sash, say these prayers, and reaffirm my commitment towards this goal.

"Also, before I went to bed at night, again I did this. And throughout the day, as much as possible, especially towards the end of my six month period of commitment, I thought about this goal."

"So what happened?" I asked. I was curious and intrigued, but at the same time, I wondered was all of this effort worth it; was this experience of unity that much of a reward?

"Well, the work was very hard," Michael replied. "It involved a great deal of patience and perseverance, and I experienced a lot of changes and sometimes a lot of doubt. But finally, after these months of focus and concentration, coupled with regular meditation and prayer, I went out to the desert with Paul. It was still dark when we arrived, and we set up our sleeping bags, planning to do the exercise at dawn.

"Then, in the morning, before the sun rose, I walked from our camp to a small valley, and took along some tools to do a brief ritual --incense, my staff, a chalice, other ritual supplies, and my red sash. Then, for the last time, I made a small circle around me and made my prayer to the divine."

As everyone listened silently, Michael paused, and then went on speaking ever more softly and slowly, as if to underline the importance of what he was going to say.

"At first, nothing much happened. The sun was coming up. I could see its light on the horizon. Then, as I watched, I perceived the rising sun not as I usually did with my ordinary perception, but now it appeared as waves or emanations of energy. Then, a the sun rose in the sky, I saw brilliant waves of bright, flashing light come up from the horizon in wave after wave.

Soon, the hills around me became a blur of double images dancing in front of my eyes.

"Then, I felt very light headed, intoxicated by the experience, and I felt a presence nearby. As I looked out across the desert, I found myself gazing at a strange beast -- a large golden red lion with wings, and it seemed very massive and fierce. It came towards me slowly and raised its paw, and I sensed that I was being challenged, that this was the last and final challenge before the vision of the deity would be granted.

"In turn, I responded by opening my heart and saying: 'Here, I am for better or for worse; and if I have any flaws, that's okay, too, because here I am.' So I opened myself fully with no reservations. Then, the lion vanished and the sun rose. As the light came out, I felt an indescribable radiance and a sense of uplift and knowing. The old texts refer to the experience of smelling the holy perfume in the presence of the divine, and perhaps this is much like what I felt. I didn't really see anything; I just sensed this tremendous power, and a feeling of knowingness filled my body, along with a feeling of tremendous release and peace.

"Then, as this sensation suffused any body, I realized that the divine is much closer than we think, and I realized that throughout my life, it was already a part of me, because this divinity is part of all of us. Though I had heard that statement before, now I had had that experience directly -- a powerful knowing and an embracing connection. It was like I had suddenly had a glimpse of the world soul, of this inner unity which unites us all – an experience which few have.

"So I found the experience very enlightening, and afterwards, I had a feeling of lightness and joy at having this fuller knowledge of the divine essence and how it was a part of my life. Yet while it was a very grand experience, it was also a simple vision of a divine messenger, along with a powerful sense of the divine energy surging through me and the world.

"Then, feeling the experience was over, I said my thanks to the divine and expressed my gratitude that as a result of my work I had been able to touch this divine essence, even if just briefly this morning. Then, I went across the desert to rejoin my friend waiting for me by the car.

"Also, I felt complete, for this was the end of one process that began six months earlier with my vow to commit myself to this practice and awareness each day, and it led to this culmination with my experience in the desert. So now I felt ready to move on to the next stage of understanding that comes after this sense of unity and connection with the divine -- the work with the elemental kings that involves getting in touch in a very deep, essential way with the positive and negative, the light and dark existing in nature."

Michael paused, looking drained from describing the intensity of the experience. He sat down, sighing deeply.

"That sounds like quite an experience," I commented.

"Yes, it was a very intense and powerful experience, almost impossible to put into words. And it's one that few people have done, though many have tried. But they failed, since their reasons were wrong. You see, many people have tried to do this just for the power, since the successful magician or shaman who makes it through this gains a great deal of power, much like the Native Americans who went on a successful vision quest experienced. So many people do this because they want that power. But that's the wrong reason to do it, and so they fail. They have a faltering of will or the divine spirit doesn't answer. For having the right attitude is everything. Only that is the key to success."

"What is that attitude?" I asked.

Michael looked at me impatiently, like he was getting tired of my questions or perhaps thought I should already know the answer.

"An attitude of openness and surrender," Michael finally answered. "Having a willingness to accept and receive. Plus there's that commitment and devotion, I spoke of. And a desire to experience understanding and the truth. Though you get power, you can't go seeking for that. It's the essential paradox. To be filled with power, you must release yourself of all power. You must learn to trust and let go."

I nodded quietly.

"And so," Michael added softly, "this experience is like crossing a border. It's realizing very directly and personally that essential spiritual and religious essence of all life. I know I came away from the experience with a larger religious focus and less of a concern with material things and power. Of course, those things are important. They are part of everyday life. Yet there is much more beneath that surface -- the very essence of divinity in life."

With that, Michael felt silent. It was time to take a break. Then he would return to complete the final lesson on the elemental kings, and we went into the kitchen to take our break.

12

LEARNING ABOUT THE ELEMENTAL KINGS AND QUEENS

After a break, Michael was ready to talk about the next stage after experiencing unification with the divinity -- experiencing the elemental kings and queens. We returned to the living room again ready to listen.

"You need to do a special evocation to contact them," Michael said, as Greta, Sara, Paul, and I sat around in a semi-circle listening. "But it's more than just an evocation, because it represents another jump in consciousness. So beyond this physical act of magic, you are reaching a greater level of awareness and power.

"This expansion and growth occurs, because essentially you are taking this knowledge of the divine and seeing how that is reflected in the world through beings that represent higher aspects of that divinity. These are the elemental kings and queens."

Michael paused thoughtfully, then continued.

"This evocation is a purely solitary experience, for from the 7th on, which begins with this unification process, you are on your own as a shaman, as you seek out your visions. Then, you succeed or fail based on your own abilities."

"But how do you know if you're succeeding if you are doing this on your own?" I asked. "Or suppose someone wants to claim he had attained all these great achievements? Who would know?"

Paul answered me. "Oe reason for a magical group is to give you this kind of feedback. It's a place to report your achievements, as well as to inspire you to higher and greater heights. You can, of course, do it on your own, without feedback from others who know what you're doing. If so, it's difficult to gauge your level of progress. But a group of other magicians and shamans can help you assess your level of performance. For example, you can describe your experiences, express your doubts, ask advice, and see what other people are doing.

"As for being able to conceal your true progress from others, that can't be done. Where you're at appears in your aura. So your ability, your level or degree is very apparent to others. An experienced seer can simply look at you and tell your level of achievement. That's because a shaman can't focus his will any tighter than his ability. So when an experienced seer looks at his hara, the center of his will, he'll see the hara focused only to the maximum degree the person has really attained."

"I see," I said, remembering how Michael had shown me how to look at people and think about how psychically developed they were by the shape of their hara. We had run around a shopping mall doing this, and then I had tried it out myself on the boardwalk in Venice. The average hara was like a ball of light energy, and as the person became more developed, it hara extended into a mushroom-like shape and finally into the shape of a rocket.

"Now I remember," I said.

"Anyway," Michael said, continuing the lesson, "ultimately, even if you have the support of a magical group, you are still on your own on doing these acts, such as going out on the desert at dawn. And your goal, after you have experienced this unification with the divine, is to look at the expression of this divinity in its many aspects in the world. And one of these forms is this high order of beings known as the elemental kings and queens."

Michael drew a triangle on the board divided up into three horizontal sections. On the top, he had written the word: "the divine." In the middle box, he had written the words: "elemental kings and queens." And in the lowest box, were the words: "elementals."

"Now the elemental kings and queens," Michael observed, "are the beings of a higher order than the elemental beings in nature -- the spirits of earth, air, fire, and water, which we have talked about. So they are much closer to the divine essence." He pointed to the top of the triangle.

"In a sense these beings are like us in relationship to the other beings in their world. That's because of our intelligence, our place in the scheme of evolution, so that we have become the keepers of our planet. We have gained so much power over all life that it has become our duty to take care of and preserve our planet. The elemental kings and queens are like that. They are in charge of their world of spirits; they are the keepers of that world. It's like they are the guiding force of the elements, for they partake more directly of this divine force or intelligence. You might even think of them as angelic forms or allies, such as described by some shamans. Castenada Castenada uses in his work on Don Juan."

I stopped writing, and look puzzled, finding it hard to conceive of these beings Michael spoke about. So Michael tried to explain some more.

"They are just very primal forces -- a more advanced aspect of the elemental kingdom, and due to their superior knowledge and intelligence, they have control of this world."

"Are they like the kings and queens of the ancient empires who were fully in charge of their peoples and considered divine?" I asked.

"Perhaps you might make that analogy," said Michael. "But they are in another dimension as very powerful spirits. They are transcendent divine forms, something you'll better understand when you experience the unification with the divine yourself."

"The point is that all things are related ultimately to the divine, and these kings and queens are aspects of the elementals which are closer to that divine force. They're like angels or watchers when conceived of in more concrete form, or viewed more abstractly, they are the intelligences that govern the four aspects of the divine as expressed in the world and known as the forces of earth, air, fire, and water. So these beings or intelligences are, in effect, in charge of the basic building blocks or forces that together create the reality and universe we know."

I nodded to show I understood,, and Michael continued.

"So, with that understanding, your next level of development as a shaman after you feel a connection with the divine is to invoke a vision of these beings, and thereby gain a great deal of knowledge and power as a shaman. However, in doing this invocation, you don't specifically ask for knowledge or power; rather you seek to experience and relate to these beings, and power and knowledge will come as part of the natural result."

To illustrate, Michael described his own experience in meeting these beings many years before. He had had four separate intense experiences, each one as a result of meeting a different elemental king or queen and the other elemental beings who came with them, much like retainers in the entourage of a Medieval lord or lady.

"My first work was with the elemental king of air," Michael said. "I can't describe the ritual or the king's name, since that is very personal. But I can describe what I experienced. It took place on a large rocky outcropping in Sequoia, high up in the hills overlooking a broad valley. I went through a period of meditation and after some invocations, this elemental appeared as a powerful manlike figure who radiated a brilliant light and was accompanied by many beings of the air, who appeared all around him. These included small air elementals, who appeared like little white balls of light in the air, bats, and some other winged beings. Like any royalty, he came with his entourage, and it was a vision granted to me alone, since Paula dn Sara who were with me, were looking in another direction when this happened, where they saw a faraway brought light. Then, after he greeted me, he gave me his name and we spoke briefly about the majesty of his kingdom. After he left in a whirlwind of air, I felt a deep awe and reverence for this vast intelligence and power that resided all about me in the air.

"Then, my next work was with the elemental lady of fire, and I could tell she was female from my familiar. In this case, the experience took place in the desert, and I drove there on my own in a jeep. After I arrived about sunset, I created an environment for the evocation by setting up an area for a special fire, and I mixed a special oil to consecrate the fire. After I did a personal ritual of evocation, I felt the being's presence and got her name."

"How did she appear?" I asked.

"It's hard to describe," said Michael "I felt a presence in the flames, like an unseen intelligence was there, so the flames glowed more brilliantly and flashed higher than ever, throwing off bright, glowing sparks that seemed to expand and perceive like eyes in the darkness. I soon felt this feeling of bonding, accompanied by a tremendous surge of energy through me, which connected me with the fire and this intelligence within it. It was hard to explain, but I felt uplifted, like I was levitating as this current surged through me, reminding me I had been in touch with this very powerful intelligence."

Michael paused while I finished writing in my notebook, then went on.

"Now my third working involved the elemental lord of the earth. For this one, I hiked up high in a rainforest in Northern California, and I followed an old dirt road to an abandoned meadow which used to be the front yard of a hunting lodge. It had this peaceful feeling that comes with great age, and I felt it was ideally isolated and quiet, so I wouldn't be disturbed.

"Then, once again I did my ritual and evocation, and this time, I found myself in touch with the guiding intelligence of earth and the many spirits inhabiting this plane of being. For example, the entourage included large hulking forms, thin wraithlike beings, and little balls of light, generally associated with the element of earth. As for this king, he was large, powerful, and looked something like a rider with a spear and shield on a horse, and I felt like he had the same kind of vibration as the powerful kings and warriors of the age of knights, although at a much higher level of being, for he was still of the spirit world.

"Then, my fourth experience was by the seashore, and though I came with several companions, it was a solitary one, because they were further away on the beach. This time, the lady of the sea appeared to me. As before, I started with a ritual and evocation, and when she came forth, she was accompanied by other lesser beings associated with the sea, including small luminous, jelly-fishlike beings that floated up out of the water, moving clouds of light energy, and humanoid-like beings that came from the sea. Then, from this group of beings, this elemental lady emerged, who looked like a golden mermaid, and again, I got her name and she pledged her relationship to me.

"Afterwards, since this was the fourth of these workings, and I had met all of the elemental ladies and kings, I had a sense of completion. I felt finished and more powerful, for I felt I could now create a more powerful circle than my regular working circle, for now I could call on these higher beings to join me at times. Also, I felt a sense of total harmony and balance, which contributed to this feeling of completion, because not only was I able to create a more powerful circle, but I felt it was fully balanced, since I was drawing on the energies of the four elemental directions. Thus, I felt I now had an especially stable and powerful base from which to work in doing future magical workings."

Then, Michael asked me to take out a small seal he had given me earlier -- a small square piece of paper, about 3" square. It was the drawing of a pentagram, with strange magical symbols, that looked like squiggles and wavy lines in each of the five arms of the pentagram. And in the center was an Egyptian eye of Horus, with a dark half-closed lid.

I fished the seal out of my wallet in my pocketbook and held it up.

"Good, you have it with you,' Michael exclaimed. "That seal you were given represents this work I have been describing. It symbolizes my relationship with these elemental kings and queens as a result of my work with them after experiencing the divine unity. So it's a very powerful symbol, which expresses the powerful balance of forces in nature, under the control of these elemental kings. I gave you the seal for protection, so you could share in a little of its power."

I looked at the symbol closely. I hadn't paid any attention to it, since after Michael gave it to me, I had filed it away in my wallet, like a membership card I didn't use very much, as I told Michael.

"That doesn't matter," he said. "The symbol has been there and its protective energies still worked regardless. Of course, if you paid attention, they would be more powerful. But even so, they can work in silence. It's like having a credit card in your wallet. You may not use it for some time. But it's there when you need it, for you can draw on it pretty much anytime."

Paul quickly related his own experiences with these beings. His first, with the elemental king of water, had been by a waterfall deep in the forest. He saw a vision of the being in the water and felt a powerful sense of knowing and understanding. His second, with the earth king, high up on a rock in the desert, where he beat on a drum, had produced a vision of strength and power, and he felt a sudden rush of acceptance, as he traveled through what seemed like a passage to another dimension.

In working with fire in the Mohave Desert, Paul had called forth the elemental king of fire from a large bonfire, as he danced around it.

"Again, I felt an acceptance, a giving of gifts, and a name," Paul said.

Finally, in working with air, Paul had climbed high in the mountains of Yosemite with his girlfriend Sara and her brother. This time, a being who came in a rush of chill air offered his acceptance. And like Michael, Paul experienced a sense of final completion.

"I felt I was now accepted as a shaman by all these beings and energies, who had the supreme ability to control all the forces of nature. So I was left with a feeling of total togetherness and completion, along with a profound sense of the underlying energy and intelligence that unites all things. Also, I felt a profound satisfaction at recognizing the harmony created by the guidance of these elemental beings in charge of all things. It was like I gained some powerful insights into the spiritual underpinnings of the operation of natural law, and I felt a great spirit of friendship and kinship to these elemental beings. Since then , whenever I have gotten out into nature, I have felt this close connection with the elements.

"Afterwards," Paul added, "this experience left me with a sense of a higher purpose and a desire to go on to new heights of knowledge, for as we open ourselves up to this spiritual universe, the desire for something greater never ends, and that keeps us learning and growing."

Michael agreed. "There are always greater quests -- quests to further explore the spiritual world; quests to seek greater unification. Though our own teachings end with the 10th degree, thereafter the personal quest for power and knowledge continues. And, as I have found, as you move on, you will find that your greater abilities to work with these larger forces will give you a greater sense of power in more mundane acts of magic and in daily life."

"What kind of advanced personal work?" I wondered.

Michael described his and Paul's explorations of the underworld and work with healing; he described his work with all types of spirits, ranging from familiars and elementals to the elemental kings and queens and even higher orders of beings.

"You see," Michael said, "each shaman, magician, or sorcerer has his own calling. Your training so far and the work you will do in seeking unification with the divine and in dealing with the elemental kings and queens will give you an overall framework. Then, it's up to you to decide on your direction, and it's hard to tell at this early stage where you will go. It's like an evolution, in which your further development will become clear as you further evolve. So seek out your own talents and affinities, and use these to help guide your way.

"In turn, the vision quest will give you some insights about where you are going. So, that's what we'll talk about next."

13

LEARNING ABOUT THE VISION QUEST

"You want to start thinking about your vision quest to prepare your way for what lies ahead," said Michael after we returned from a brief break. "Basically, the quest is to help clarify your thinking about the divine, so you have that framework to bring to your meeting with the elemental kings and queens, who are much closer to divinity that ordinary spirits. Your quest will help you seek your relationship to the divine."

Michael circled around the room, while Paul, Sara, Greta, and I listened quietly, and continued: "You'll find your vision quest a little like your first solo..."

I quickly flashed back to the scene three years ago, where I had sat quietly under a tree in a wide meadow in the darkness, imagining a protective bubble of energy around my circle, while I sat there receptive to whatever I might experience.

"You also want to open yourself up to the universe and be very receptive," Michael explained. "Then, let the divine speak to you in whatever form it appears -- in the form of gods or goddesses, forces of nature, omens or symbols, or whatever. The vision quest is much deeper, more profound than your initial solo, because you are not only out there longer, but you are more isolated, since you do this on your own. Also, you are asking more profound questions about your personal path of power -- such as: What kind of magician or shaman am I? Where am I going? What kind of road will it be?"

Michael paused to let the importance of the quest sink in, and then went on.

"Now, as to the procedures for going on this quest. First, this vision quest must be something special, something set aside from your everyday life. You can't just go to your local park to do this. With that little commitment and dedication, you won't have the same quality of vision as you would if you make it a special part of your life. In effect, you need to conduct the quest as a special ritual.

"So make it a journey. Plan to go to a special locale -- someplace especially inspiring, such as a desert or mountaintop. Also, it's especially important to do this in isolation. So your vision quest shouldn't involve any other magicians or shamans. Rather, it should involve only you seeking information. You don't even want to go to a place where you know another magician has worked, because it will interfere in your own magic.

"Instead, do something like driving to the desert or climbing to a mountain top to have your vision. Or go to an isolated section of a rainforest or to a stretch of deserted sea shore.

What's of crucial importance is that you should be away from the works of humans or other humans. Because your quest must be totally private and isolated. So seek out a place in the wilderness alone to do it."

The wilderness alone! "But what about safety." I wondered, and I express my concerns about being very new to this and not very active outdoors.

But Michael and Paul reassured me.

"There are many things you can do to help prepare," said Michael. "Go to some local parks, take some hikes to get in physical shape, and learn about outdoor safety procedures."

"And maybe do some informal short-term local vision quests," said Paul. "Consider this quest like an extended version of your solo, so you need to feel more comfortable being out in the wilderness alone. Then, when you feel ready, you can do the real thing."

"What's that?" I asked.

Paul described the classical system used by some American Indians and other groups.

"In the traditional system, the person on the quest would go to a place carrying four days of water and a blanket, and that's it. Then, he would sit there for four days and nights, depriving himself of sleep. He would drink his water and bless it as holy, and then, he would take care of any personal hygiene outside this blessed circle. The goal was to culminate the ritual at dawn on the fourth day, so any vision would be received then."

"Is that what I'm supposed to do?" I asked.

"No, not necessarily," Paul said. "Your level of involvement is up to you, although your level of achievement will correspond to what you do and your level of commitment. So while four sleepless days is the classic form, the key to a successful vision quest is to deprive yourself sufficiently, so this isolation and deprivation enable you to achieve the purpose of the quest, which is to rid yourself of impurities and receive the divine. In other words, the ultimate goal is to be like a divine receptacle, where you make yourself worthy of the divine through self-purification and open yourself up to be whatever the divine chooses – like discovering your life's calling or purpose. So it's just you and the divine there together, in whatever form the divine chooses to manifest itself."

"What was your own quest like?" I wondered, and Paul described it.

"I went out for four days into a wooded rainforest, but instead of no sleep and no food, I had limited sleep -- three hours a night, and limited food -- about 250 calories -- for the first three days. On the last day, I had no sleep and ate nothing. When I came down from my isolation, I had people waiting for me who could drive back and they had food for me, too. However, while I was on the quest, they were several miles away, so I really did feel isolated and alone, and the vision I had, which is really personal, was very powerful. So even though you don't exactly follow the classical shaman form, the results can be very powerful."

Just as I started wondering if I could really do this, Michael cut in:

"Now for your own trip, it should be at least 24 hours, more if you feel comfortable. The point is to have enough time so you feel some sense of deprivation and isolation and can feel the closeness of the divinity to you. But you don't need to do this with the same intensity as in the classic trip to gain a vision. For example, you might go to a national park, set up a base camp, and hike a few miles from there to pick out a site that feels right for you, as well as safe. Then, you can conduct your quest there. Use a limited fast or full fast, as you choose. What's most important is the physical isolation. You need to be alone."

After some discussion of the logistics of going on a quest and preparing for it -- "You should plan well in advance"... "Check out the weather"... "Take the proper supplies"... "You don't normally have to worry about the animals, though you can take some precautions"... "You can take some courses on outdoor skills and camping," Michael turned to the ritual and spiritual aspects of such a quest.

"The point of all this," he emphasized, "is you are going on not just a physical journey, but a journey into yourself and the deeper levels of being and meaning in the universe. Then, if you do this with full dedication and the proper attitude and take the necessary precautions, you will come away with a deeper vision and an understanding of who and what you are.

"Certainly, there may be some risks, because you are in a strange, isolated environment. But you can take some simple precautions, such as having a jacket with you in case you get cold and having extra food in case you are hungry. So you want to be sensible and take care of yourself. But at the same time, having a little risk is part of the process -- part of this rite of passage to this new level of experiencing and being. And any rite of passage involves overcoming some challenge or passing through some barrier. That's the way we grow and learn.

"In fact..." Michael swayed back and forth on his heels, holding his hands in a "V" to underline his point, "...you might see the process of gaining education and experience to work up to this quest as part of your quest. So as you gain knowledge in such things as how to fast, safely backpack, and camp out, consider doing each of these things as another step on the path to bring you closer to reaching your quest.

"In turn, such an outlook is important, because as you learn new things to prepare yourself, you must realize and reaffirm that what you are doing is a spiritual act towards your spiritual goal. So you see all these preparations along the way as an exciting step towards this goal and not a burden."

"In other words, once you decide you want to do this quest and decided on your setting, there are logistical questions to take care of so you can make this journey, such as finances, the time needed to do it, the education needed to prepare, and the like. But most important is your spiritual focus -- what you will do, for this is the driving force behind these preparations.

"So, for this spiritual focus, you must affirm to yourself that you are embarking on a journey that will lead to your interaction with power. Think of it like having an appointment with power and from that you will gain mastery. To this end, on your journey you will isolate yourself in a conducive setting and use the exercises and disciplines you have been taught to perceive and interact with this power, as it presents itself to you in various forms.

"Thus, when you stand there alone wherever you have chosen – be it a deserted beach, isolated mountaintop, wherever -- you are very receptive to power, because you have been fasting and using your seeing exercises, your circle, your power object, and your communication with the other world to heighten your receptivity. Then, too, you are not only focused on communicating with a specific being or a set of beings, but you are directing your focus and intention outward and making a request to power as a whole."

"Power as a whole?" I interrupted.

"In other words," Michael explained, "you are making your request to that divine force that links and binds all of the forces in the universe together. You are making this request like a prayer for a vision of power for yourself or a vision of something which you will guide you to further visions of power.

"Then, as you wait for your vision, keep in mind that the manifestation of this vision of power may take many different forms. For example, it may take the form of an animal or several animals. It may take the form of supernatural visions or phenomena. It might appear as an entity or force. It may take the form of a sequence of events. Or it could manifest as a combination of these things.

"So the key to successful vision quest is to regard the entire event as a magical occurrence. Everything on the quest has significance from the moment you begin by stepping in your car or boat to go wherever you are going to the moment you come back. For everything is part of the vision, although the most intense part will come when you perform the ritual and you ready yourself for magical seeing."

Again, Michael walked around the room thoughtfully, now almost a silhouette in his black uniform in the dark candlelit room. I tried to imagine what it must have been like for him on his own quest for power in the darkness of the desert where he first worked.

Michael went on. "As for the significance of the vision or visions you receive, these are interpreted through your heart. On one level, all of these visions, omens, power animals, and other things you see may be exciting and wonderful. In fact, these fantastic events are rather commonplace on these quests. But the real significance of this journey is only felt in your heart, which places these events in a context which gives them meaning. The reason for this is that you have set out on your journey saying that, 'I want knowledge from these events I experience. I want to know something about myself.' As a result, your experience of these events becomes personally oriented, so you receive this illumination about yourself.

"In short, you need to make the entire event a ritual and act of power, and you need to seek significance in even the smallest things that happen. For these are the basic keys to a successful vision quest. If you don't do that, even the most fantastic experience won't mean anything. So, an essential thing to understand as you go on this quest is that there is no coincidence. All that happens has a reason and a meaning, and you need to know that in your heart and interpret that meaning for yourself."

On that note, Michael ended the lesson and turned on the lights. My own journey to L.A. to further explore the ways of the shaman warrior were now over, and Michael pulled out two gold star-shaped pins from his pocket and pinned them on my shirt collar to symbolize this achievement.

"Congratulations for passing your 5th and 6th degrees here," he said. "You have completed your gateway; you have contacted your familiar. Now you are ready to go on further."

Quietly, I got up and gathered my things. Paul, Sara, and Greta said their goodbyes, and Michael walked me to the door. It was hard to believe the training was really over; but now our parting had a strong sense of finality about it, as Paul, Sara, and Greta hung back in the living room, almost like they were in another dimension, as Michael and I walked towards the door.

At the door, we paused.

"Now as you go on," Michael continued, "the first door is the vision quest, which will show you the divine presence. We may call it the 7th degree, but you can think of it as a door. Afterwards, you can seek to realize that in everyday life, and then seek the unification with the divine. Finally, you can learn how to contact the higher manifestations of that divinity, such as the elemental kings and queens. Then, you can further explore. So there's much to do. You may think your journey here is over. But now your further journey begins."

Michael shut the glass door and waved goodbye. I saw him engulfed in darkness as I left, and I started my car. In many ways it was just like another night of driving back to my hotel in Santa Monica on the freeway. Everything certainly looked the same.

Yet it was different. I felt like I was in that center point between two realities, between two worlds. Behind me lay this shamanic reality I had been exploring for three weeks at Michael's. Around me lay the day to day freeway and city. And ahead lay even further vistas of other dimensions to explore.

I imagined myself like a point of consciousness about to jump from one world to another, and with that image, I drove on in the night. There was much to think about and explore, and this journey to work with Michael in L.A. had been one more step along the way.

About the Author

GINI GRAHAM SCOTT, Ph.D., J.D., is a nationally known writer, consultant, speaker, and seminar/workshop leader, specializing in business and work relationships, professional and personal development, social trends, popular culture, lifestyles, and criminal justice. She has published over 50 books on diverse subjects. Her websites are at www.changemakerspublishingandwriting.com and www.ginigrahamscott.com.

She has written five books on shamanism, including SHAMAN WARRIOR, SECRETS OF THE SHAMAN, SHAMANISM AND PERSONAL MASTERY, SHAMANISM FOR EVERYONE, THE COMPLETE IDIOT'S GUIDE TO SHAMANISM. FURTHER JOURNEYS WITH A SHAMAN is a continuation of her studies with a shaman described in SHAMAN WARRIOR and SECRETS OF THE SHAMAN.

Her books on business relationships and professional development include: WANT IT, SEE IT, GET IT!; DISAGREEMENTS, DISPUTES AND ALL-OUT WAR; 30 DAYS TO A MORE POWERFUL MEMORY; A SURVIVAL GUIDE TO MANAGING EMPLOYEES FROM HELL; A SURVIVAL GUIDE FOR WORKING WITH BAD BOSSES; and A SURVIVAL GUIDE FOR WORKING WITH HUMANS (all from AMACOM 2004-2009).

Scott's books on social trends and popular culture include: THE VERY NEXT NEW THING, PLAYING THE LYING GAME, YOU THE

JURY, CAN WE TALK? THE POWER AND INFLUENCE OF TALK SHOWS, MIND YOUR OWN BUSINESS: THE BATTLE FOR PERSONAL PRIVACY, and PRIVATE EYES (with Sam Brown).

Her books on marketing include: LET'S HAVE A SALES PARTY, BUILDING A WINNING SALES TEAM, SUCCESS IN MLM and GET RICH IN PERSONAL SELLING (Self-Counsel Press).

She writes books and book proposals, articles, scripts, and other materials for clients, and writes books and does workshops on writing and promoting books and films. These include: SELL YOUR BOOK, SCRIPT OR COLUMN; USING LINKEDIN TO PROMOTE YOUR BUSINESS OR YOURSELF; DOING YOUR OWN PR; and WRITING, DIRECTING AND PRODUCING A LOW-BUDGET SHORT FILM. Her books for clients include books on work and business, professional and personal development, self-help and relationships, psychology, sales, marketing, and money, health and beauty, memoirs, crime, social trends, and popular culture, novels, and specialty books. Her scripts include book adaptations and screenplays from original ideas.

She is founder and director of Changemakers Publishing and Writing and Changemakers Productions and has taught classes at several colleges, including Cal State University, East Bay and Notre Dame de Namur University.

She has published over 30 POD and E-Books in various formats, and has licensed several dozen books for foreign sales, including the UK, Russia, Hungary, Lithuania, Korea, Spain, and Japan.

Scott has received national media exposure for her books, including appearances on Good Morning America, Oprah, Montel Williams, and CNN. She has been the producer and host of a talk show series,

CHANGEMAKERS, featuring interviews on various types of change. Additional information is at www.changemakersradio.com.

Scott's screenplays, mostly in the crime, legal thriller, and sci-fi genres, include RICH AND DEAD, COKE AND DIAMONDS, DEADLY AFFAIR, THE NEW CHILD, and NEW IDENTITY. UNBALANCED is expected to be completed in 2011. She produced, directed, wrote, cast, and sometimes directed over 50 short films and trailers, which can be viewed at www.youtube.com/changemakersprod.

As a game and toy designer, Scott has had over two dozen games with major game companies, including Hasbro, Pressman, and Mag-Nif. Two new games were introduced by Briarpatch in 2007. She licensed GLASNOST: THE GAME OF SOVIET-AMERICAN PEACE AND DIPLOMACY to John N. Hansen (1988).

She received a PhD in Sociology from the University of California, Berkeley, a JD from the University of San Francisco Law School, and MAs in Anthropology; Mass Communications & Organizational/ Consumer/Audience Behavior, and Popular Culture and Lifestyles from Cal State, East Bay. She will be getting an MS in Recreation and Tourism at Cal State, East Bay in 2013.